THE CONCEPT OF SOCIALISM

THE CONCEPT OF SOCIALISM

EDITED BY BHIKHU PAREKH

HOLMES AND MEIER PUBLISHERS, INC.
NEW YORK

Published in the United States of America 1975
by Holmes and Meier Publishers, Inc.
101 Fifth Avenue, New York, N.Y. 10003

© 1975 by Bhikhu Parekh

Library of Congress Cataloging in Publication Data

Parekh, Bhikhu C
    The Concept of Socialism

    1. Socialism and society.   2. Man.   3. Sociology.
I. Title.
HX542.P27 1975   335.4'01   74-28393
ISBN 0-8419-0190-2

Printed in Great Britain

CONTENTS

INTRODUCTION

Discussion of political doctrines such as Liberalism, Conservatism and Socialism is an exceedingly hazardous enterprise. There are no clear criteria by which their identity can be determined, and this unavoidably leads to their caricature. F. A. Hayek, for example, presents an extremely odd picture of Conservatism when he asserts, among other things, that the Conservative is 'essentially opportunist and lacks principles', is not much interested in limiting the powers of government, 'does not really believe in the power of argument', and rejects well-substantiated new knowledge simply because he dislikes some of the consequences which seem tò follow from it.[1] David Spitz goes even further.[2] He conveniently defines the liberal as a man whose 'basic value is the value of free inquiry, his basic attitude the skeptical or at least the inquiring mind . . .' As he defines him, the liberal rejects all claims to absolute truths and always keeps an open mind, accepting only the results of rational inquiry. He thinks that Conservatives and Socialists do not share this attitude, and therefore dismisses them both as 'fanatical men', who 'claim possession of the truth . . . (and) are both impervious to the results of scientific inquiry, to the tests of reason'.[3] Spitz's equation of the Liberal with the rational man and his dismissal of all non-liberals as bigoted fanatics is not peculiar to him; it is to be found in many a liberal writer.

The fallacy is not peculiar to the Liberal; it is committed by Conservative and Socialist writers too. Several Conservative philosophers have conveniently defined their doctrine in terms of political realism, sense of history, appreciation of the role of passions in human life and love of order, and have directly or by implication so defined other political doctrines as to make one wonder how any decent human being could ever subscribe to them. Socialist writers too have sometimes defined socialism in terms of equality, justice, decentralisation of power and protection of minorities, thus depriving rival political doctrines of almost all humanistic content. Each political doctrine defines itself, and is defined by others, in a manner that suits their respective interests. It may or may not be true that to a Westerner all Chinese look alike, but certainly it seems true that to a political doctrine all its rivals look more or less alike.

Why this is so is a very difficult question that we cannot pursue here in detail. Excepting cases where writers deliberately use their theoretical analysis as a vehicle for subtle and not so subtle ideological propaganda,

1

or where they lack adequate knowledge of the history of a doctrine, two factors seem responsible. First, social and political thought has an inescapable ideological basis, and a writer's thought - his definition and analysis of concepts included — is unavoidably influenced by his moral, cultural, political and other biases. Second, we have not so far devoted enough thought to the analysis of the logical structure of political doctrines and inquired where precisely to locate their identity. Political doctrines are highly complex and fluid conceptual structures, with one foot in the world of abstract ideas and the other in the humdrum world of human practice. Unless we know where to look for their identity, we are bound to end up misunderstanding them. Of the two factors, nothing more can be said about the first than that each writer should be rigorously self-critical and that others should criticise and expose his biases. Developing criteria for determining the identity of political doctrines cannot by itself of course put an end to the caricature referred to earlier, but it can at least minimise it.

Broadly speaking, a political doctrine such as Conservatism, Liberalism and Socialism is an attempt to present a specific conception of man and society — the type of creature man is, his basic needs and motivations, the way he is and ought to be related to other men, the form of life best suited to him, the role of government in the life of community, etc. A conception of man raises two types of problems: first justificational or philosophical, and second, implementational or programmatic. It competes with others for the loyalty of men and is therefore required both to justify itself and to show why it should be accepted in preference to others. Further a political doctrine by its very nature is practically orientated and seeks to achieve a particular type of society. It therefore needs to work out concrete policies, proposals and the organisational structure needed to realise them. Every carefully worked out political doctrine therefore has a tripartite structure. First, it has a more or less well articulated metaphysic, a general view of the universe, that provides justification for its conception of man and society. Second, it has a specific conception of man and society which constitutes its core. And third, it has a programmatic content intended to show how its view of man and society is to be realised.

The relationship between a doctrine's conception of man and society and its programmatic and philosophical content is necessarily contingent. The policies and the institutional structure recommended by a political doctrine are inescapably conditioned by the circumstances and the stage of development of the society in which the doctrine operates, and sometimes by the tactical need for expediency. As society changes, it throws up new problems and changes the context of old problems, and requires new solutions. Liberalism, for example, is not

2

necessarily committed to *laissez-faire* because under certain circumstances, it might find that liberal values can be preserved only by state intervention; nor is it committed to argument and persuasion, since it may at times have to resort to other methods to make the voice of moderation heard, as liberals in the developing countries and in America and elsewhere are beginning to realise. No political doctrine can therefore remain committed to and defined in terms of a particular policy or method of social change.

The philosophical part of a political doctrine is more tightly related to its conception of man and society than the programmatic content. No specific political doctrine is *necessarily* entailed by a metaphysical system, and nor does a political doctrine *necessarily* presuppose a particular metaphysical system. Liberalism can find its philosophical justification in Aristotle, Christianity, Aquinas, Hobbes, Locke, Bentham, Mill or Hegel; and conversely Aristotle, Aquinas, or any one of these eminent philosophers can be so interpreted as to justify conservatism, socialism or even Fascism. A metaphysical system necessarily deals with extremely general statements from which, directly or with the help of low-order secondary assumptions, different concrete views concerning man and society can be deduced. Thus, for example, Aristotelian metaphysics enunciates the doctrine that each being in the universe naturally strives to realise its potentialities. One can accept this metaphysical principle but define and grade human potentialities differently, and arrive at conservatism, liberalism or socialism. No political doctrine therefore can be equated with and defined in terms of a particular philosophical system. Conservatism, for example, cannot be defined in terms of Christian metaphysics, because liberals and socialists can invoke it too; nor can socialism be defined in terms of the Hegelian dialectic (as some Marxists do), or Christian metaphysics (as christian socialists do), or Kantian metaphysics (as German Utopian socialists did), because liberalism and conservatism can invoke them too.

The identity of a political doctrine is to be found neither in its philosophical nor in its programmatic part but in its conception of man and society. It is this 'middle part' that provides the most fruitful point of entry into its complex structure, and the most useful vantage point from which to trace its changing history. I propose to show this with reference to one political doctrine − socialism.

Socialism began as a revolt against capitalism, and its conception of man and society was initially developed as an alternative to the one which in the socialist view underlay and reinforced capitalist society. Socialist writers have not been unanimous in describing the conception of man they reject, and have variously labelled it liberal, individualistic or bourgeois. To avoid confusion we shall use the last description.

Socialists articulated the bourgeois view of man and society as follows: The bourgeois conception of man, took the isolated individual as its starting point and glorified him. It defined him as a private, self-enclosed, socially exclusive and basically egoistic being, who possessed sovereign power over his body and its constituents which he was free to dispose of as he pleased, consistent with the minimum necessary limits imposed by social existence. Society is seen as essentially a series of exchange relationships voluntarily entered into by sovereign individuals. It is external to the individual, not an expression of his very being, and therefore more or less a consciously designed mechanism. Since the individual is regarded the master of himself, he is considered to have a right to the products of his labour. Thus private property is given the status more or less of a natural right. The self-interested individual, the bourgeois view of man asserts, can produce his best only when guaranteed the full reward of his labour and only under competitive conditions. Competition is considered necessary both to spur man into action and to limit his excesses and thus is an indispensable means to both social progress and stability. Capitalist economy is therefore sacrosanct and in accord with the demands of human nature. Since individuals are rational and responsible adults, the government has no right to interfere with their actions except to the extent necessary to maintain peace and order. The bourgeois view of man is fearful of the government, sees it principally as a source of security of life, liberty and property, and rejects all attempts to turn it into an instrument of social change. It is admitted that in an 'energetic', competitive, 'dynamic' society, some men might prove misfits and suffer. Such tragic casualties are considered a small price to pay for the 'enormous' benefits of the capitalist economy, and are either accepted as unavoidable or are deemed to warrant limited remedial action.

Socialists rejected the bourgeois view of man and offered an alternative: Human beings, far from being independent atoms related to each other in certain limited ways, were necessarily interdependent not only in the obvious material sense but also in the cultural and spiritual sense. They need each other to help them acquire abilities and skills which each of them by himself cannot hope to develop. Indeed, none of them can fulfil himself as a human being unless others are able to do so as well. Some went even further and contended that the individual, believed by the bourgeois view to be soveriegn, was in fact a social product. He owes his existence to others. He cannot think without a language which is a social institution. He owes his skills, abilities and knowledge to formal and informal education, a cooperative enterprise in which several men and generations participate. He needs incentive, encouragement and opportunities to work, and these are socially provided; the ambition to achieve something

4

great or create something new is not inherent in man but a product of social structure. Socialists therefore concluded that man is essentially a social being, not only in the obvious and superficial sense that he likes human company, or needs others' help, but in the profound sense that he is totally unintelligible outside of society. Since the individual's abilities, skills and indeed his humanity have a social basis, they are not his private property to be used as he pleases. He holds them in trust for society and should use them for the well-being of his fellow men. Each individual is his 'brother's keeper' and ought to take an active interest in his well-being.

Socialists rejected the bourgeois view that the pursuit of self-interest was natural to man and maintained that it was planted by capitalist society. Some argued that man was social by nature and even postulated a social 'instinct' in him, whereas others were content to maintain that man could become social and altruistic in a differently organised society. But they were all agreed that 'selfishness' was a perversion of human 'nature' and condemned it vehemently. Robert Owen called it immoral; Fourier called it a perversion; E. Belfort Bax called it unnatural; Marx thought it was worthy of an animal; William Morris equated it with 'hell'; and in recent years Mao has called it 'poison', and Fidel Castro 'the beast instinct'. Since selfishness, also called 'individualism' and 'individuality', was for early socialists (and for all socialists since) the essence of capitalism, they called their own doctrines 'socialism', centred around the principle of human sociality. For Owen, Fourier, Bax, Robert Blatchford, Morris and others, 'social' was the opposite of 'selfish', and socialism of individualism.[4]

Since they rejected the bourgeois emphasis on self-interest as the predominant human motive, they rejected competition as the basis of social organisation and emphasised cooperation. They argued that competition was wasteful of human energy and resources; militated against human solidarity and turned men into enemies, led to the exploitation of man by man, created discord and conflict, and was therefore not in harmony with man's true nature. By contrast cooperation created harmony and 'concord', drew men closer together, was economical, and expressed and developed man's social nature. Socialists were not all agreed as to whether competition might not be retained in some form. Some such as Owen rejected it altogether, while others such as Saint-Simon and Fourier retained it, provided that it was subordinated to the superior principle of cooperation.

Socialists, further, contended that man was an intelligent or rational being who could and should take conscious charge of his destiny. He has a unique ability not shared by any other being in the universe which enables him to become a 'sovereign of circumstances'. For him to remain a plaything of impersonal forces was therefore to live a life unworthy of his nature: it was to live like an animal. He must plan his life, decide what type of life he wants to live, and consciously design and regulate his environment accordingly. The idea of social planning seemed to socialists to be inherent in their definition of rationality, indeed, in their definition of man. To be human was to be rational, and rationality consisted in planning one's conduct and environment in a way that helped realise one's consciously formulated purpose.[5] The bourgeois view of man also defined him as a rational being, and rationality as a capacity for planning, but for socialists there was a contradiction. They thought it odd that men should plan their lives individually but not collectively, that they should live as men individually but as 'animals' collectively, and wondered if it was ever possible for an individual to act rationally in a society that was not itself rational.

Socialists therefore rejected the bourgeois view of man (and the capitalist society) because they thought that it was totally false and perverted man's true nature and his relations with his fellow men. While man is essentially a social being, the bourgeois view takes him to be essentially selfish; while man is a cooperative being, the bourgeois view takes him to be competitive; while man is essentially outgoing and seeks the company of his fellow men, the bourgeois view takes him to be socially exclusive; while man finds fulfilment in sharing, the bourgeois view emphasises his possessive nature; while men are essentially partners in a common enterprise, the bourgeois view sees them as rivals; while man is a brother to his fellow men and a source of strength and encouragement to them, the bourgeois view sees them as his enemies ready to swindle him at the first available opportunity; while man ought to love and be concerned about his fellow men, the bourgeois view sees him as basically self-absorbed and callous. Again, socialists argued, instead of creating social harmony by consciously planning and coordinating human energies, the bourgeois view of man relies on creating equilibrium by the wasteful and inhuman method of interpersonal jealousy, suspicion and rivalry. Instead of creating a society where man can fulfil himself, the bourgeois view creates one that is no different from a 'jungle' where 'beasts' roam in human garb. Given the socialist conception of man, it is not surprising that socialists almost invariably refer to the capitalist society in animal terms.

The socialist vision of man appeared on the European scene in the nineteenth century, spread all over the globe with the spread of European ideas and institutions, and has continued to dominate human conscious-ness ever since. During its not very long history, socialist thought has retained its vision of man as an essentially social, rational and cooperative being and has given its history coherence and continuity. But socialist thought has undergone important changes too. These have been of three kinds corresponding to the tripartite structure of political doctrines discussed earlier.

First, although the socialist vision is *prima facie* plausible and attractive, like all political doctrines it needs philosophical justification and this has had to be reconsidered. The early socialists had only two political doctrines to contend with, conservatism and liberalism. Since then a number of others, such as anarchism, fascism and nazism have appeared and commanded the allegiance of large sections of mankind. Again, socialism has become established in several societies and their experiences have highlighted some of its ambiguities and contradictions. Again, capitalist society itself has changed; new problems have appeared and some of the old problems have vanished. The intellectual climate has changed and new ways of talking about man and society have appeared. For these and other reasons socialists have felt compelled to offer new and relevant justifications of their view of man and society. Some have tried to anchor socialism in Christian metaphysics; some others in Darwinian naturalism; some such as Marx in radical humanism; and some have questioned the very possibility of its justification and made its acceptance a matter of personal commitment or taste. Unfortunately socialists have paid little attention to their philosophical basis, and the history of this aspect of its thought contains few new departures, the only outstanding exception being Marx.

Secondly, the socialist vision of man has been refined and made clearer and extended into new areas. This is the most fascinating part of the history of socialist thought and deserves to be considered in some detail. It will not have gone unnoticed that the socialist vision contains a powerful collectivist element. In reacting against the lean and barren individualism of the bourgeois view of man, some of the early socialists such as Owen and Saint-Simon clearly swung to the other extreme and almost totally ignored the demands of human individuality — his freedom, his uniqueness, his need for privacy, his desire to develop his capacities in a distinctive way. Marx was one of the first to see the danger of collectivism, and to protest against the early socialists' tendency to see society as an abstract and independent entity and to set up a false antithesis between it and the individual. However, even he did not give the problem the attention it merited. He continued to emphasise the features men share in common at the expense of those that distinguish them, and provided little institutional protection for individuality in his sketchy outline of the communist society. Communists, reverted to the collectivism of some of the early Socialists, thereby provoking some socialists to rush into the arms of the self-righteous liberals and even conservatives, some to go back to Marx, some to seek inspiration in other socialist writers, and some to reappraise the entire socialist tradition itself. Although all this has produced a great deal of intellectual ferment in socialist circles and generated some new insights, no outstanding statement of the socialist vision has so far appeared that comes to terms with the familiar and tragic problems raised by the practices of Russian and other socialist societies.

The socialist vision during its short history has been extended into new areas and has produced some fascinating perspectives on social life. From the very beginning, socialist writers have been interested in the institution of the family and the conventional bourgeois views on love and marriage. Nearly all early socialists advocated equality of women, only Proudhon being the most notorious antifeminist. For him, women were congenitally inferior to men and occupied an intermediate position between the animal and the male; he even 'calculated' that the 'total value' of man to woman was in the ratio of 27 to 8.[6] Many of the early socialists attacked the family as a bourgeois institution breeding selfishness, 'individualism' and exclusiveness. Marx was ambiguous, sometimes attacking the institution itself and sometimes only its bourgeois form. Engels rejected it altogether and advocated a 'communist household'. Russian communists attacked it in the beginning but later idealised it as a nursery of socialist virtues. In recent years some socialists such as Marcuse have stressed its vital role in building up powers of critical thought, while others have dismissed it as a mere unit of consumption, serving the nefarious interests of the consumption-orientated bourgeois society. As to sexual love, many early socialists such as Saint-Simon, Cabet and Fourier, and even Owen rejected the Christian degradation of the flesh and insisted that the sexual desire was as essential a part of human fulfilment as the so called spiritual desire. In his Harmony, Fourier guaranteed a 'sexual minimum' and offered institutional assistance to lesbianism, pederasty and exhibitionism.[7] The Saint-Simonian 'church' under the leadership of Le Pere Enfantin shocked Paris by their profession and practice of 'religious' promiscuity. Indeed, Enfantin thought that God was androgynous by nature, and his disciples resolved to die with the words 'père-mère' on their lips.[8] Marx took little interest in sexual love, condemned all forms of non-heterosexual relations as most early socialists had done, and insisted that sexual love must be practised within the framework of marriage. Among contemporary socialists, the theme of 'sexual liberation', meaning not merely feminine equality but also rejection of almost all forms of sexual taboo, has reappeared but has remained confined to the periphery of the socialist movement.

From the very beginning socialists, again, took keen interest in the abolition of the distinction between the town and the country, and explored the possibility of new residential units with new types of buildings based on the socialist principles of communal and cooperative living and man's unity with nature. Ebenezer Howard's 'garden city of tomorrow', Fourier's design of his phalanstery, More's description of his ideal city on an imaginary island and Robert Owen's 'New Harmony' are all well-known examples. Marx and Engels reiterated the need to abolish both urban 'slums' and rural 'idiocy,' but took little interest in new forms of architecture and new territorial units. In their early years Russian communists experimented with interesting ideas, more or less dropped the subject for several decades, and have now begun talking about it again. In recent years French socialists such as Manuel Castelle[9] have launched a powerful attack on the 'bourgeois' theories of town planning and architecture reflected in some of the recent works on urban sociology, and have offered interesting perspectives based on the socialist idea of the 'social origin of space'.

While these themes have continued to interest socialists, there have also been new departures. Most early socialists showed little interest in abolishing division of labour; indeed some of them, for example Saint-Simon and Fourier, idealised it as the most effective way to secure human interdependence and solidarity. Having rejected the collectivism of the early socialists Marx, on the other hand, thought that the division of labour was one of the most obnoxious sources of man's dehumanisation and placed its abolition on the socialist agenda where it has remained since. Early socialists did not show much interest in political and industrial participation; Marx stressed its desirability and socialists since have emphasised its role even further. Again, the early socialists did not think much of the idea of the whole man. For Marx, on the other hand, it was crucial. In his view the greater the range of a man's interests and abilities, the greater the area of human achievement that he was able to appropriate, and therefore the correspondingly lesser was his degree of alienation from the species.

Some of the most fascinating changes have occurred in the socialist moral vocabulary. Some of the early socialists took a rather puritanical and serious view of man. Marx revolted against some aspects of it and taught socialism to appreciate the value of 'middle-class' culture and the romantic ideal of guiltless self-enjoyment. In other respects, mainly sexual, Marx remained a rather prudish Victorian, despite his life-long interest in pornography and an affair with his maid servant. Russian communists, and indeed communists everywhere, reverted to the puritanical and humourless moralism of the early socialists, against which some socialists such as Marcuse and the student left have recently revolted. Following Marx, Marcuse dismissed morality itself as a punitive expression of human self-alienation — although he has in recent years begun to emphasise the need of a moral perspective on society — and followed Schiller in placing 'playfulness' at the heart of the socialist vision of man. Again, some of the early socialists such as Babeuf considered equality a most desirable ideal. In his imaginary Icaria Cabet rejected all forms of social inequality, down to differences of clothing. Saint-Simon, Fourier and others disagreed and called equality 'a poison', although it must be remembered that they did not reject social responsibility for the equal well-being of all its members but only the mechanical and extreme equality of Babeuf and Cabet. Marx too condemned it as a bourgeois principle, although, again, he was not opposed to the equal development of all but only to the individualistic basis of equality. Socialists in recent years have considered it one of the most important, indeed, even the most important moral and political ideal. Like the concept of equality, the concept of justice too has aroused strong feelings among socialists. Many early socialists considered it the most important principle of socialist morality and attacked capitalist society for its injustice and unfairness. Marx, on the other hand, attacked it for its bourgeois-individualistic basis. For him it was a distributive principle that in no way changed the form and quality of interpersonal relationships. The idea of justice, he thought, presupposed isolated and possessive individuals, each of whom claimed a right to the rewards of 'his' labour, to use them 'as he pleased'. Since a socialist sees man as a social being and his labour as social labour, and rejects the idea of private ownership, he can have nothing to do, Marx argued, with the language of claims and rights in which the principle of justice is rooted.

We said earlier that the third area in which the history of socialist thought reveals interesting changes is in its programmatic content. The programmatic part is divisible into two broad categories, one relating to the policies and the institutional structure appropriate to the socialist society, and the other to the method of overthrowing capitalism. Since socialism began as a reaction against capitalism, and since it considers work a most important aspect of man's life, economic problems have naturally engaged most of its attention. All socialists emphasise planning, but they disagree on its form and extent. Some insist on collective national ownership of all the productive resources of the community, some on the collective ownership of the commanding heights of the economy, and some are content with the ownership of a few key industries. Some socialists are opposed to collective national ownership and prefer localised ownership by the workers of their respective industries. Some socialists reject the idea of ownership altogether and rely on fiscal and other regulatory devices for making capitalism socially accountable. As to political organisation, most socialists favour participatory democracy but disagree on its form. Some would break up the existing state into loosely related self-governing units; others urge greater central coordination; while others are content to democratise the existing state by plebiscitary and other devices. As to social organisation, we have already mentioned their views on the family and marriage.

As to the second aspect of the programmatic part, socialists have been generally agreed on the methods of persuasion, political education, electoral pressure and peaceful protest for overthrowing capitalism. Most early socialists rejected violence either in principle or for its alleged inefficacy. Marx justified violence only when used to deliver a new society about to be born. In democratic societies such as Britain, America and Holland, he generally considered its use unnecessary. Within the Marxist tradition, the problem of violence has been and is being discussed in two separate contexts: the developing nations of the Third World and the developed societies of the West. All marxists are agreed that the use of violence is justified in the former where regimes are generally oppressive and do not allow nonviolent means of protest. The most agonising problems arise in relation to developed societies. The rigid party system, the parliamentary emphasis on conciliation and compromise, and the relative political and ideological emasculation of the proletariat with its attendant problems of cooptation and false consciousness, have led some marxists to ask if extraparliamentary methods, including violence, may not be necessary. For the most part, however, the marxian emphasis on the inherent self-negation of capitalism, on the objective ripeness of the revolutionary situation, and its rejection of 'elitism' have dissuaded all but extremists from resorting to large-scale violence. Excepting its anarchist and extreme juvenile wings, no socialist, marxist or otherwise, has ever glorified violence and sought in it a short-cut to the immensely complicated problems of social change.

This then is the brief account of the problems and concerns of socialists over past hundred and fifty years. Some of these problems have disappeared and new ones have taken their place. Socialism has sought both new philosophical inspiration and new practical ways to actualise its cherished values. Amidst all these changes, however, its basic vision of man and society has persisted, and therein lies its identity. Schematically, the following four values or principles are integral to its vision and distinguish it from all other political doctrines. First, the recognition of man's essential *sociality* and the implied notions of human brotherhood and man's abilities and powers as a social trust; second, *social responsibility* for the well-being of all its members and the implied rejection of the doctrine of self-help; third, extension of *cooperation* in all areas of life, above all, the economic; and fourth, the idea of *planning* as an expression of man's conscious control of his resources and destiny. It is, of course, true that no political doctrine can claim monopoly of a particular value. All political doctrines aim to achieve a good society as they see it, and therefore endeavour to accommodate all or at least most values. The need to win over men's allegiance ensures that they will at least *claim* to subscribe to them. Nevertheless the four values mentioned above are central to the socialist vision of man in a way that they are not to any other. They are to be found in all socialist writers, past and present, and appear only marginally in non-socialist writers. A liberal or a conservative may, for example, recommend planning, but feels apologetic about it and thinks that it needs special justification. For a socialist, the reverse is the case; it is competition that needs special justification. What is true of planning is also true of the other three principles. Detailed demonstration of this thesis is clearly beyond the scope of this introduction.

We outlined above some of the socialist concerns and preoccupations. Most of the problems that worried our socialist forbears are still with us, and in some cases we have not come any closer to their solution. It is about time that we took stock of contemporary socialist thought, and examined over again some of the themes of continuing interest to socialists. The task can be best undertaken only from within the socialist tradition itself, for the obvious reason that socialists can bring to it a sense of personal commitment and a better appreciation of their heritage, avoiding the type of caricature referred to at the start of this introduction. It is against this background that the following essays should be seen. Each author is a socialist and brings to the discussion of his theme the detachment of an academic and the passion and conviction of a socialist. With the exception of Victor Kiernan who traces the important stages in the development of socialist thought, particularly in Britain, each contributor explores a specific theme; he analyses its nature and place in socialist thought and grapples with some of the problems raised by it. Between them the authors cover most of the central themes in socialist thought, such as the conception of man, the nature of knowledge and its relation to action, the division of labour, the nature of rationality, the nature of the state, marriage and family, and the relation of the marxist sub-tradition to the larger socialist tradition. As the conception of man is central to an understanding of socialism, it naturally receives greater attention. Four papers are devoted to it, each exploring a particular aspect of it. Contemporary socialist thought is obviously dominated by Marx who, although not the only source of inspiration, is still the greatest philosopher the socialist tradition has produced. Naturally he dominates the book and is not only mentioned or discussed in most papers but also has three papers specifically devoted to him. I am aware that some of the important themes in contemporary socialist thought that I mentioned earlier are not adequately discussed in the book. I had planned to include three papers dealing with the socialist critique of contemporary moral thought,

12

and the socialist theory of equality and of town planning and architecture, but for unavoidable reasons the contributors had to withdraw at the last minute. If the collection stimulates the reader to undertake a more thorough-going appraisal of the socialist tradition than can be afforded in a small collection such as this, the contributors and the editor would deem their efforts well-rewarded.

I am grateful to John Rees, David McLellan and Bernard Williams for commenting on the initial outline of the book, to all the contributors for preparing their papers, and to David Croom for inviting me to edit the volume and bearing with its slow progress.

NOTES

1. F.A. Hayek, *The Constitution of Liberty* Routledge & Kegan Paul, London, 1960, pp. 401ff.
2. David Spitz, *Essays in the Liberal Idea of Freedom* The University of Arizona Press, 1964, pp. 4 f.
3. Spitz's analysis and his treatment of its rivals is a poor advertisement for liberalism.
4. George Lichtheim, *The Origins of Socialism* Frederick A. Praeger, New York, 1969 pp. 120ff. Bax maintained that the ultimate aim of socialism was to absorb the individual 'in a corporate social consciousness'. *The Ethics of Socialism* Swan Sonnenschein, London, 1893, pp. 28ff.
5. For Saint-Simon's view of rationality, see Frank E. Manuel, *The New World of Henri Saint-Simon* Harvard University Press, Cambridge, 1956; For Fourier, see Charles Gide, *Fourier précurseur de la coopération* (Paris, 1922-3). For Marx, see Chs. 2 and 3 below. G.D.H. Cole's *History of Socialist Thought* Macmillan, London, 1953-60 brings out well the reasons for the emphasis on planning in socialist thought.
6. Lichtheim, *op. cit.,* p.254.
7. J. Beecher and R. Bienvenu, ed., *The Utopian Vision of C. Fourier* London, 1972, pp. 68 f, 333f, and elsewhere.
8. Frank E. Manuel, *The Prophets of Paris* Harvard University Press, Cambridge, 1962, pp. 162 f.
9. See, for example, his 'Y a-t-il une sociologine urbaine' in *Sociologie du Travail,* 1968, no.1, pp. 72-90.

1 SOCIALISM, THE PROPHETIC MEMORY

Victor Kiernan

1

Buddhist metaphysics, the highest wisdom of Asia, solved the paradox of our isolated yet incomplete selves by dismissing the 'self' of consciousness as an illusion, and seeing all 'true' being as part of one Unity. Marxism, the highest achievement of Western thought, agrees — at least in regarding human beings not as mutually exclusive atoms but as entities continually borrowing and giving, and in this sense each infinite as well as finite. It is the heir of a long European evolution where the relationship between individual and social has always been a practical as well as a philosophical issue. Here from very early times there has been a dual, antiphonal development, nowhere else nearly so pronounced: on the one hand the single human integer with its rights and claims, on the other the collective organisation. In place of the Asiatic State, external in nearly every way to its subjects' lives and impinging on them only by magical pretension or by compulsion, there arose in Europe the Mediterranean city-state, the *alter ego* of each citizen, a partnership extending, at any rate in the lofty conception of a Pericles, to every corner of life. It raised natural gregariousness to a higher plane, elevating man from a merely social being to what Aristotle called a political animal. Both individual and collective were thereby enlarged: a genuine political spirit can arise only through interaction between the two. Since then the two have been growing, through interplay or collision. Today finds us in another of those recurrent epochs when their rival demands are felt to have become incompatible. To escape from this by abolishing the collective, as Anarchism desires, would enfeeble the individual; to suppress the individual, as Fascism desires, would stultify the collective.

From the point of view of socialism, it is a question of depriving a limited number of men of a 'freedom' based on a bloated power over the community's economic life, in order to liberate the growth of countless others, both as individuals and as members of a meaningful community. Property has always been the vital third term. The ancient *polis,* and its successor the medieval city-republic, both of them ancestors of the nation-state of western Europe, were collective owners on a large scale of land, food reserves, public buildings sacred or profane; above all, perhaps, of the town walls and forts which

14

guaranteed their security. Such common possessions did much to generate the concept of a *res publica*, a 'commonwealth', scarcely glimpsed outside Europe, and with it that of a *patria* for the citizen to identify himself with. But within this whole the unfolding of individuality was being furthered, on some sides of its complex structure, though on others hindered, by the proliferation of private property. The Greeks, who debated everything, debated this explosive force, generated within the late clan and the early city-state growing out of it, which threatened to disrupt them. In Sparta the dominant class practised a kind of State communism; it could be admired by conservatives elsewhere like Plato, whose ideal Republic reflected an aristocratic disdain of vulgar competition for wealth. In a more democratic spirit a dislike of private property, as an unnatural novelty, was perpetuated by the Stoic philosophers, and outlived its Attic cradle. 'A broad current of communistic sentiment runs through the mental life of the Roman Empire in the age of Christ.'[1]

At the opposite pole was an unbridled competition for wealth, as the empire obsessively expanded and the republic degenerated; along with this expansion, property was coming to be endowed by Roman law with a mystically absolute, unfettered right. Social conditions bred mass resentment and calls for the land to be taken back from its greedy monopolists and reallocated as the common good required. These calls for an 'agrarian law' were among the spectres haunting nineteenth-century Europe. Property triumphed, but the memory of a time before its advent, before class division, lingered, bathed in a sentimental glow, in legends of a golden age of the dim past. There was no way for men to find their way back to it, or resurrect it; they could only wait for the 'great cycle' of time, the endless return of things, to restore it, as Christians were to await their less remote Millennium. Collective ownership of land may never really have existed, at least after land came under regular cultivation, and before that time what men had to share was mostly hunger. Educated Romans knew enough about Goths or Scythians to be realistic about primitive poverty; but they could imagine no other refuge from the corruptions of wealth and sophistication than the daydream of primitive simplicity. They drew a nostalgic picture of an existence full of hardship and of virtue, free and equal and fraternal.

The common man was less apt to hanker for austerities that he was only too well acquainted with. His daydream of the past was the one romanticised by Virgil, of a time when nature produced unbidden, and men enjoyed plenty without the curse of toil. It was compounded of the genuine fellowship of older days, and of modern wealth, the happiness of the rich man who neither toiled nor span and yet was arrayed like Solomon. A like illusion showed itself in the New Testament

15

maxim that men should take no thought for the morrow, but trust to luck. Primitive man to this day has had no need to be taught such fecklessness; it is fostered by habits of group life and dependence, which only the stern discipline of individual work and self-sufficiency has been able to counteract. A Frenchman living among Eskimos, in the harshest of environments, was astonished at their inability to practise self-restraint by rationing their food supply on a long journey.[2] Chinese communists found it hard to introduce tribesmen like those of the Cool Mountains to any orderly routine: they were accustomed to work by fits and starts, and as seldom as possible, and the notion of a team reckoning up its members' quota of labour and sharing the produce in proportion to work done struck them as mercenary, unfeeling.[3] Communism was having to bring them the work ethic of Calvinism or capitalism. Something of the same childlike irresponsibility was to be seen in the loafing Sicilian or Catholic Irishman of the last century, by contrast with the north Italian or the Ulsterman. Each type suffers from its own maladies, which socialism hopes to cure by merging the two in one.

2

Like nations, classes have perpetuated something of the old social bond of the undivided clan, though at the cost of mutual hostility. Each maintained or created forms of association within which their members could enjoy a sense of partial reabsorption into a community. Sparta's collective land-holding found a counterpart, on a far greater scale and in more complex forms, among the feudal ruling classes that emerged from Germanic tribal infiltration into the western Roman provinces. Feudal land ownership, by contrast with Roman property right, was indeterminate: the same acres belonged to a multiplicity of persons, with conjoint though very unequal claims; even the cultivators had some share. Monasteries and military orders were brotherhoods of members of the elite, holding land and buildings in trust. The same medieval spirit, of the privileged group leading its own corporate life, was to be seen in the town guilds and fraternities, which were professional associations and mutual benefit societies combined; they too owned collective endowments, much as the village had its common lands.

Templars and Teutonic Knights provided a model for the later officer corps of modern Europe, the Prussian above all, with their common table and identical costume; monasteries were to live on in colleges like those of Oxford and Cambridge, resolutely anti-socialist in our times while practising a version of socialism of their own. Aristocracy in modern Britain has herded together in the public school – in the exclusive club safeguarded by the democratic weapon of the blackball –

and in a semi nomadic lounging from country house to country house. Its men, though not its women (whether or not this proves women to have less of socialist instinct in them), learned to wear identical clothes every evening, a costume marking them out as society's officers or superiors. While the rich exchanged entertainment, the poor exchanged aid. The same custom of everyone within a social group being entitled to a share of whatever was going, which struck William Penn among the Red Indians,[4] likewise struck Dr Chalmers and his Kirk deacons exploring the bottomless poverty of Glasgow.[5] But the poor too have practised forms of social extravagance; a funeral in Lancashire, or a wedding in an Indian village — a feast due from the family to all its neighbours, the *baradari* or brethren. In all these shapes an ingrained collectivism, truncated and often rendered noxious by class division, can be seen asserting itself.

It was left to religion to prolong, in a more ghostly fashion, the lost integrity of the social whole. All the 'founded' religions have begun with an emphasis on their followers, as children of God, being of one family. Early Islam had a *bait-ul-mulk* or treasury of the people, replenished by plunder taken from non-Muslims. Christianity grew up with an exceptional measure of this 'social' sentiment, thanks to its complex inheritance of ideas, and its setting in a cosmopolitan society torn by class strife as well as strife of peoples, full of slaves and other expatriates to whom it offered a compensation for lost roots. Some of them in the early days pooled their resources and had common funds. Christianity was faithful to what may already at that date be called the European spirit, in being at once strongly individualist and strongly associationist; it endowed each man and woman with a precious soul, but this soul was to find salvation by doing good to fellow creatures. This helped to qualify the new faith presently for official adoption, and for eminent service as reconciler or harmoniser of classes, the prime social task in historical times of all religions.

This European religion was to be the parent or fosterparent of socialism, if a reluctant and even unnatural one. Not only did it preserve and deepen men's recognition of their interdependence, but more remarkably even if only abstractly, it also kept alive through many ages the belief, a legacy of the philosophers of antiquity, that private ownership was a corrupting innovation, and communal ownership the natural usage of mankind. Ideas when sanctioned by religion can have an astonishing tenacity. This one must have helped to keep the Church's conscience uneasy, and the duty of charity in mind. But the Church studied and prayed in a dead language, and presided over a society where literate and illiterate were very far apart. So far as carrying the principle into practice was concerned, it was satisfied with a symbolic, merely negative parade, the joint renunciation of wealth that monks were supposed to make. Monkish austerity seldom lasted long; and when envy of the rich by the poor sharpened, it was time for a more striking exhibition of voluntary poverty, as vicarious atonement for the sins of an unjust world. This was provided not by the clergy, but by St Francis, who dedicated himself from the moment of his conversion to the quest for *Sancta Paupertas,* as for a blessed lady.[6]

Embracing and idealising poverty, Francis tacitly rebuked envy or hatred of the rich. The Church would know how to exploit his cult, and turn it into one more device for bamboozling the poor and reconciling them to their lot. Meanwhile Aquinas, born in 1227, the year after Francis's death, came to the rescue of orthodoxy by explaining that communism was, indeed, the ideal, but had only been practicable in the state of innocence: in man's fallen condition its place must be taken by legally sanctioned private property.[7] Property was thus smuggled in as a regrettable necessity. A line of descent can be seen here from the thinking of the upper classes of antiquity, uneasy under the burden of their wealth; the Christian doctrine of man's sinfulness and fall from grace had offered them a sort of comfort. By the propertied classes of his own time Aquinas might well be hailed as the 'Angelic Doctor'. He was in a way anticipating the Marxist historical scheme of primitive communism followed by an era of private ownership, but he was ruling out its sequel, the return to communism on a higher level, discovering the modern objection, so dear to conservatives that human nature is not good enough.

3

Francis came to terms with the Church, and was rewarded with a title and a gaudy tomb. Other zealots refused to do so, and were persecuted as heretics;[8] to wealthy prelates any preaching of poverty sounded like a reproach. In the later Middle Ages there was a proliferation of sects with a leaning towards sharing of goods, or more frequently, towards rejection of any goods. The name of one of them, the 'Family of Love', is revealing. They were trying to hold on to the brotherliness of a social order partly remembered, partly imagined, in an epoch when it was being eaten away by the search for money and luxury. Their emotional fervour was kindled by the sight of selfish riches which seemed to show that all property, even the least, must in some degree corrupt men and set them against one another. In moods of religious exaltation stimulated by economic and social tension, acceptance of shared penury as the best of blessings, because it preserved human brotherhood, could be very potent.

But many ideas or sensations must have jostled together in discontented minds, among them the thought of relieving the rich of their superfluity in order to relieve the hunger of the poor. To the healthy materialism of the ordinary man, with his utopian daydreams of ease and plenty,[9] pauperism however spiritual would have little appeal. Its attractions may have been strongest for those already penniless. Rebels like Wat Tyler's men in England in 1381 had something to defend against their rulers. After the revolt John Ball, the democratic priest who took his Christianity too literally, was hanged. In the Hussite national resistance in Bohemia in the first half of the fifteenth century a species of war communism was practised by the most extreme faction. Social unrest and mystical doctrines often intertwined as the Middle Ages neared their end, as in southwest Germany. Mysticism has been serviceable to all religions, but also perturbing, because by removing barriers between man and God it may undermine those between man and man, and cast doubt on the solidest of them, private property.

In western Germany the disturbances which culminated in the Peasants' War of 1524-25 were largely, like the risings in England in the same period, a defence of village commons — pasture and woodland — against encroachments by the lords. In other words they were a defence of a socialist element embedded in the traditional economy, threatened now in Germany and elsewhere by neofeudalism, in England by nascent agricultural capitalism. Newer experiments in common ownership were tried by groups of craftsmen and mine workers, under pressure of nascent industrial capitalism such as had already provoked a blend of religious and social unrest in the Flemish manufacturing towns of the later Middle Ages. Anabaptism, that loose array of left-wing movements demanding a far more radical reformation of Church and Society than either Luther or Calvin contemplated, was hunted down everywhere. It was denounced for wanting abolition of private ownership, as well as for pacifism and other mortal errors. For good measure, Anabaptists were charged, like the early Christians they sought to emulate, with wanting wives in common as well, and with enjoying them in common during the outbreak at Munster in 1533 led by John of Leyden. Classes, like nations, have been fond of accusing each other of degrading women (a modern British critic of socialism maintained that it would turn women into 'brood mares').[10] Perhaps some sectaries really did hanker after communal marriage, if only because their women might be almost the only belongings left them to share. Whether for women this would have been a step towards or away from emancipation may be debatable.

4

The same epoch of groping and confusion that gave birth to modern capitalism was also giving birth to its antithesis, modern socialism, though this was to be pushed for long into the background. And if new forms of Christianity, notably Calvinism, were mixed up with the beginnings of capitalism, others had as close links with those of socialism. Fresh interest in common ownership, as the means to overcome men's perennial discords, showed itself in speculation among thinkers as well as in action by the people. The two were far apart, but socialism as a conception might unfold the more readily for this. It was turning away from archaic reverence for poverty towards the thought of common ownership for the sake of the well-being of the majority. This thought showed itself in the 'Utopias' that were being written in the sixteenth century, efforts — encouraged by the expansion of Europe's geographical horizons and contact with far-off civilizations — to transpose the never-forgotten golden age of legend into sketches of how society might be reconstituted.

More's *Utopia,* most famous of them all, was written in 1516. As a churchman employed by the State, More belonged to a type which might be said to float above private property in its ordinary manifestations: it was supported by public funds of diverse origin. Disgusted by the spectacle of rampant greed, and the expropriation of the English peasantry already under way, he repeated with renewed force the old conviction that private property was the root of all evil, that land (and everything else) should be collectivised. He was thus going far beyond the peasants, still struggling to defend their mixed economy. To Shakespeare, nearly a century later, Utopian bliss could be no more than amiable fantasy, like the worthy Gonzalo's talk for the amusement of his companions on Prospero's island about how he would direct a commonwealth, where all should enjoy plenty without toil. In the forest of Arden Shakespeare conjured up a retreat where men could 'fleet the time carelessly, as they did in the golden world', but he did not disguise the ruggedness of this flight to the wilderness. Yet no invective of reformers against human greed for wealth and power has ever gone beyond Shakespeare's in the tragedies; in *King Lear* above all his vision of the social problem, unsoftened either by hope of possible change or by religious illusion, is abysmally pessimistic.

It was in Catholic Europe, where capitalism was developing much more slowly, that religious illusions could loiter longest. More gave his life for the papacy, not for the peasantry, but he was a precursor of the Counter Reformation not only in its theology but in its social thinking, which revived here and there the old patristic mistrust of property. On this plane, ideas resembling those of Anabaptism could emerge at the opposite pole. Catholic writers reminded themselves that Christian tradition (like Islamic) regarded the land as belonging to God, and that it condemned private ownership as a man-made and malignant thing. In the Spain of the early seventeenth century, sinking into decay while landowners piled up huge estates and reduced the cultivators to pauperism, the churchman Pedro de Valencia called on the King to protect the poor against the rich, *los poderosos,* and to compel the proper cultivation of all land, even if it meant expropriating absentee owners and planting agricultural colonies.[11] Philip III had other things to do with his time. These finer flights of the Counter Reformation were bound to be ineffectual, because they were merely appeals to the conscience of the great, divorced from any protest by the poor. More wrote his *Utopia* in Latin. Once more Catholic revival was utilised, instead, by the rich to quieten the poor.

With the fading of the old order its collectivist ingredients were disappearing or shrinking. Unleashed individualism could not be held in check by any prophetic images of socialism drawn on the clouds; it was something more crude and earthy that arose in the sixteenth and seventeenth centuries, to impose limits and keep social conflict within bounds. This was the emergent modern State, most often in the guise of absolute monarchy. Equipped with standing army, secret police and firearms, and with greater coercive strength than any before, it was further fortified by close alliance with churches everywhere directed by it; with its aid these churches were themselves armed with a power of persecution — its acme the Spanish Inquisition — on a scale virtually unknown in history outside Europe. There could be no more complete negation of individualism than all this dragooning, no clearer illustration of how much else has to be sacrificed to untrammelled pursuit of happiness, when happiness means money. Yet the State and its ecclesiastical partner obscured the dominant economic interests which they largely served, and popular feeling could come to identify itself with them. Nationalism was far less natural or wholesome than the civic spirit of the old city-states, but it was growing far stronger than any sentiment resembling it outside western Europe. It could preserve, however distortedly, some part of a collectivist ethos which would one day help to make western Europe the cradle of practical socialism.

5

Human aspirations represented today by socialism have been in great measure constant through the ages, but the means men have looked to for their fulfilment have varied widely. For a long time after the opening of the modern era the belief that brotherhood among men requires community of wealth was overlaid by a new faith in private ownership and free enterprise. This could include a democratic leaven of peasant proprietorship, and fortunes, except in land, were still usually moderate. Mentally as well as economically the self-assertion of the individual was necessary for progress, but it was always haunted by a Faustian aura of guilt, of a primordial social compact violated. However heroically the new man has dramatised or romanticised himself, he has always suffered from misgivings about his wilful self-isolation; it has been the source of the travail, the *Angst,* of modern Europe. In the eighteenth century, whose laborious optimism hid a great deal of hypochondria, Pope tried to believe that there was no real contradiction, because Providence had bidden 'self-love and social be the same'.[12] Poetry was showing the way to laissez-faire economics, and reversing the old Christian tenet that a man could only do good to himself by serving others: he was now to do good to society by serving himself. Such sanctifying of egotism bore a resemblance to Paley's argument from design, which proved the existence of a benevolent Deity from the care he had taken to provide for his creatures' sustenance by arranging for them to eat one another.

In the bourgeois revolutions, in 1789 above all, the eagerness of an inchoate social order to appear as reconciler of personal and public welfare was carried to the most ambitious point. The messianic complexion of all grand revolutions, the desire of a class intoxicated by the sense of leadership to deem itself the vanguard of humanity, its own interests universal, is a familiar phenomenon. It is not all hypocrisy, for the bourgeois idealists who have inspired enthusiasm and made sacrifices were for the most part quite different men from the profiteers who carried off the spoils. 1789 may have opened the door to unrestricted capitalism, but its intentions were at least as much in harmony with socialism, and their frustration led at once to the first active attempt at socialism, the 'Conspiracy of the Equals' of 1796.

All the values that classical antiquity ascribed to its golden age, or to its noble savages, can be seen again in the three grand if vague watchwords of the Revolution. *Liberty* extended to various 'freedoms' that we have since then been compelled to distinguish more closely, among them 'freedom from want'. 'Tis against *that* that we are fighting', an ardent Frenchman exclaimed to Wordsworth as they watched a 'hunger-bitten girl' knitting with 'pallid hands' by the banks of the Loire, and Wordsworth joined him in looking forward to 'better days to all mankind'.[13] 'Equality' stood for another complex of associations, old and elemental or new and sophisticated. Burns with his 'A man's a man', Mozart's Sarastro with his call to every man 'to be a man', were paying tribute in almost the same words to the worth and the rights of the ordinary human being, which the Revolution undertook to vindicate; theirs was an individualism with higher, socialist overtones, like all the best in bourgeois ideology. In the subsequent passion of the middle-class Frenchman for equal civic and legal status it took on more cramped dimensions, behind which lay the glaring absence of any material equality. 'Fraternity', the third dimension of the Revolutionary trinity, was like that of the Christian hardest of all to define; yet it could be the most emotive and unbounded of all. The word 'brother' as used among Wesleyans or trade unionists perpetuates an older and commoner usage, still current in lands like India. In 1524 the German peasants argued that no man should be another's serf, because all men were children of God and therefore brothers. The kernel of George Eliot's humanist faith was a prayer for 'energy of human fellowship'.[14] It was an often repeated story among socialists in the late nineteenth century that a Communard prisoner, derisively asked by his captors what he was going to die for, answered: 'Pour la solidarité humaine'.[15]

Ideals soon to be taken up by socialism can be recognised among the quickly blighted hopes of 1789, alike in the microcosm of the family and the macrocosm of world relations. One of these aspirations was for a freer, more equal bond between men and women, and parents and children, with more even sharing of family goods. It found its way into the Civil Code, but was sadly warped by Thermidorean reaction and Bonapartist dictatorship. In 1789 the National Assembly formally renounced war as an instrument of policy, and Europe applauded. Nations like individuals, it was assumed, had only to be relieved of the incubus of monarchy and aristocracy to get on happily with one another ever after. In 1792 a far from unwilling French government took up a European challenge to war, and France embarked on two decades of conquest. It has been left to socialism to fulfil all such disappointed hopes; it is the New Testament that supersedes all old ones — though like all scriptures, it is still a very incomplete one.

6

In the Paris of Georges Sand, she says, sooner or later in any conversation someone would say: 'Posons la question sociale'. It was the social problem engendered by industrial revolution, along with a new proletariat, and a new concreteness and immediacy of the socialist idea. This could not blossom in the countryside, even in England with its unique capitalist agriculture; though after it appeared it could be received eagerly by some rural workers, like the gangs of labourers on the *latifundia* of Andalusia. The rise of large-scale capitalist industry to a dominant place in the economy was polarising society on fresh lines, and bringing in sight a possible future of machines owned and worked for the good of all. This could not only reduce labour and increase well-being, but could constitute a new bond of combination among men, and at the same time a release from the servitude of the factory run for private profit.

Socialism was indeed as obviously necessary, once steam machinery came in, as the replacement of private armies by a single armed force of the State had been three centuries before, when gunpowder came in.

Without the driving force of private profit industrialism might have spread much more slowly, but in a far more orderly, rational style. Yet after another century and a half, in most of the world socialism is still only knocking at the door – in many countries, like Britain, not very insistently.

The idea made its way spasmodically, here quickly, there more sluggishly, and frequently taken up only to be forgotten. It had attractions for both the more progressive (morally progressive) of the educated classes, and the new working class, but they were still – like their ancestors, and too often their descendants – far apart, and each weakened by the lack of contact. Among the literate, some of the pioneers had no notion of converting society to their views, but like the Anabaptists before them were separating themselves from it, to make a life of their own. Disillusion following the too sanguine hopes of 1789 helped to inspire small groups to retreat as far as the American wilderness where the socialist cream of the Revolutionary milk could, so to speak, be strained off. Two years before Babeuf's Conspiracy of the Equals, the youthful Southey and Coleridge were planning a 'Pantisocratic' settlement beyond the Atlantic, whose name proclaimed the same principle. These Utopias had a long lease; as late as 1881 we find a socialist refugee from Germany joining a colony in Tennessee, but soon quitting it.[16]

When it was time to think of remodelling society, instead of hiding from it in little oases, it was tempting to suppose that socialism could come about by peaceful penetration, here and there. That was, after all, how capitalism had been and still was developing. Cooperation, or 'Association', seems to have been the original meaning of socialism when the word came into use in the 1820s. It could be started by small groups, but these would be living among their neighbours, and trusting to force of example to bring others eventually to emulate them, leaving capitalism to wither away. Only while industrial technology was still rudimentary could the programme be at all realistic; after this stage socialism could only be established by the taking over of existing factories and mines. Another 'Utopian' thought was of socialist measures, sweetened by a religious infusion, being adopted by governments, in the spirit of the enlightened autocrats of the eighteenth century, just as they could be induced to assist capitalism. Saint-Simon's disciples made some impression on Napoleon III, when in his days of exile he was looking round for a cure for the social problem, a nostrum to be his passport to the throne. They even thought it worth while to make approaches (so she told Kinglake) to that minor autocrat Lady Hester Stanhope, self-appointed ruler of a patch of the fabled East.[17] In China the same impulse showed itself when the reformer K'ang Yu-wei sketched out in 1884-85 a Utopian programme of universal peace, emancipation of women, and socialism.[18] A dozen years later he tried to carry it out, with the support of a youthful emperor; the latter was promptly dethroned, the reformer had to take flight.

Working-class responses were equally variegated. Capitalism took on differing complexions in different regions, under the influence of their past and of their social structure, and its proletariat, which Marxism was to think of too much as everywhere one and the same, was in reality at least as diverse. Neither self-conscious classes nor their political parties can come into being without a heavy admixture of features carried over from earlier times, or moulded by national temperament. The ironclad socialism of the Third International was to be very much the offspring of the First World War, and could only have grown from a soil as stony, as indurated to battle and martial discipline, as Europe's; outside Europe it has transplanted itself with most success in the Far East, in so many ways a second Europe by comparison with the rest of Asia. In the formative years of capitalism much, in the reactions of any work-force to industrial conditions and in its receptivity to socialist thinking, depended on how far it was made up of women and children; on its national or religious composition, which might be as little uniform as in Glasgow or Manchester or eastern France; on how many recruits were coming straight from the village, and what their status there had been, and what they had known of agrarian resistance; and on how many had been craftsmen. It would be affected also by the extent to which other artisans managed to hang on to their independence, as they did in London or Paris. All this heterogeneity of the labouring masses, in the crucial first generation or two, did as much as anything else to allow capitalism to consolidate its position.

7

Before the end of the 1820s there was 'an indigenous English Socialism', and writers like Gray and Hodgskin had 'laid down the main lines of Socialist thought'.[19] In England as elsewhere the movement was taking shape on two levels, which have never come very close together, that of the mainly middle-class thinkers — or dreamers — and that of the working people. Among the workers there was a medley of jostling sects, a millennarian ferment with all sorts of freakish religious notions once more mixed up in it,[20] heaven and earth churning together as in one of Turner's landscapes. Little by little amid this turmoil there dawned first a longing to destroy the machines before these monsters could gain sway over mankind — then an ambition to win control over the monsters, and make Steam a boon to all instead of an enrichment to a few.

Heaven and earth jostled together in the mind of Robert Owen, an outstanding 'Utopian' in every sense of the term, who did nevertheless drift towards a recognition that the blight of capitalism would have to be eliminated to make the world safe for something better. He drifted therefore into collaboration with a young trade union movement, a few of whose leaders envisaged the overthrow of capitalism by means of a general strike. But by this time British capitalism was so firmly in the saddle that to overthrow it must mean also overturning the State. William Morris was to dwell on Owen's failure to understand the impracticability of hopes like his 'as long as there is a privileged class in possession of the executive power'.[21] This country's relatively low concentration of State authority helped to conceal its decisive importance from socialists, most of whom have never yet fully opened their eyes to it; whereas over most of the continent the bureaucratic, military structure could no more be overlooked than the pyramid of Cheops in its desert. Local amateur magistrates, Yeomanry, special constables, could provoke class resentment without this crystallising into political hostility to the class State.

Chartists did recognise the vital need of political power for any new social dispensation. Many of them, however, when they thought of social change looked backward rather than forward. They wanted to resettle the people on the land, giving each family a farm of its own. This seems strangely atavistic, considering how long it was since most Englishmen had possessed any land. Peasant proprietorship was particularly dear to Feargus O'Connor, and one may wonder how much of its popular appeal entered England with the flood of immigrants from peasant Ireland, a country of land-hungry rack-rented tenants. The British Isles had to wrestle with the ailments of several eras of history at the same time. Later leaders of Chartism like Harney and Ernest Jones reached more modern and socialist conceptions, not without some help from Marx, but they came too late, when the mass movement was about to crumble. After 1850 industrial capitalism in Britain was strong enough to enforce acquiescence, flourishing enough to win it by doling out its proceeds a trifle more liberally, but above all perhaps established for long enough to achieve it by simple force of habit. The chaotic protest it aroused when its whips and scorpions were new died down as it became a thing of use and wont, and could seem the only imaginable mode of life. Socialism as an alternative had been a compound of many remnants of social life and experience now fading into the past. It was painfully slow to develop a new, autonomous consciousness; in this it has been more tardy than the march of capitalist technology, always lagging at least a stage behind.

8

Marx and Engels were fixing their hopes on the working class before the defeat of the revolutions of 1848 on the continent, and of Chartism in England. When they worked out their doctrine, in the following years, it was to counteract a mood of failure, by furnishing a guarantee of ultimate success for socialism, as well as to exorcise 'Utopian' notions about socialism arriving by amiable agreement. Their 'scientific' teaching fused economics and politics. Its essence was the conviction that socialism must come, not from men acquiring any ideal preference for it, or resenting capitalist injustice, but because capitalism would be brought by the laws of its own nature to the point of collapse, and thus enable, or compel, the working class to put socialism in its place. It followed, or seemed to follow, that socialist teaching ought to be addressed to the working class alone. Others might sentimentalise, but only a class driven by economic compulsion could be the reliable vehicle of change. Part of this calculation was that the working class was destined to become a bigger and bigger part of the total, as the strata above it were proletarianised each in their turn, and that it would be burdened with increasingly unbearable conditions. As things have turned out, the manual working class has come to be a diminishing part of the population, in America less than half, and conditions have not forced it willy-nilly towards socialism. Its worst miseries, those brought by wars, have been shared with other classes, and capitalism's responsibility for them has been successfully disguised by its apologists.

Marxism always disclaimed any necessitarian belief in revolution coming of its own accord, but it was led by its 'scientific' logic into some undervaluing, not of the factor of human will, but of the ideas and ideals, the emotional wants left by religion and many other things of the past, which are needed to create the will to socialism. All these it was too much inclined to ignore as Utopian fancies. In the process, intellect and emotion were too strictly set apart. Countless men and women have been able to identify themselves with the Marxist cause (though not always for very long) by an unconscious blending of their own emotions with its rigorous argumentation — as Marx himself must have done; the mass of mankind, and of the working class, may have required something more romantic, such as religion or patriotism offered. Tom and Dick are as much Don Quixote as Sancho Panza, and readier to follow rainbows and will-o'-the-wisps, crusades or football pools, than sober sense.

Earlier on Marx had made a forecast which turned out to be correct, but which later Marxism has never taken adequate account of: that in all coming social revolutions the petty-bourgeoisie would play its part.[22] Unlike Calvin, who confined salvation to the chosen, Marx looked to socialism to enfranchise all mankind, by abolishing all classes. But in counting on the working class to perform the task virtually single-handed, he was making another dichotomy, akin to that between thought and feeling. There may have been a miscalculation here on a par with Mazzini's belief that Italy could free itself unaided. Marxism has had a keener eye for the weaknesses than for the better qualities of the middle classes. In the shadow of 1848 and the years that followed, when everyone from millowners to professors displayed a timid incapacity to complete their own bourgeois revolution, it must have seemed hard to suppose that any of them would ever be useful allies in the struggle for a socialist revolution. In any case most of them were supposed to be doomed to disintegration and absorption into the proletariat.

Marx and Bismarck both dismissed the middle-class 'ideologues' from history with something like the same contempt, as mere blowers of soap-bubbles. Certainly among such an assemblage as Owen's respectable well-wishers, cranks and religious oddities abounded,[23] and it has often been the case at other times when middle- and lower-class progressives have been in conjunction. Yet the Utopian sects proved at least that there was an instinctive hunger for socialism among some of the middle, or literate, strata, as well as among the workers; that they too harboured aspirations which socialism alone could realise. They were dreaming, that is, of betterments in the human condition that their own historical trajectory could never bring about; all their idealists, from Hamlet on, suffered an acute sense of social disharmony, of the times being out of joint with no remedy in sight. And the paradox remains that Marx was devoting his best energies to a book which only very well-educated readers would ever understand, while he was impatient of efforts by self-taught workmen to devise a philosophy for themselves. Late in life Engels lamented a proneness of the workers to 'ineradicable suspicion against any schoolmaster, journalist, and any man generally who was not a manual worker as being an "erudite" who was out to exploit them'.[24] He considered that it was being left behind by then, but to this day it has never been fully overcome; and Marxism with its depreciation of everything 'bourgeois' must be said to have helped to foster the prejudice. In this alienation of classes lay another disunity that has helped capitalism — 'With all its crimes broad blown, as flush as May' — to divide and rule, to prolong its reign and multiply its ill-gotten gains.

9

Marxism shared with the later phase of Chartism the fate of appearing on the scene when in Britain a tide of mass militancy was about to ebb. Having been pioneer first of machine industry, then of the first struggles to get rid of it or to take it into custody, this country was to lead the way in reconciling itself to capitalism. Disputes over wages and hours could be energetic without threatening to upset the system. Similarly in the Middle Ages dogged defense of rights by a peasantry rooted in the soil was of a different character from the more desperate revolts of the disinherited. As time went on, indeed, trade union pressure could stimulate the economy into expansion, instead of paralysing it, by compelling it to widen its home market.

A brief fresh glow of socialist enthusiasm was marked by the founding in 1881 of Hyndman's Social Democratic Federation, which Morris joined in 1883 and left two years later to start his Socialist League. It was the time when cyclists made weekend forays into the countryside with leaflets to stick on cows' horns, for the edification presumably of farm labourers. Belfort Bax rejoiced in the thought that socialist ideas were finding their way even into the trade unions. 'The solid front of true British stupidity, of which, unfortunately, hitherto, they have been the embodiment, has at length, to say the least, been broken.'[25] But the antidote was to hand in the Fabian Society, formed in 1884, which speedily guided the movement back into safe conventional channels. One of its hallmarks was a thick-skinned indifference to foreign and imperial affairs; the same attitude has always been typical of British labour.

When Kautsky lived in England in the early 1890s he gained the worst possible impression of the working class, as more apathetic and inert even than in Russia; incapable of rousing itself to anything higher than football or horse racing, because it had renounced the goal of a transformation of society in favour of mere bread-and-butter 'practical politics', and by so doing had given up its soul.[26] Renewed combativeness in the years before 1914 was soon to show that British workers were anything but inert or submissive, but no economic struggles can rise, except in the moment of conflict itself, above a certain height. They could be no substitute for the sense of historical mission that Marxism had sought to kindle. Instead the working class was turning in on itself, forming an Estate with a culture and social life of its own, coexisting with the capitalist realm. In short, it was relapsing into 'labourism'.

'Utopian' habits of mind of one sort lived on in the political attitudes of what it would be a misnomer to call a 'movement', in the Labour Party's easy confidence in its ability to extract socialist tunes from the capitalist hurdygurdy, or turn the grizzly into a tame performing bear by a wave of the electoral wand. John Strachey remarked on the propensity of British and American socialism to forget all lessons of history, all hard-won ideas, and be obliged to start from scratch over and over again.[27] (He was soon to forget some of them himself.) This is only a special case of the inability of men in the mass to remember and profit by experience: we retain only the most generalised impressions, and have very little hold on the facts or events that gave birth to them. While capitalism has had a continuous development, and piled up an armoury

of argument and expedient as well as a mountain of profit, socialism
has come and gone, wearing all kinds of guises. This may have conferred
on it each time renewed hopeful freshness, but has also rendered it
liable to youthful illusions. Marxism has maintained continuity at some
cost in over-fidelity to obsolescent ideas.

10

Rulers and ruling classes did not sponsor socialism, as optimists had
expected them to do, but in face of the danger of socialism making its
way without them they were edging towards the 'State socialism'
patronised by Napoleon III and adopted by Bismarck, the 'collectivism'
fashionable in late nineteenth-century England. 'We are all socialists
now', said Vernon Harcourt with humorous resignation. This was the
starting-point of our Welfare State, the most effective substitute for
socialism yet invented, often reminiscent of the philosopher's maxim
in ancient China: 'Fill the people's bellies and empty their minds.'[28]
It was a secularised rendering of the old religious acceptance of a duty
of the rich to take some care of the poor, combined with the feudal
paternalism not yet extinct in Europe's aristocracies. When Winston
Churchill as a bright young Liberal politician toured Uganda on a
bicycle, the duke's grandson indulged in a benign flight of fancy about
this secluded bit of Africa as the right place for a trial of socialism, with
all selfish money-grubbing businessmen kept out. 'The first, and perhaps
the greatest, difficulty which confronts the European Socialist', he
observed (and history must be said to bear out his words), 'is the
choosing of Governors to whom the positively awful powers indispensable to a communistic society are to be entrusted.' In Uganda there
could be no such obstacle, for it already possessed in its British officials
a perfect set of governors — perfect because as aloof from their subjects
as H.G. Wells' invaders from Mars.[29]

Europe it may be remarked was frequently disposed to look at itself
like this in the mirror of a wider world. When the western hemisphere
was discovered, reports of its tribal customs reinforced the conception
of communal ownership as being part of the law of Nature. When
Marxism was mobilising its arguments it soon delved into primitive
society, as well as into history, for evidences of a prehistoric communism
of which modern socialism was to be the dialectical completion. Anti-
socialist anthropology took up the challenge. Earlier on there had been
a preoccupation with untutored man's notions about God, now there
was more concern with his view of property. Conservatives in every
country have liked to think of socialism as an alien importation (as all
patriots have liked to think of sundry diseases) and they were anxious
to confirm from the behaviour of man in the state of nature that

socialism was unnatural. To the same observers nothing has appeared more 'natural' than the Stock Exchange, or the House of Lords. In mid-century China they could not fail to notice and dislike symptoms of a rough and ready communism in the programme of the great Taiping rebellion;[30] and in our epoch Western determination to suppress any growth of communism in the backlands by armed force marks a continuation of the academic debate about primitive society with new weapons.

Catholic Europe in the last century was less fully exposed to industrialism, and its reaction to it amounted to nothing more constructive than 'Christian Socialism', a species of feudal demagogy laughed at in the Communist Manifesto. (Today we are told of an 'Islamic' and even a 'Buddhist Socialism' of even cloudier complexion.) It resurrected the social teaching of the Counter Reformation, but in a still more abstract, unmeaning fashion. Which way it was likely to turn under stress was made clear by the spread of 'clerical fascism' in the late 1920s and 1930s; and 'welfare' societies, of the more undemocratic or 'Martian' type at least, have been all too ready to lurch in the same direction. William Morris foretold something very like fascism in his picture of the 'Friends of Order' banding together to crush social revolt,[31] much as Jack London foretold it a few years later with his 'Iron Heel'.[32] If socialism is the legitimate heir of the bourgeois revolution on its ideal side, the inheritor in our times of its sordid impulses, its violences, has been fascism. But this too has been a perverted species of socialism, as its title in Germany implied. It was a socialism for the middle classes, morbidly divided from and set against the working classes, but wanting, like them (though by very different means) to break out from the crisis of an anarchic egotism and find shelter within some organic society. There the workers themselves, after submitting to the loss of their selfish trade unions and parties, and being forcibly merged in the *Volksgemeinschaft,* would have their modest share of the rewards.

In the long run the masses were intended to get their share out of the loot of foreign lands. Nazi imperialism had a barbarian analogue in the tribe, when it took to preying on its neighbours. War has always owed much of its charm to its power in bringing men closer together: in an army at war both food and danger have to be shared, and all its members dress alike and strive for the same ends. It was in modern Germany that the doctrines both of socialist internationalism and of the armed people, the nation in arms, grew most readily. They were rivals, but also mutual reinforcements. Fascism has been the climax of all the diseased striving of modern Europe towards an artificial restoration of social union.

11

In the sharp air of 1938, when his Marxism was at its keenest, John

Strachey found fault with Fabians for putting the socialist case on grounds 'humanitarian, moral and aesthetic, rather than scientific or economic'; and for addressing it to all classes, instead of specifically to the working class.[33] Such an attitude has been recurrent at times when great events have been in the making. Talk about ethics and human duties has then seemed, as it did to Kirk zealots in Scotland, no better than 'a blether of cold morality'. In other, less urgent hours dogma has been felt to matter less, moral considerations more. But arguments like those Strachey deprecated have not always gone with a watered-down socialism. If Fabians used them, so did William Morris. And in a press interview in 1893 Engels jubilantly asserted that in Germany 'our ideas make headway everywhere, as much among teachers, lawyers, etc. as among the workers. Tomorrow, if we had to take over power, we should need engineers, chemists, agronomists. Well, I am convinced that we should already have a great many with us.'[34] In practical politics Engels was anything but a doctrinaire.

To call up new horizons something wider is needed than the self-concern of either a class or a nation. On the whole, socialism in Europe has been allowed to appear too closely linked to a single class and its bread and butter, or beer and tobacco; and paradoxically, a class not always showing much interest in it and scarcely entitled — or eager — to speak for all. Bax looked on the socialist workman as, by virtue of his socialist enlightenment, rising above his narrower class self to shoulder human aspirations at large;[35] but this workman has remained an exception, and 'labourism' has not been confined to Britain. On the other side, in the student or youth movements of recent years something of the inveterate confused excitement of middle-class efforts for progress has shown itself once again, fed by a curious medley of grievances over trifles and fundamental discontents. With all this, partnerships across class boundaries have continued to be fumbling and ineffective.

A way forward must take account of Europe's perennial groping towards a balance between individual and collective, a harmonious development of both. At various times our unstable continent has gone to both extremes in sacrificing one to the other, but in its healthier moods it has recoiled. It censures an aberration to which it is more liable itself than Asia, when it condemns 'Asiatic uniformity', the spirit of the ant heap. Its intellectuals have felt as strongly as its plutocrats a horror of being swallowed up in an anonymous mass. With well-educated Germany in mind, Kautsky could be hopeful of this reproach to socialism fading, in face of 'the rapid and unbroken rise of the proletariat in moral and intellectual relations'. Half a century before, he admitted, even socialist intellectuals might fear, as all the bourgeoisie did after the Paris Commune, that the coming to power of the proletariat would be a barbarian invasion, bringing a new Dark Age.[36] Some similar advance must be hoped for again, but a broader and deeper one.

So far as the ant heap — instead of chaos — is concerned, we may trust that individuality is by now sufficiently adult to dispense with the artificial brace of the ownership of fields or factories. Most men have always had to do without it; and for the majority to let their economic life be run by a few is as much an abnegation of responsibility as to let political life be run by monarchs or dictators, or moral life by bishops. We may also recall that just as the 'liberal' outlook has always contained a dash of social thinking, in the working-class outlook there has always been a dose of individualism, a hatred of factory regimentation and the reduction of craft skill to mechanical repetition. This disgust is being revived in our day by the spread of automation. An assembly belt is closer even than a barrack drill ground to the 'Asian ant heap'. Generations of embittered artisans looked to cooperation or socialism to deliver them from enslavement to the machine; and today socialism ought to be better able than capitalism to guide industrial life away from this nightmare.

Forms of workers' control will be needed as well as technological changes. Ownership of all means of production by the State, as proposed by Marxism, is no doubt essential, but it has had a forbidding look to workers as well as others: syndicalism, guild socialism, have expressed the desire to belong to a small tangible community, instead of to the 'broad masses' that Marxism has been too fond of talking about. Stalin was making a far too mechanical distinction, as he and many others often did, in his polemic against Anarchism, which invites comparison with Calvin's against Anabaptism. 'The cornerstone of Anarchism', he wrote, 'is the *individual,* whose emancipation, according to its tenets, is the principal condition for the emancipation of the masses . . . The cornerstone of Marxism, however, is the *masses*, whose emancipation, according to its tenets, is the principal condition for the emancipation of the individual.'[37]

Morris was again seeing clearly into the future when he foresaw a capitalist world where all human values will be debased and 'the earth's surface will be hideous everywhere, save in the uninhabitable desert'.[38] With this other nightmare, on its physical side if no more, we have lately been coming face to face. There has been looming up too the prospect of exhaustion of raw materials, and, between this danger and that of global pollution, the prospect that capitalism is leading us into a blind alley, or across a broken bridge; that it *must* be working out its own nemesis, as Marx prophesied, though not for Marx's reasons. All this affects all classes (much of it affects all industrial civilizations, capitalist or other), and ought to convince anyone not shackled to vested interests of the necessity of thoroughgoing change. It may be that the evolution of the human race has not equipped it to disentangle itself from such a situation, and that even *in extremis* only an ineffective minority will try, amid the labyrinth of official deception and mystification, bribery and corruption, force and intimidation. If there is to be any hope, it must depend on a reawakening of ideas and ideals, the common inheritance to a great extent of the middle and working classes which Marx, himself steeped in them, took for granted or left in the shade in his 'scientific' *schema*. Engels wasted time when he tried to apply the laws of social dialectics to the inanimate world; and to scan human affairs by the measuring rod of physical science is equally futile. Marxism counting on the working class, but this, too much turned in on itself, is evidently in need of fresh inspiration; though it remains true that no progressive impulses outside it will get very far if they are not in league with a strong and intelligent mass movement.

Middle-class man in the West has lost most of his religious ideology; ironically, Christianity and socialism have been drooping together, and the new-old faith of humanism has a message for both. Christianity has been catching fire again, here and there in the world, from contact with socialism, or with the problems that socialism brings forward; but socialism is in need of intercourse with the Christian ethic that ushered it into the world. 'Materialism' in the sense of mindless egotism is as much an enemy of socialism as materialism in a philosophic sense of religion. Many older socialists or communists now living (how many, it would be worth while to enquire) came from religious backgrounds, Christian or Jewish; not a few of them have found themselves wondering whether a new generation, of whatever class, growing up cut off from it, will be likely to feel as they have done.

Rosa Luxemburg declared long ago that socialism could not be reached without a great moral renewal, which she feared Bolshevik rigidity might hinder.[39] Communist China with its small working class has been obliged to rely more heavily on human will and idealism. Its Cultural Revolution has been at bottom a design for a vast moral rebirth; it has sought to persuade hundreds of millions that they can live better and more happily by agreeing to live as one great family — to make real what religions have only dreamed of. Cabral in his little corner of Africa, with scarcely any working class to take part in the rising against the Portuguese, confronted a still more acute dilemma. There was only a petty-bourgeoisie with 'the historical opportunity of leading the struggle', but this class could 'strengthen its revolutionary consciousness' only by aligning itself with a working class. His final conclusion was that 'if national liberation is essentially a political problem, the conditions for its development give it certain characteristics which belong to the sphere of morals'.[40] These cautious words can be repeated more boldly about every progressive cause everywhere.

34

12

When 'revolutionary' socialism is talked of, either of two meanings may
be intended: the aim of a sudden catastrophic overthrow of the old
order, or a reconstruction of society that may be slow and piecemeal
but will in the end be all-embracing. As to the first, European socialism
for the most part settled down early to acceptance of patient legal
methods, in contrast with middle-class Liberalism which, often in
alliance with national revolt, had a long and adventurous history of
plots and uprisings; they find an echo today in the student movement,
with its taste for direct action. In other regions socialism has displayed
a similar fighting spirit, often again in partnership with national
rebellions, because there it has been allowed no choice. To Marxists it
has often appeared that radical change could only be brought about
suddenly; slow sapping and mining may be unable to rouse the required
fervour. Soviet experience may suggest, on the other hand, that forcible
seizure of power, against not merely the will of the few, but a large dead
weight of inertia or conservatism as well, must perpetuate evil features
of the old order, beginning with a secret police. Idealistic socialism
curdled into Stalinism, as naive Anabaptism was superseded by
authoritarian Lutheranism and Calvinism.

It is another good reason for spreading socialism as widely as may be
among the middle classes before it comes to power, that once in power
it seems to find it harder to convince them. Altogether, the task of
fitting men's minds and dispositions to a genuine new life has turned
out to be a much harder one than socialism expected. China's self-
imposed and heroic, if at times freakish ordeal, the Cultural Revolution,
was recognition that genuine socialism can only be built from below, by
a people roused to wish and work for a new society. At the opposite
pole is what E.P. Thompson, speaking of Robert Owen's paternalism,
has called in one of his many happy phrases 'planning society as a
gigantic industrial panopticon'.[41] That Owen and Stalin thought so much
alike suggests that the antithesis of 'Utopian' and 'scientific' socialism —
in many ways an unsatisfactory one — has less meaning than that of
'artificial'and 'organic'.

H.G. Wells in 1905 sounded extraordinarily like a forerunner of Mao
when he insisted that socialism was no mere 'odd little jobbing about
municipal gas and water', but meant 'revolution', 'a change in the
everyday texture of life. It may be a very gradual change, but it will be
a very complete one.'[42] There was a blind thirst in Europe for some
sweeping change, some apocalypse; the middle classes, straggling along
their road towards war and fascism, were fascinated by Nietzsche's
gospel of a 'transvaluation of all values', his fantasy of a transfigured
mankind with its economic system untouched. Fabians and kindred

'reformists', oblivious of all transcendental goals, suffocated socialism under the plodding humdrum business, the 'little jobbing', of today and tomorrow. A Dutch social democrat has eloquently dwelt on the loss of dedication and fire that overtook socialism when it exchanged the image of a new heaven and a new earth for the mess of pottage of small repairs to an old, worn-out dwelling. 'Socialism's worst enemy is its own cultural blindness and deafness.'[43] He reproached Marxist 'scientific' formulas with helping to cripple it by darkening its vision of Utopia, the very thing to which it owed and still owes its own 'tremendous and revolutionary influence'.[44] More recently E.P. Thompson has written of how the New Left endeavoured 'to rehabilitate the utopian energies within the socialist tradition'.[45]

In 1898 Bernstein told the German Socialist Party that he no longer credited any sudden coming collapse of capitalism, but that he still held to the aim of the conquest of political power.[46] His doubts were repudiated, and he and his associates failed to discover an alternative route. In effect Western communism since 1945 has been setting itself the same purpose as Bernstein's, of keeping alive the goal of a fundamental renovation of society and all human relationships, while discarding the prospect of a cataclysmic transition. How far it has been or will be able to keep clear of the creeping parochial numbness that goes with philosophies of gradualism, is still to be decided. It may fortify confidence to recall that socialism in its human essence was a fact long before it was an idea; it is already very old, private ownership by comparison newfangled, capitalism a usurper of yesterday.

NOTES

1. M.Beer, *A History of British Socialism* 1929 vol.1, p.3.
2. G.de Poncins, *Kabloona* 1942, p.101.
3. See A.Winnington, *The Slaves of the Cool Mountains* 1959. Cf. the passage of Virgil in *Georgics*, I, 121 ff. – in strong contrast with Eclogue IV – where Jove terminates the golden age in order to force men to toil, suffer, invent and develop.
4. William Penn, *Pennsylvania . . . a General Description* 1683, XIX.
5. Thomas Chalmers, *Problems of Poverty* ed. H.Hunter, 1912, pp.342 ff.
6. See the *Sacrum Commercium,* written by a disciple of Francis, para.1,2. When the saint went to the 'optimates et sapientes' he was roughly repulsed, and his ideas declared 'nova . . . doctrina' (para.3).
7. Beer, *op.cit.,* vol. 1, p.14.
8. See Chaps. II, III of Rev.M.Kaufmann, *Socialism and Communism* 1883, a work reflecting the revived interest of its period in socialism.
9. See A.Morton, *The English Utopia* 1952, especially Chaps.1,2.
10. Quoted in H.G.Wells, *New Worlds for Old* 1908, p.192.
11. See Pedro de Valencia, *Escritos Sociales* ed.C.Vinas y Mey, 1945.

12. *Essay on Man,* Epistle III, 318.
13. *The Prelude,* Book IX.
14. J.W.Cross, *George Eliot's Life* 1885, vol.III, p.141.
15. E.B.Bax, *The Ethics of Socialism* 2nd ed.,n.d.,p.19.
16. *George Gissing and H.G.Wells* Correspondence, ed.R.A.Gettmann, 1961,p.49n.
17. A.W.Kinglake, *Eothen* 1844, Chap.8. Lady Hester seemed to have some notion of becoming 'mystic mother' to the Saint-Simonian sect, but on this she bound him to 'eternal silence'.
18. See V.Purcell, *The Boxer Uprising* 1963, pp.102 ff.
19. R.H.Tawney, Introduction to Beer, *op.cit.,* p.xviii.
20. E.P.Thompson, *The Making of the English Working Class* 1965, pp.799 ff.
21. William Morris, *Signs of Change* 1888, pp.102-3.
22. Marx, letter to P.V. Annenkov, 28 Dec.1846.
23. Thompson, *op.cit.,* pp.797-8.
24. Engels, 'On the History of Early Christianity', in *K.Marx and F.Engels on Religion* 1957, p.319.
25. Bax, *op.cit.,* p.iv.
26. Karl Kautsky, *The Social Revolution* English ed., 1916, pp.100-2.
27. J.Strachey, *What Are We to Do?* 1938, p.114.
28. Quoted in W.A.P.Martin, *Hanlin Papers* 1st series, 1881, p.99.
29. W.S.Churchill, *My African Journey* 1908, pp.71-2 reprint, 1972.
30. W.S.Gregory, *Great Britain and the Taipings* 1969, p.158, discounts the argument that it was the socialist of the Taipings that turned the West against them. But some Western strictures which he cites suggest that the argument has some force.
31. See William Morris, *News from Nowhere* 1890.
32. See Jack London, *The Iron Heel* 1907.
33. Strachey, *op.cit.,* pp.83, 90.
34. *Correspondence* of Engels with Paul and Laura Lafargue, vol.3 (n.d.), p.394.
35. Bax, *op.cit.,* pp.102-3.
36. Kautsky, *op.cit.,* pp.44-5.
37. J.Stalin, *Anarchism or Socialism?* English ed., 1950, pp.9-10.
38. Morris, *Signs of Change* pp.138-9; cf. p.29.
39. Rosa Luxemburg, *The Russian Revolution* 1918; English ed., 1961, p.71.
40. *Selected Texts by Amilcar Cabral. Revolution in Guinea* 1969, pp.88-90.
41. Thompson, *op.cit.,* p.781.
42. H.G.Wells, 'This Misery of Boots' 1905; (turned into a Fabian tract, 1907), Section V.
43. F.L.Polak, *The Image of the Future* 1961, vol.II, pp.309,322. Cf. p.326: 'the childlike and eternal longing for human fulfilment in another and better future is basic to man's mental structure'.
44. *Ibid.,* p.308.
45. E.P.Thompson, 'An Open Letter to Leszek Kolakowski', in *The Socialist Register, 1973* ed.R.Miliband and J.Saville, p.1.
46. E.Bernstein, *Evolutionary Socialism. A. Criticism and Affirmation* 1899; English ed., 1961, p.xxiv.

2 MARX'S THEORY OF MAN

Bhikhu Parekh

Marx's theory of man can be best seen as an attempt to integrate the radical humanism of Fichte and Hegel on the one hand, and the naturalism of Feuerbach on the other. Fichte and Hegel were right, Marx thought, to place man in the centre of the universe and to see history as a process of man's self-creation. Following Feuerbach, however, he objected to their attempt to identify man with his consciousness and to explain human history in terms of its independent dialectical movement. It is man who possesses consciousness and not the other way round, and therefore not human self-consciousness and Absolute Spirit but the sensuous, empirical man which ought to be made the explanatory principle of history. Since Fichte and Hegel took a 'topsy-turvy', 'Idealistic' and 'speculative' view of man their account of human history remained abstract and false. Further, since they denied the reality of nature, human freedom, which they so cherished, lacked a medium of objectification and therefore remained illusory and unreal. Marx thought that Feuerbach's naturalism avoided the Idealist mistake and was more satisfactory. It acknowledged man's essentially sensuous nature, recognised his membership of the natural world, and stressed the empirical basis of all human knowledge. However Feuerbach's naturalism was static and unhistorical, and did not recognise that both nature and man were constantly evolving. It took a passive and 'contemplative' view of man and did not stress man's power to create both himself and nature. It remained unable to explain human history. A view of man was therefore needed, Marx seems to have thought, that satisfied two conditions. First, it must combine the valid humanistic insights of Fichte and Hegel and the naturalistic and empirical orientation of Feuerbach. Second, it must combine them not mechanically but dialectically; that is, it must not combine them in the 'insipid' (Marx's favourite expression) spirit of 'Bourgeois' compromise but in a truly dialectical manner. What Marx meant was that it must be a view of man in which humanism and naturalism interpenetrate, so that it is not merely humanistic *and* naturalistic but humanistic in its naturalism and naturalistic in its humanism. Marx set about to develop such a view.

To anticipate, Marx viewed man basically as a dialectical unity of certain powers or qualities that he shares with other beings in the universe, and certain others that are unique to him. In Marx's own language, man is a dialectical unity of his natural and human being or essence. For analytical convenience we shall therefore divide this paper into four sections. In the first two, we shall examine man's natural and human being respectively. In the third section we shall outline the nature of their dialectical integration, and in the fourth, we shall sketch the 'fully' developed human being as he emerges from the preceding discussion.

1

Man as a natural being

Marx maintains that sense perception is the sole criterion of reality. Only what is 'visible to senses', 'observable, visible and therefore beyond all doubt' is real and can be said to exist.[1] Marx calls an object of sense a sensuous or natural being. A sensuous or natural being alone is therefore 'real'. A non-natural object, an object that is not an object of sense, is 'an imaginary being, a being of abstraction' and therefore 'a non-being'. God, angels and ghosts are by definition non-natural beings and therefore do not exist and are human fantasies. Natural beings are for Marx the sole constituents of the universe.

In places, Marx inquires if all natural beings can be reduced to some underlying ultimate reality of which they are so many diverse forms, and concludes that matter is such an ultimate reality. However, for the most part Marx found the answer and indeed the inquiry itself pointless and uninteresting. Matter was, he thought, an unreal abstraction, never to be encountered in human experience. We see trees, stars, fruits, animals, humans, etc. but never matter as such. Again, to say that everything is matter, Marx thought, was to stress an abstract similarity between vastly different objects at the expense of their differences which alone made them the sort of object they are. He also seems to have thought that the preoccupation with the so-called material substratum tended to the 'one-sided' 'mechanical and mathematical' view of matter dominant in Hobbes and others, depriving matter of 'impulse, vital life spirit' and 'sensuousness'.[2] As the term 'materialism' has a specific meaning in philosophical circles to-day and can more properly be ascribed to Engels's philosophy, Marx's ontology might be better described as naturalistic rather than materialistic.[3]

Natural beings are basically of three kinds, Marx suggests. First, there are inanimate natural beings, such as the sun, stars, planets, mountains and rivers, that have neither life nor consciousness. Second, there are natural beings that have life but not consciousness. Plants, trees, etc. belong to this category of 'living natural beings'. Finally, there are natural beings that have both life and consciousness. Animals and humans fall within this category of 'conscious natural beings'. Marx's use of the term 'natural being' is not consistent. Sometimes he refers to all three kinds of being as natural beings; sometimes he confines the term to the last two. Sometimes, again, he calls the last two 'living natural beings' and by implication the first, non-living natural beings.

Every natural being, Marx argues, is a specific and determinate being, and therefore has a definite character or nature which constitutes its identity or essence. Marx defines the character of a natural being in terms of the concepts of power (*Kraft*) and need (*Bedürfnis*) and contends that every natural being has powers and needs. Marx does not define powers but seems to use the term to mean a faculty or ability to act and to produce certain results or consequences. Thus the plant has power to grow, the sun has power to help it grow, and man has power to see, to think, to smell, to eat, etc.[4] Marx takes a vitalist, Aristotelian view of nature and contends that every natural being *strives* to realise its powers. He therefore views 'powers' as not merely capacities but 'impulses', and argues that every power of a natural being has an inherent dynamism. It *strives* to realise itself, and suffers when it is frustrated. For Marx to say that X possesses a power to do Y is to say not merely that he can do Y but also that he *strives* to do Y. A being with eyes not only can see but wants to, has an urge to see, and feels frustrated when blinded or otherwise prevented from seeing. Need, as Marx understands it, corresponds to power and refers to the conditions a natural being must have to express and realise its powers. Once a natural being's actual and potential powers are identified, that is, powers it at present possesses and is in principle capable of acquiring, we can determine its needs. Powers of a natural being are objectively identifiable, and so therefore are its needs.

Marx explains the point by an example. A plant has the power or 'faculty' of growth, of acquiring leaves and flowers. Not only can it become a fully fledged plant in all its beauty but also *strives* to become one. When it grows into a fully developed plant, it manifests all its powers, and can be said to have realised its being, its essence. A plant, however, cannot develop its powers without the help of the sun, the soil, water, etc. These objects are required by its very nature or being, and therefore constitute its needs. Without them its powers remain barren possibilities, and its being remains unactualised and eventually withers away. Even as a plant has the power of growth and needs the sun, the sun too has powers and needs appropriate objects. The sun has the power to confer life on living things, the plant included, and this power remains unactualised in the absence of the plant. The sun therefore *needs* the plant in order to actualise its being. To talk of the sun *needing* the plant is obviously odd. While the vitalist view of nature is *prima facie* plausible with respect to organic nature, it makes little sense when applied to inorganic nature. One can interpret a plant's growth in terms of actualisation of its possibilities and say that it suffers when thwarted; but it is difficult to take such a view of the sun, which cannot be said to be *striving* to actualise its potentialities or to *suffer* in the absence of plants. Marx seems aware of this and for the most part confines the vitalist view to organic nature.

To continue with our example: the plant needs the sun, and the sun needs the plant. They are thus interdependent. Each, further, needs other objects as well. The plant needs not only the sun but also soil and water, and likewise the sun needs not only the plant but also soil, flowers, animals, etc. by means of which to demonstrate its powers. Nature, for Marx, is an interlocking system of interdependence, and each natural being is involved in a series of complex and interlocking patterns of relationships with other natural beings.

Since the being of a natural being can be actualised only with the help of objects existing outside it, we can say that the essence of each natural being resides outside itself.[5] In isolation from external objects, it not only cannot develop its powers but cannot even exist. Every natural being is therefore a relational being, and its nature *is* its relationship to external objects. We know a natural being through its relationships to external objects and have no other privileged access to it. Since the nature of a natural being thus lies outside itself, every natural being is an objective being, a being that cannot exist without the presence of natural objects outside it. A non-objective being, a being that is totally self-sufficient, is a non-natural being, and therefore a non-being, a fantasy. Marx concludes that every natural being, by its very nature, is first an objective being, second, a relational being, third, a dependent being, fourth, a needy being, and, fifth, a suffering being, who can suffer when the objects required by its very nature are not available.

Animals can be dealt with in a few words since they are not central to our discussion and are covered by what we shall later say about man. Like any other natural being, the animal is a specific and determinate type of being. It therefore possesses certain definite powers and needs and has its own distinctive ways of relating to external objects. It is more complex and differentiated than a plant but less developed than a man, and therefore has more powers and needs than a plant but less than those of a man. The animal has a definite physiological structure and distinctive sense organs, each of which in turn has a determinate power, a determinate mode of gratification, and distinctive needs. It has eyes and therefore power to see, and needs external objects over which to exercise this power. Similarly it has nose, ears and other sense organs and therefore appropriate powers and needs. As a living being, the animal further has 'natural powers of life' — energy, vitality, the power to be active, — and therefore needs the scope to be active, 'to hunt, to roam' and to engage in varied types of activity. The animal has the power to recognise other animals of its species, and finds pleasure in their company, and therefore has 'the need of companionship'. Since the animal as we shall see later, lacks the capacity for consciousness, it cannot and does not possess intellectual powers and therefore its needs are extremely limited. The animal's being embodies a limited range of powers and capacities, and these determine its needs and the range and quality of its relationships.

Qua natural being man is not substantially different from the animal. He too is 'a living, real, sensuous, object being' endowed with wants, drives, faculties and powers that can be gratified only through the necessary existence of external objects. Like any other natural being he tries to realise himself, that is, to appropriate objects related to his powers and tendencies. Marx does not draw up a list of these powers and tendencies and gives only a general indication of what they are. Like an animal, he has several sense organs and the powers associated with them. He has eyes and therefore power to see, ears and therefore power to hear, genitals and therefore power to procreate. He is endowed with 'natural powers of life' and therefore finds 'joy', 'pleasure', 'merriness' in being active, in playing with nature and its objects, in 'exhaling and inhaling all the forces of nature'.[6] Like animals, man *qua* natural being has the power to recognise other members of his species and therefore to enjoy their companionship.

Each of these powers and facilities strives for realisation, for fulfilment. Each is an active power, an 'impulse', a 'tendency', a 'disposition' as Marx calls it. It constantly impels man to go out and secure objects with which to gratify it. In Marx's view human senses and their powers are necessarily outgoing. Man's stomach, whose need for gratification we call hunger, impels him to go in search of food; and his genitals, whose impulse and mode of gratification we call sexual impulse, 'urge' or 'impel' him to look for the person with whom to copulate. Likewise, his eyes and ears have no meaning in the absence of external objects which they can see and hear, and are therefore necessarily outgoing. Like his sense organs, man's natural energy and vigour make him outgoing. A 'real man of flesh and blood' bubbling with 'energy and life' requires the 'living world' of nature whose powers he can breathe and from which he can derive nourishment. As to man's power and need of companionship, it by definition requires other men.

As we observed earlier, for Marx each human faculty, power and need is unique. Each of them has its own 'essential being' and a determinate and distinctive mode of appropriation and gratification. Each requires a different object for gratification, and can only be gratified in a manner dictated by its own unique nature and that of its correlative object. Take hunger, for example. It requires edible objects, and cannot be gratified by any other kind. Further, these objects, like hunger, possess a distinctive character and must be appropriated in certain ways. Some must be eaten with hand, some with a knife and fork, and so on. Even as hunger by its very nature can appropriate its objects and gratify itself in a limited number of ways, other impulses too can gratify themselves only in certain ways. What is more, the mode of gratification is unique in each case. Sexual urge cannot be gratified in the same way as hunger, for the obvious reason that the two do not and cannot relate to their different objects in the same way. A woman cannot be appropriated in the same way as an edible object. Following this line of argument Marx argues that each sense organ and faculty relates to and appropriates its objects in a totally different manner from every other.

Man then is a being naturally endowed with certain faculties and powers and therefore with definite and identifiable needs. He needs specific objects appropriate to his natural powers and drives, as well as needing the entire world of nature. Because the objects that satisfy his needs lie outside him, he is by his very nature an outgoing, active and striving being, driven by his impulses and needs to explore and manipulate the external world. Since passion 'is man's faculties energetically striving after their object' man is by nature 'a passionate being', a creature governed by passions.[7] A striving being constantly runs the risk of failing to obtain the objects it needs; man is therefore a suffering being, capable of pleasure and pain, joy and sorrow. As we observed earlier, man's faculties and desires are of a determinate kind and can appropriate their respective objects only in certain ways. Since limitations are thus built into the very structure of human desires and faculties, man is a 'limited and conditioned being'.

It is man's needs, which Marx appropriately calls 'inner necessity', that constitute the dynamics of human action and give his activity a direction. Because he is a needy being and his needs are objective, man is not and cannot be a purely passive and contemplative being as Feuerbach had imagined, and because his needs have a built-in objective structure, man is not and cannot be a purely active being, furiously and aimlessly going out into the world to appropriate it in its entirety as Fichte had imagined. Human needs are needs for specific objects, and therefore man cannot have a need for something as abstract as wanting to appropriate the world. Man's needs, further, are not contingent, something he happens to have and can do without, but are rooted in his very being. They are, as Marx puts it, 'not merely anthropological phenomena . . . but truly ontological affirmations of his being'.

Marx's analysis of need and the way he relates it to passion throws an interesting light on the mode of operation of human passion. As we saw above, passion refers to the strivings of human faculties to attain their objects. It is not, therefore, some mysterious force or a chemically produced urge existing independently of concrete faculties and driving them in certain directions. It is at bottom a mode in which a faculty affirms itself. A faculty, in turn, is not an independent and isolated power, but a particular way in which the human person affirms himself. There is, for example, no entity called sexual passion, but only a passionate way in which a human being strives to gratify his sexual impulse. There are therefore as many passions in man as there are faculties. Marx thus does not confine the term passion to the so-called biological passions such as sexuality but uses it to cover every faculty that strives for its object in an intense way. One can have a passion for music or art or natural beauty just as much as for a woman or a man. Marx does not seem to think that some one or more of these passions are naturally stronger than the rest. As all organs are equally natural and important, so are the impulses located in them. If a particular passion is dominant in an individual or society and absorbs its consciousness, that must be due to undesirable social influences and is a cause for concern.[8]

2

Man as a Human Being

We have so far examined Marx's concept of natural being and outlined what he means by it. As we remarked earlier, man is not merely a natural but also a human being. It is to the analysis of this concept that we should now turn.

Like Hegel and Feuerbach before him, Marx argues that Man's humanity, his human character, consists in those qualities that distinguish him from all other natural beings, above all the animal, which comes closest to him. The discussion of man's distinctive human character therefore involves Marx, as it had involved Hegel and Feuerbach, in tracing the basic differences between man and the animal.

In Marx's view we can discover the essence of a being by examining its behaviour, the way it lives. As he puts it, 'The whole character of a species is contained in the character of its life activity.[9] Of 'the totality of life-activities'[10] a living being has to undertake in order to stay alive — such as eating, sleeping, drinking and defecating — the one concerned with gaining its sustenance is the most important. It is the activity that it *must* undertake; it occupies most of its time; and in it are absorbed most of its energies. Marx therefore concludes that the way a species produces its sustenance provides a clue to its essential character and identify. As he puts it, 'As individuals express their lives, so they are. What they are therefore coincides with their production, both with what they produce and how they produce.[11] The distinctive character of the human species is therefore to be found in man's productive activity. According to Marx, if we compare man's productive activity with that of the animal we find that he differs from it in four basic respects, — that his humanity consists in his possession of four basic features or capacities.[12]

1. Man is a conscious being.
2. Man is a free being.
3. Man is a universal being.
4. Man is a species-being.

1. Man as a conscious being

Like Feuerbach, Marx uses the term consciousness in its rather specialised and narrow sense of self-consciousness. In its ordinary and broad sense consciousness is not distinctive to man. Animals too are conscious. They can and do recognise other animals, distinguish between members of their own species and outsiders, apprehend danger, etc. Feuerbach, however, thought that animal consciousness was so 'limited' that it could more properly be called instinct, and that the term consciousness should be reserved for human consciousness. Marx does not argue the point and implicitly accepts Feuerbach's usage.

The animal, he says, is 'directly identical' with, 'directly merged' into, its life-activity, and is unable to distinguish itself from it. It is unable to see itself as a separate being from its environment and to detach itself from its activities. Unlike the animal, man is able to distance and distinguish himself from his activities, his environment, and even from himself, and is therefore aware of himself as a subject. This is the familiar Hegelian view that man is not a being-in-himself but a being-for-himself and is capable of subject-object distinction.

2. Man as a free being

Man is a free being and the animal is not in two senses. First, Marx argues, an animal produces only when compelled by immediate physical needs, while man can not only produce when he is free from physical needs but produces better when he is so free. What this presumably means is that man can anticipate his needs and therefore produce in advance of his wants, and that he can produce better when he produces at his own pace and at the time of his own choosing than when compelled to do so by immediate needs.

Second, an animal's 'product' belongs immediately to its physical body, while man freely confronts his product. What this means is not very clear, but presumably what Marx intends to say is that the animal cannot see its 'products' as separate from itself in a way that man can, and that it sees them as in some sense parts of its own body and not as objects in the external world to which it can freely relate.

3. Man as a universal being

The animal's productive activity is confined to a limited part of nature, while man can take the entire world of nature as his field of action. The animal has a natural *Wirkungskreis,* a hermetically sealed circle of activity that exhausts the totality of its life-activity and within which 'it acts calmly . . . not striving beyond, not even surmising that there is another'.[13] Its 'consciousness' is 'merely an awareness of the *immediate* sensible environment'. Human consciousness, by contrast, knows no such limits. Man can make the entire universe the object of his consciousness and will, and can study and manipulate it.

4. Man as a species-being

Man has a number of capacities not to be found in the animal. These, which Marx sometimes calls 'mental' or 'spiritual' capacities, include the capacity to think, reason, judge, act, know, will, imagine, plan, anticipate, etc. Man can for example visualise the end-product of his activity and direct the latter accordingly, while an animal cannot. To use Marx's example,

> 'A spider conducts operations that resemble those of a weaver, and a bee puts to shame many an architect in the construction of her cells. But what distinguishes the worst of architects from the best of bees is this, that the architect raises his structure in the imagination of the laborer at its commencement. He not only affects a change of form in the material on which he works, but he also realizes a purpose of his own that gives the law to his *modus operandi,* and to which he must subordinate his will.'

Of all these 'mental' capacities, the most important is that for conceptual thinking. It is this that Marx wishes to emphasise in calling man a species-being. Marx's concept of species-being is highly complex; he does not always use the term in the same sense, and he is not always aware of its implications. Although he abandoned the term later, he retained the concept; and the term social being that he later preferred had all the force and meaning of its predecessor. Marx's concept of species-being therefore deserves close analysis.

Marx took over the concept of species-being from Feuerbach, purged it of part of its meaning and invested it with nuances of his own.

He used it for the same purpose as Feuerbach — to define man and distinguish him from the animal. Marx was struck by the fact that unlike the animal, man has generic consciousness, the consciousness of being a man like other men, a member of a species, and he felt that this difference could be best conceptualised in terms of the Feuerbachian notion of species-being. Evidently he found the term extremely useful, as he used it on every conceivable occasion during his Feuerbachian period and derived a number of terms from it that are not to be found in Feuerbach. Thus he used such terms as species-life, species-activity, species-powers, species-capacity, species-consciousness, species-object-ivity, species-relationship, species-act, species-will, species-bond, species-action and species-spirit.

Let us begin with a few of Marx's remarks where these terms are most clearly explained.

'Man is a species-being not only because in practice and in theory he adopts the species as his object (his own as well as those of others) but, this is another way of expressing it, also because he treats himself as the actual living species, because he treats himself as a universal and therefore a free being.' (Quote 1)[14]

'Conscious life activity distinguishes man from the life-activity of animals. Only for this reason is he a species-being. Or rather he is only a self-conscious being, that is, his own life is an object for him, because he is a species-being.' (Quote 2).[15]

'In creating an objective world by his practical activity . . . man proves himself a conscious species being, and as a being that treats the species as its own essential being, or that treats itself as a species being.' (Quote 3)[16]

In his several other uses of the term, Marx refers to the sexual act as a species-act and man's relation to woman as 'a natural species-relationship'. He calls the family, community and state 'species-forms'. He says that in a properly constituted political society, the legislature is the 'representative of the people i.e. of the species-will', and remarks that a will 'has its true existence as species-will only in the self-conscious will of the people'. He says that man's 'species-spirit' finds satisfaction only in cooperation between men. He says that the object of man's labour is 'the objectification of species-life' and that being alienated from it deprives him of 'his real species objectivity'.[17]

Quote 1 above is one of the few clearest definitions Marx ever gives of the concept of species-being and reveals a deep tension in his thinking. We shall therefore examine it in some detail.

Marx is here saying that man is a species-being, and the animal is not, in the sense that man can undertake the following five activities which the animal cannot.

First, he can make his species an object of his consciousness; that is, he can study it theoretically. Marx often identifies consciousness with theoretical study.

Second, he can make his species an object of his will. That is, he can pursue its well-being. Marx often identifies practical action with an exercise of will.

Third, he can make the 'species . . . of other beings' an object of his theoretical study.

Fourth, he can make other species an object of his practical concern.

Finally, he can treat himself 'as the actual living species'. That is, man is a being 'that treats the species as its own essential being, or that treats itself as a species being'. (Quote 3) In other words man is not only conscious of the fact that he belongs to a species but also of the fact that he derives his essence, his distinctive human powers, from his species. Every being in the universe is a species-being in the sense that it derives its being, its essence, from its species. Man differs from them all in recognising this and in being able to act as a conscious representative of his species.

Marx says (Quote 1 above) that the fifth power is 'only' a way of expressing' the first four. He does not elaborate this remark and it is difficult to see what he means. He could mean that the fifth power *means* (is the same as) the other four. But this is odd, since man's capacity to treat his species as his own essential being and his ability to study and manipulate other species are clearly different powers. It is more likely that he meant to say that the fifth power is a *source* of the other four. There is some evidence to support this view. First, Feuerbach had taken this view, and it is likely that Marx was following him here as elsewhere during his Feuerbachian period. Feuerbach had argued that it is because man is aware of himself as belonging to a species that he acquires the ability to think in terms of species and therefore to classify natural objects. In other words, it is because man can make his own species an object of his thought and will that he can make other species objects of his thought and will. Feuerbach never clearly explained how man acquires the consciousness of belonging to a species in the first instance, and argued rather feebly that he does so by observing that all men share certain features in common, concluding that they constitute a species.

Secondly, Marx says, at one point: 'since the human being does not come into the world bringing a mirror with him, not yet as a Fichtean philosopher able to say "I am myself", he first recognises himself as reflected in other men. The man Peter grasps his relation to himself as a human being through becoming aware of his relation to the man Paul, who with flesh and blood, and with all his Pauline corporeality becomes for Peter the phenomenal form of the human kind'.[18] Although the remark is not as clear as one would like it to be it could be read to mean that for Marx man acquires awareness of himself as a human, i.e. a species-being, by detecting similarities between himself and others, and that it is the species-consciousness so acquired that enables him to deal with the species of other objects in the universe. Marx's reference to 'the consciousness which man derives from the species' seems to reinforce the point.

Whatever the origin of man's species-consciousness and the relation between the first four powers and the fifth, it is interesting to examine the totality of the five powers. Man cannot deal with diverse species, including his own, either theoretically or practically unless he is able to group individual objects into species or classes[19] in the first instance. Man's five powers *qua* species-being therefore presuppose a more general power to classify objects on the basis of their shared character-istics. Marx is saying in effect that man is a species-being because he has the power to classify objects into species. The ability to classify is ultimately the ability to form concepts, to abstract the shared features of a group of objects and to make statements of differing degrees of universality. In effect, man is a species-being because he has a capacity for conceptual thinking, for abstraction. We can go even further. For Hegel and for Feuerbach, to formulate the concept of a thing is to pick out its essential features, so that the concept of a thing is a theoretical statement of its essence. Marx shares their Aristotelian view that the essence of a thing lies in its differentia. Man is a species-being because he can comprehend the essence, the being, the species-character, of all the objects in the universe. In other words, the capacity to grasp the essence (or species-character) of all beings, himself included, constitutes man's essence (or species-character). It would seem that Marx, like Feuerbach, is suggesting that man's five species-powers are 'differentiations' of his more general power to comprehend the species-character of each being in the universe. In other words, it is because man has this general power that he has the power to make the species-character of his own and other species the object of his theoretical and practical concern.

Feuerbach had described reason, will and love as man's essential and distinctive human powers.[20] Marx's five powers can, with some qualification, be reduced to Feuerbach's three. Of the five, the first four powers are clearly reducible to two, viz. theoretical and practical powers or reason and will. The first and the third refer to man's theoretical capacity, the second and the fourth to his practical capacity. Theoretical intellect or reason enables man to understand the species-character of beings in the universe and the will enables him to subordinate them to his practical purposes. Thus Marx is saying that reason and will are man's powers *qua* species-being and are derived from his more general power of conceptual thinking. Marx does not examine the relationship between reason and will,although he does at one point claim to enunciate 'a psychological law that once the theoretical intellect has achieved freedom within itself, it turns into practical energy and directs itself against the exterior reality of the world'.[22] His general view of the relationship between theory and practice also indicates that he would link reason and will very closely. Unlike Feuerbach, Marx does not list affection or love as a separate power, but it is implicit in the fifth power listed above. A being who knows his species to be his essential being is naturally capable of treating all its members as his own essential being and therefore of loving them.

Marx analyses the nature of reason further. It is, he says, a source of two other powers. First, it enables man to identify, abstract, analyse, compare and relate general features of objects and to formulate general laws about them; it is therefore a source of man's scientific capacity. Second, it is also a source of man's artistic capability. Since reason can comprehend the species-character of each being, it is able to grasp the distinctive and unique character of each species. It is therefore able to deal with it according to its own 'inherent standard', the norms implicit in its nature.[23] In other words, reason enables man to deal with each species in its own terms, without imposing external, *a priori* and alien standards on it. The animal, not a species-being, cannot do this. It lacks the capacity to respect the character and uniqueness of each species. Presented with pearls, for example, it will play with them, but will not appreciate their distinctive character. That is, it deals with each species of beings and objects according to the demands of its own and not their nature. It is this capacity to deal with each species according to its own inherent standards, that is the source of artistic creation. Man alone therefore is able to form things 'in accordance with the laws of beauty'.[24] For Marx the capacity for conceptual thinking is a necessary presupposition of the capacity for artistic creation.

For Marx, man is a species-being in the sense that he is capable of elucidating the differentia or the essence of objects and of classifying them. By definition he is also therefore capable of elucidating his own essence and of acting as a representative of his species. Sometimes Marx uses the term species-being in its first, wider, sense (for example Quote 1 above); more often, however, he uses it in the second, narrower, sense. This is evident in the second part of Quote 1, in Quote 3, and in almost all other remarks where he uses the derivatives of the term listed above. Thus the term species-consciousness refers to man's awareness of being a human being, a member, a representative, of the human species. The term species-power refers to that power which is distinctive to the human species. The term species-act refers to acts such as loving, cooperating, exchange and sexual intercourse, in which man affirms his species-being, that is, in which he reveals his distinctive human capacity and 'completes' or complements other men. The term species-activity refers to those organised forms of activity, such as science and art, and, at a different level, 'shoe-making' and other activities in which distinctive human capacities are revealed and human needs served. The term species-form refers to those organised forms of interpersonal relationship, such as the family, the state and the community, in which men cooperate with each other to realise common objectives. In the same way the term species-will refers to the will formed by men in the light of their species-consciousness, that is, the will that aims at the good of humanity; and the term species-existence refers to man's existence not as an isolated individual, but as a member of the human species.

We observed above that Marx uses the term species-being in two senses. The failure to see this has been largely responsible for the mistaken view taken by many commentators[25] that, for Marx, man is a species-being only in a communist society. Marx does occasionally make remarks that lend credence to this view, but they must be seen in their proper context. If man is a species-being only in a communist society, it would follow that he lacks the capacity for conceptual thinking and is therefore no different from an animal, in precommunist societies. But this is absurd since, however alienated capitalist and other societies might be, they could clearly never have been created by animals, and are distinctively human achievements. Further Marx himself says that man 'proves' his species-being in controlling nature; since precommunist societies, above all capitalist society, have clearly controlled nature, they have 'proved' beyond doubt that their members are species-beings. When therefore Marx remarks that man will be a species-being in the communist society, implying that he is not yet one, he means to use (or must be taken to mean) the term in its narrow sense. That is, he is saying that, although man in the precommunist society has understood and controlled the species of other beings in the universe and thus proved his species-being in the wider sense of the term, he has not so far understood his own essence, and pursued the well-being of his own species, and has therefore not yet become a species-being in the narrow sense of the term. In all precommunist societies man has remained, and will continue to remain, an egoistic, insulated, selfish, individualistic atom lacking full awareness of the fact that he derives his distinctive human powers from his species.

We have seen that for Marx man is a conscious, free, universal species-being. The question then is how these four capacities (powers, characteristics, or differentia) are related. Marx's answer — such as it is —

is ambiguous and somewhat muddled. He says (Quote 2 above) that man is a conscious being *because* he is a species-being, but in the previous sentence and elsewhere[26] he says the opposite — man is a species-being because he is a conscious being. Again, Marx seems to be vaguely aware that the animal too is a species-being (in the narrow sense of the term) at least to a limited degree. As he says in *The German Ideology*, the animal has 'herd consciousness' and knows which herd it belongs to. A lion, for example, knows that it does not belong to a flock of sheep, and copulates only with a lioness and not with a goat or a cow. The animal has a 'need of companionship' and it seeks its companions only among its kind. As if realising this, Marx describes man not as a species-being *simpliciter* but as a 'conscious species-being', without appreciating that he cannot then keep referring to man as a species-being *simpliciter* and also that he cannot then derive man's consciousness from his species-being. He says (Quote 1 above) that man is a universal being and therefore a free being, deriving his capacity for freedom from his universality. But he also says (Quote 2) that man is a conscious being and therefore a free being, deriving his capacity for freedom from his consciousness. Quote 1 continues that man is a species-being *because* he is a universal being; but then to say that man is a species-being *is* to say that he can deal with universal features of different species, so that his universality instead of being a source of his species-being, is partly entailed by it.

It is clear that man has certain powers that are his as a member of the human species. They include power to conceptualise and theorise, power to will, to plan, to anticipate, to create space between himself and the object of his perception, to act as a representative of his species, to produce according to laws of beauty, etc. In the course of exercising these powers, man develops countless others and builds 'the whole world of culture and civilisation'. He is able to develop other powers only because he has these basic powers in the first instance. They are therefore his 'essential' or 'species powers', characteristic of his species and constitutive of his essence. A man who lacks them is not a proper human being and it is only when an animal equipped with these powers evolves that a proper human being can be said to have appeared.

3

The Dialectical Integration

We saw above that man has certain distinctive species-powers. Since they constitute his human essence, he lives a truly worthy human life, only when he develops and exercises his distinctive species-powers and all other powers that grow out of them. The more powers he develops, the more of a human being he is; and he is fully human when he develops all the powers of which the species is capable. As we saw earlier, Marx takes an Aristotelian view of man and his powers. Man not only *ought* to develop and exercise his powers, he in fact *wants* and *strives* to develop them. Man can develop his powers only when he is free to plan his life as he chooses, only when he is 'the sovereign of circumstances'. As long as his will is subject to restraints imposed by external factors he remains restricted and unable to make free choices. Freedom, meaning absence of all forms of limitation on the human will, is for Marx the most basic demand of human nature and the most essential condition of a fully human life.

Man's striving for freedom brings him into inevitable conflict with nature which necessarily imposes limitations on him. These limitations are of two kinds, external and internal. External nature is not hospitable to human needs; it is harsh and does not sponteanously produce means of man's material sustenance. Its wild and unpredictable forces constantly threaten his existence. Rivers and mountains create natural barriers to man's free physical and social intercourse with his species. Nature has planted limitations in man's very being and thus his internal nature too mocks at his striving for freedom. As we saw in the first section man's natural being is no different from that of the animal. His natural senses are limited, primitive, confined to narrow perceptual areas and guided by crude and immediate needs. He has limited physical strength, limited capacity to anticipate events, and a narrowly circumscribed life-activity. Marx concludes, 'Neither nature objectively nor nature subjectively is directly given in a form adequate to the human being'.[27]

If man is to live a free and fully human life, he must overcome these natural limitations. He must use his human powers to reshape nature — both external and his own — in the light of his needs. In other words he must humanise nature. It is only as he humanises nature that man properly becomes a human being. The limits of humanisation are the limits of man's freedom and humanity. He can humanise nature by using his theoretical and practical powers of knowledge and will. He can study nature and use his 'theoretical knowledge of its independent laws' as 'a stratagem for subjecting it to human needs'. He cannot change it all at once, because this requires an Archimedean point in some supranatural world, and such a world is not available. What he can do is to change it gradually, consolidating the parts already won and using them as a basis for further conquests. In this way over centuries man becomes a free being. Although Marx is somewhat ambiguous, he seems to think that man can never humanise nature completely. Notwithstanding the fact that nature might one day cease to be a 'power in its own right' and man become able to alter its 'forms', Marx is convinced that its 'particles' or basic 'stuff' will always retain their inherent character and continue to be governed by their own 'independent' laws. Man's body will always need food, whether he likes it or not. It will continue to feel tired, grow old, decay and die, thus flouting human will. Human freedom is therefore necessarily hedged in with a number of inescapable limitations, eloquently summed up by the phrase, the 'realm of necessity'. However, man can and ought to try to subdue nature. As his knowledge grows, the limitations that had appeared 'natural' and inescapable to one generation will be transcended in another. In this way man constantly pushes the boundary of nature further and further and correspondingly expands the area of freedom.

It is from this perspective that Marx views human history. Its dialectic is the dialectic of the battle between man and nature, between freedom and constraint. Ever since his first historical appearance as a human being proper, man has striven to recreate, to humanise, both his own and external nature. In the beginning his successes were limited; building on them, he was able to conquer further areas of nature, and this enabled him to extend his mastery even further. Over the centuries generations of men, standing on the shoulders of their predecessors, have subdued the wild forces of nature, subordinated them to human needs, eliminated physical and other barriers imposed by nature, transformed their own nature, developed new needs, civilised their intercourse, and have in general brought nature in harmony with their human powers. Human history, to express the point differently, is a story of human 'autogenesis', or human self-creation, of man's continual self-transcendence and 'coming to be'; it is a story of 'the continuous transformation of human nature' and of the universe.[28] To avoid misunderstanding, Marx is not saying that human self-creation is the end, the *telos*, of history. Contrary to the opinion of his critics, Marx firmly rejects all such attempts to anthropomorphise history and to convert a way of seeing it into its hidden aim or end.[29]

Marx's highly suggestive idea of humanisation of nature raises a number of questions. For example, what precisely does it mean? How precisely are the humanisation of man's own nature and of the natural world related? How far can the humanisation of nature go and what are its limits? How is fully humanised nature achieved in history? Who are its agents and what is the logic of its progression? We do not have the space to pursue these fascinating questions and shall have to be content with exploring in some detail the question most relevant to our discussion, viz. the process by which humanisation of nature is achieved and Marx's conception of the fully humanised man.

Marx takes the view that man humanises nature through labour, a purposive and planned activity in which he uses his knowledge of nature to change and modify it. Although Marx is not entirely clear on this point he seems to say that labour involved in the humanisation of nature is of two kinds. Its first and most well-known form is, of course, industry, in which man 'works over' external nature and humanises it. Its second and less well-known form is culture, the term which Marx uses a few times in his early writings and not much thereafter and which in my view best describes the type of activity he has in mind.[30] Industry and culture are, of course, intimately related. Industry creates the basis on which culture arises, and conditions its form and structure. Nevertheless I think it is important to realise that Marx assigns culture a distinct role in the process of humanisation of nature.

The way in which industry humanises nature is obvious and need not detain us long. By cultivating land, by building dams, bridges and tunnels, by taming nature's wild and explosive forces, by building machines and factories etc, man subordinates external nature to his needs. He relieves nature of its naturalness, and makes it an integral part of the human world. Man's humanisation of external nature humanises his internal nature too. He develops new interests, new powers, and new needs, and learns to concentrate, to plan, to discipline and regulate his conduct, to cooperate with his fellow men, and to subordinate his fleeting whims and moods. Above all, the humanisation of external nature develops his species-being and unites him with his species. Humanised nature embodies man's human and species powers. In it therefore man encounters not nature but himself, not a nonhuman power but his own species. In dams, fields, bridges and machines, for example, he sees the efforts and creative powers of his fellow men, and feels both a sense of admiration and gratitude to them and a sense of pride in being human. They thus affirm his species-being and give it an objective and secure expression.[31] That nature does not act as a bond between man and his species in capitalist society is a separate question and does not concern us here.

Industry humanises external nature and through that, man's own nature. Man humanises his nature in another way too. He has, as we have seen, several natural senses and powers. In themselves they are primitive. They are gratified by crude objects; they appropriate them in crude ways; they are compelled by needs and approach them in a purely utilitarian manner. Man must therefore humanise them. Marx calls the process of humanising them culture or humanisation of the senses. Although his concept of culture is highly complex and relatively unexplored, we shall deal with it rather briefly.

Even as man has humanised external nature over the centuries, he has also learnt to humanise his internal nature. He has developed culinary skill, the art of painting, music, architecture, games, literature, dancing, etc., all of which collectively constitute culture.[32] These are all different ways of exercising his natural senses in a sophisticated, skilful, human and therefore free manner. Thus the species has developed culinary skill and produced different types of food and different ways of eating them. Man's palate is therefore humanised, and appropriates its objects in a human way, when it is able to appreciate the quality of the food it eats and the culinary skill embodied in it. A man who lacks a sense of discrimination, and sees food as no more than an edible lump, is no different from an animal. His relation to this food is not culturally mediated, and therefore not human but animal. Man's eyes too are humanised[33] when they appreciate beautiful objects — paintings, sculptures, etc. — with a sense of discrimination, feel at home with them, demand to be surrounded by them and feel outraged and insulted by anything that is ugly. An eye to which beautiful and ugly objects look alike and which sees them only as use-objects, is a 'crude' 'nonhuman' eye and is no different from that of the animal. Man's ears are similarly humanised when they are able to distinguish between noises and harmonious sounds and feel offended by all that is coarse and discordant. Human sexuality is similarly humanised when it does not simply aim at *secretic mechanico* and follow the printed instructions of sex, but is accompanied by romantic love and variation in love-play. Humanised sense is in other words a 'cultivated', 'refined' or 'cultured' sense, a sense that has incorporated within itself all the relevant achievements of the human species and that relates to its object not merely because of its ability to serve a raw human need but 'for its own sake', that is, because of the kind of object it is. A cultured man, a man of humanised senses, is for Marx a free man, a man who has emancipated his senses from the tyranny of nature and turned them into organs freely expressing his human powers.

Like his physical or natural senses, man's mental or practical senses such as 'feeling, thinking, being aware, wanting, loving' and imagining are humanised when they respond to their appropriate objects in a human way. Marx does not elaborate the point, but it is not difficult to see what he means. Thus man 'feels' in a human way when the character, object and mode of his feeling are determined by human considerations. To respond to man's exploitation of or cruelty to his fellow men with a sense of indignation is to feel in a human way; to respond to it with indifference or to seek to justify it is to feel in an inhuman way. To will an object or a state of affairs because it promotes human well-being is to will in a human way; to will an object that causes suffering to others is to will in an inhuman way. To be 'aware' of the human power embodied in an object and of the human needs it serves is to be aware of it in a human way; to be aware of it only as an object of utility is to be aware of it in an animal *and* nonhuman or even inhuman way.

In a fully humanised man, the senses 'have therefore become directly in their practice theoreticians'.[34] Although Marx does not elaborate this interesting and rather puzzling observation it is not difficult to see what he means, especially as Feuerbach, from whom he borrowed both the concept and the phrase, had explained it in some detail. As we saw earlier, theory, for Marx, refers to the capacity to understand objects not merely in their natural particularity but also as members of a class. In that the senses of the humanised man do not simply grasp the particularity of objects but also the general species-skills and powers embodied in them and the general human needs they serve, they are appropriating their objects in a theoretical manner. They do not merely perceive their objects but understand them, and see their point; that is, they see through them just as a theoretician does. Human senses, no doubt, do retain their particularity: eyes, for example, can only see and not hear or smell, but their particularity has become infused with universality. In other words they have become what Idealists call a concrete universal. In becoming universal, man's natural senses have become adequate vehicles of his universal nature, 'truly ontological affirmations of his essence' and no longer merely his anthropological characteristics.[35] At the end of a long historical process, his natural existence would at last have caught up with his human essence.

From what Marx has said so far, it follows that humanisation of nature, human self-creation is a cooperative process involving the entire species. It is not achieved by a single individual for obvious reasons; nor by a single nation which by its very nature can develop only some human powers and not others and depends on international commercial and cultural intercourse, thus presupposing humanisation of nature in other countries. As Marx puts it 'the liberation of every single individual is achieved proportionately to the extent in which history is completely transformed into world history',[36] to the extent that the species as a whole has humanised nature. Marx demonstrates this on the basis of a most impressive doctrine that has received surprisingly little attention from his commentators. Marx calls it the doctrine of 'mutual completion' and contrasts it with the bourgeois doctrine of 'mutual exploitation' or 'mutual enslavement'.[37]

Man is capable of developing countless human powers, and cannot be said to have become fully human unless he has actually developed them. The individual by himself, however, is too limited to do so, and needs others to 'complete' him. I may, for example, be good at painting but have no 'sense' for sculpture or poetry. Left to myself I would therefore remain artistically impoverished, unless someone else who was good at sculpture or poetry produced a beautiful object and thereby enabled me to cultivate the relevant capacity. Marx gives the example of a pianist. The 'pianist produces music and satisfies our musical sense; perhaps to some extent he produces this sense . . . he raises our individuality to a more active, livelier level'.[38] Any individual who produces something new educates his fellow men, gives them new capacities, deepens their imagination, and raises their level of existence. In giving them a new 'sense', he recreates his fellow men, and brings them closer to becoming species-beings.

Marx develops the point beautifully in his essay on James Mill.[39] Imagine an individual, he says, who produces a beautiful object. His act has four consequences. First, he has objectified his individuality in this object. In the object his personality has become 'objective, visible to the senses and thus a power raised beyond all doubt'. This is a source of pleasure to him and enriches his life. Second, others will enjoy the object he has produced, and thus he will have the further pleasure that he has satisfied a human need. Third, he has helped others acquire new senses, a new capacity of appreciation, a new power. He has thus been a 'mediator' between these men and the species and would be acknowledged by them as 'a completion . . . and a necessary part' of their essence. He is thus 'confirmed' in their 'thought' and 'love'. Finally, in objectifying a human power, a species-power, he has realised his 'human' and 'communal' essence. He has created an object that all can collectively share and cherish as an expression of their common essence. It is like a 'mirror' out of which human essence shines.

Men become humanised, Marx maintains, through each other's help. In expressing your powers, you benefit and enrich me. Enriched, I am better able to appreciate and criticise your products and to set you higher standards at which to aim. In educating me, you do not suffer any loss; on the contrary you benefit as much as I. Thus we grow together. In human life we constantly appropriate each other. In appreciating your music, e.g., I appropriate your musical sense which now is as much mine as yours. In giving me new senses, you have refined your own. If you had withheld your powers, I would no doubt have suffered a loss, but so would you. Properly defined, individual and social interests always coincide. In helping me become a human being, you become one yourself; in destroying my humanity, you destroy yours too. As Marx puts it, 'mutual completion . . . leads to the species-life, to the truly human life'.[40] It is therefore as much in my interest as in yours that I should encourage you to become a unique and 'truly individual' being. It is only when an individual is unique that he can 'complete' others, and both become and help others to become a species-being.

4

The Communist Man

In the light of the preceding discussion it is easy to see what a fully humanised man, a communist man, is like for Marx. He is a man united with himself, with his species and with nature. He is not a self-divided being caught up in the morbid and paralysing conflict between his flesh and spirit, or between his natural and human being. He does not deny the demands of his nature, but his behaviour is not dictated by them. He has humanised his nature and acquired the capacity to anticipate its demands and to gratify them in a cultured way. He therefore accepts his natural desires but satisfies them as he freely chooses. Ascetic self-denial on the one hand, and indiscriminate self-indulgence on the other, are both alien to his way of life.[41] He lives a balanced and integrated life in which each dimension of his being finds its proper satisfaction and none is allowed to dominate. Marx's man, further, is united with his species. He possesses all the basic powers distinctive to the human species — the power to conceptualise, theorise, desire, to concentrate and coordinate his energies, to form independent judgments, — and many others that the species has developed subsequently. Although not entirely clear on this point, Marx does not seem to wish to say that every man should become capable of pursuing science, writing poems and novels, composing music, constructing beautiful buildings, painting pictures, etc. He seems to want to distinguish between power and sense, and to suggest that a fully fully developed man should have the 'power' to undertake some of these activities and the 'sense' to appreciate the rest.

The communist man is energetic and active, constantly striving to objectify his powers. He is a 'demanding'[42] man who requires opportunities both to exercise his powers and to acquire those that the species is constantly developing. He is capable of making his own distinctive contribution to the enrichment of his fellowmen and of mediating between them and the species. He has humanised all his senses and relations to the world and is revolted and outraged by anything that reflects inhumanity, meanness, cruelty, suffering and ugliness. He is, further, united with nature and finds delight in its beauty and diversity. Above all, he has 'pride' in being human, a sense of 'worth' and self-respect, a love of 'independence' and a 'sense of dignity'.[43] He refuses to subject others to his power or to be 'subject, devoted, and obedient' to them himself. He is, in short, a cheerful, well-integrated, expansive, outgoing, loving, inwardly rich, cultured, social being who sums up in his life the greatness and wealth of his species. As long as any individual in any society fails to live this kind of life, the species suffers a loss, and its historic task of humanising nature remains unfulfilled.

On the basis of his conception of man Marx works out a fascinating theory of human needs and sketches the outlines of a society in which a fully humanised man is possible. On its basis he launches a powerful and, in my view, essentially sound attack on the christian, liberal and primitivistic conceptions of man. An examination of all these and other aspects of Marx's theory of man is beyond the scope of this essay.

NOTES

1. *Economic & Philosophic Manuscripts of 1844* Tr. Martin Milligan, Foreign Languages Publishing House, Moscow, 1961, pp.111, 155f, and p.170. This work is hereafter referred to as EPM. See also David McLellan, ed., *Karl Marx – Early Texts* Basil Blackwell, Oxford, 1971, pp. 202 and 203.
2. *The Holy Family* Foreign Languages Publishing House, Moscow, 1956 pp. 172ff. In all the bibliographies of Marx's writings that I have seen, this work is listed as authored by Marx and Engels. For the sake of historical accuracy and the light it throws on the two men's initial relationship, it must be observed that the title page of the first 1845 edition states that it was written by Engels and Marx.
3. Z.A. Jordan in *The Evolution of Dialectical Materialism* Macmillan, London 1967 pp. 11ff takes a similar view.
4. Bertell Ollman offers a careful analysis of Marx's concepts of power and need in his *Alienation* Cambridge University Press, 1973, pp. 75ff.
5. *EPM*, pp.156f.
6. *EPM*, p.155. See also Marx's description of Fleur-de-Marie in *Holy Family*.
7. *EPM*, p.158. I have preferred McLellan's translation in *Karl Marx: Early Texts*, *op.cit.*, p.168.
8. *EPM*, pp.73 and 116f.
9. *EPM*, p.75.
10. *ibid*. p.112.
11. *The German Ideology*, Tr. R. Pascal London, 1942, p. 7.
12. *EPM*, pp. 75-6.
13. *Writings of the Young Marx on Philosophy and Society*, ed. and Tr. by Loyd D.Easton and Kurt H. Guddat Doubleday Anchor Book, 1967, p.35.
14. *EPM*, p.74.
15. *ibid.*, p.75. I have preferred Bottomore's translation in his *Karl Marxm Early Writings*, p.127.
16. *EPM*, p.75.
17. *ibid.*, p.76. Also *Critique of Hegel's Philosophy of Right*, ed. Joseph O'Malley, Cambridge University Press, 1970, pp. 27, 58, 65 and 119; and *Karl Marx: Early Texts, op.cit.* pp. 193ff.
18. *Capital* Everyman ed. p.23.
19. Marx uses the two terms interchangeably.
20. *The Essence of Christianity*, Tr. George Eliot Harper Torchbooks, 1957, p.3.
22. *Karl Marx: Early Texts, op.cit.*, p.15.
23. *EPM*. p.76.
24. *ibid*.
25. Ollman, *op.cit.*, p.116.
26. *EPM*. p.58.
27. *EPM*, p.158.
28. For the socialist man, 'the entire so-called history of the world is nothing but the begetting of man through human labour'. *EPM*, p.113.
29. See, e.g., pp.57, 58 and 63 in T.B. Bottomore and Maximilian Rubel, eds.,

Karl Marx: Selected Writings in Sociology and Social Philosophy, Watts and Co., London, 1961.

30. *EPM.* pp. 100, 108f, 117, 118f; *cf.* McLellan, *Early Texts, op.cit.,* p.147.
31. Marx's constant reference to the human essence of nature shows clearly that nature for him has no rights against man. Its purpose is to serve man's material and 'spiritual' needs.
32. *EPM,* pp. 118f.
33. *ibid.,* p.107.
34. *EPM,* p.107.
35. *EPM,* p.136.
36. Quoted in Helmut Fleischer, *Marxism & History,* Tr. Eric Mosbacher, Allen Lane, The Penguin Press, London 1973, p.23.
37. *Karl Marx: Early Texts, op.cit.,* pp.194 and 200f. See also his criticism of Bentham and Utilitarianism in general in *German Ideology.*
38. *Grundrisse,* Tr. David McLellan, Paladin, London 1973, p.94.
39. *Karl Marx: Early Texts, op. cit.,* p.202.
40. *ibid.,* p.194.
41. The attack on asceticism is a recurrent theme in Marx's writings: see, for example, *EPM,* p.118; *Holy Family,* particularly his sympathetic characterisation of Fleur-de-Marie and denunciation of Rudolph's 'moral theology'; and those parts of *Grundrisse* and *Capital* in which Marx makes a powerful case for full satisfaction of human desires.
42. *EPM,* p.100, where Marx attacks the 'poor and understanding man' who does not ask to appropriate 'the entire world of culture and civilisation'.
43. *Karl Marx: Early Texts, op. cit.,* pp.75f, 189.

3 MARX AND THE WHOLE MAN

David McLellan

'At early stages of development the single individual appears to be more complete, since he has not yet elaborated the abundance of his relationships, and has not established them as powers and autonomous social relationships that are opposed to himself. It is ridiculous to wish to return to that primitive abundance as it is to believe in the continuing necessity of its complete depletion. The bourgeois view has never got beyond opposition to this romantic outlook and thus will be accompanied by it, as a legitimate antithesis, right up to its blessed end.'

Karl Marx

This essay centres on the problem of potential human nature in socialist thought — and particularly in Marx's thought. I aim briefly to investigate the question of what is meant when socialists talk of an all-round personality. Does Marx's thought imply a definite view of human nature? And, if so, are some qualities more essential to this human nature than others?

This problem was posed by the first socialist thinkers — the Utopian Socialists writing around 1800. Indeed it was an obvious and urgent question in the light of the impact of the industrial revolution and its seeming to narrow the possibility of self-fulfilment for the average worker as opposed to what seemed the more integrated and varied life of the Middle Ages. Of the great Utopian socialists, there is little of this pessimism in Saint-Simon — one would not expect to find much in a thinker who believed so strongly in the virtues of what he called 'industrialism'. There is something of this in Owen, but the chief representative of the view I am concentrating on is Fourier. Fourier began a central theme in socialist thinking by locating successfully organised labour as the key to human happiness. Not so socialist was his rejection of industrial civilization, his advocacy of a social system based on agriculture and his view that nature was always more than generous if not abused. His extraordinary perceptions on sexual repression have no parallel in socialist literature until Marcuse's *Eros and Civilization,* but his insistence on harmony in the fulfilled man and community in the fulfilled society found a ready echo in Marx.

Many of these criticisms of the industrial revolution were, of course, not confined to the socialists: there was, at the beginning of the nineteenth century a general nostalgia for the Middle Ages that was most clearly articulated by the Romantics. In his *Letters in Aesthetic Education,* for example, Schiller wrote:

'. . . enjoyment is separated from labour, the means from the end, exertion from recompense. Eternally *fettered* only to a single little fragment of the whole, man fashions himself only as a fragment; ever hearing only the monotonous whirl of the wheel which he turns, he never displays the full harmony of his being . . . 'the aesthetic formative impulse establishes . . . a joyous empire . . . wherein it releases man from all the fetters of circumstance, and frees him, both physically and morally, from all that can be called constraint.'

Both of these viewpoints – that of Fourier and that of Schiller – had, I believe, an important influence on Marx. That of the German Romantics was possibly even stronger as we have to remember that Marx enjoyed the classical education common to all the German middle class youth of his time, an education that was centred on an admiration for Antiquity. It is not surprising that the Marxian ideal of the freely developed all-round personality has much in common with the ideals of the aristocratic society that produced the Greek *polis*. To this must be added the more immediate influence of the company Marx was keeping while in Paris: the two poets Heine and Herwegh were Marx's most intimate friends during the summer of 1844 and did a lot to embody the kind of personality outlined in the *Economic and Philosophical Manuscripts.* However that may be, both the Fourierist and the Romantic strain are present in Marx to whom most of this paper is devoted in the belief that – in most respects at least – there is no socialist or Marxist theoretician who has been able to go beyond Marx in depicting a conception of human nature. What follows, therefore, is an exposition and evaluation of Marx's views on this question followed by some suggestions of those areas where Marx (and Marxists) have failed to come to grips with real questions.

Firstly, then, a word about the tradition to which Marx's views seem, at first sight, to be in fairly stark contrast. For Plato, in the *Republic,* the soil was tripartite and he was in no doubt that the rational element should rule over both the high and the base desires. Morality, goodness were closely bound up with the intellect and the best person to rule the city was a philosopher: virtue = knowledge, in the Socratic equation. And however much he criticised Plato's views, Aristotle held firmly to the belief that the good life consisted in an exercise of the intellect. In the tenth book of the Nicomachaean Ethics he talks of life according to the intellect – as constituting happiness.

And his forceful conclusion expressed literally is that 'the bounds of happiness stetch as far as those of contemplation. I believe that this view is very deeply rooted in the Christian tradition where contemplation of one sort or another was said to be man's highest goal: Aquinas roundly declared in the second part of the Summa that *vita contemplativa simpliciter melio est quam vita activa.*

This current is also present in Hegel with his view of Spirit as the central force in man's history. But there is also in Hegel the radically different emphasis on self-creation — man as an historical being who creates his own destiny. Now with regard to Marx's views on this question I wish to distinguish three periods in his thought: (1) the early Marx, the Marx of the 1844 manuscripts, (2) the Marx of *The German Ideology,* when he is in the process of formulating his ideas on historical materialism. And (3) the mature Marx of the *Grundrisse* and *Capital.* Of course, this may imply a view of the periodisation of Marx's thought which is contestable, but I am presupposing some sort of continuity of basic concepts.

In the early Marx we get a view of man as capable of living in spontaneous cooperation with his fellow men, self-consciously deter-mining himself in a free society where there is no exploitation and no unsatisfied natural need. In his society the individual will have the two essential qualities of being a 'complete' individual, all-round (*allseitig* in Marx's word) and also being harmonious, capable of integrating the many facets of his personality. This is achieved in a context of work, cooperative work in which men act together to change the world around them and in so doing change and develop themselves. Instead of being alienated in the sense of dominated by external objects, they themselves will eliminate the objects and this constitutes their true nature and vocation. Productive activity is the fundamental feature of human nature. Marx, however, cannot quite abandon his feeling of the primacy of the intellectual over the practical. In the passage on 'Alienated Labour', for example, what is said by Marx to distinguish man from animals is that 'man makes his life-activity itself an object of his will and conscious-ness . . . conscious life activity distinguishes man from the life activity of animals . . . only for that reason is he a species-being'. Nevertheless, the general impression given in Marx's 1844 writings is that the funda-mental activity appropriate to human nature is a practical one — or at least one in which theory and practice are inextricably combined. After all, Marx's whole criticism of Hegel at the end of the *Economic and Philosophical Manuscripts* consisted in Hegel's misconception of labour as 'abstract and mental'. Marx's critique of alienated man in the Paris manuscripts is fairly well-known and I will not rehearse it now. What is perhaps less well-known — and of more relevance to my theme — is that

Marx did give a picture of unalienated man, not in the Paris manuscripts, but in the Notes on James Mill written about the same time. It represents, in many ways, the nearest Marx ever came to describing a communist society and, as such, deserves lengthy quotation:

'Suppose we had produced things as human beings: in his production each of us would have twice affirmed himself and the other. (a) In my production I would have objectified my individuality and its particularity, and in the course of the activity I would have enjoyed an individual life; in viewing the object I would have experienced the individual joy of knowing my personality as an objective, sensuously perceptible and indubitable power. (2) In your satisfaction and your use of my product I would have had the direct and conscious satisfaction that my work satisfied a human need, that it objectified human nature, and that it created an object appropriate to the need of another human being. (3) I would have been the mediator between you and the species and you would have experienced me as a reintegration of your own nature and a necessary part of yourself; I would have been affirmed in your thought as well as your love. (4) In my individual activity, I would have immediately confirmed and realised my true human and social nature.'

'Our productions would be so many mirrors reflecting our nature. What happens so far as I am concerned would also apply to you . . . My labour would be a free manifestation of life and an enjoyment of life . . .'

'Furthermore, in my labour the particularity of my individuality would be affirmed because my individual life is affirmed. Labour then would be true, active property. Under the presupposition of private property my individuality is externalised to the point where I hate this activity and where it is a torment for me. Rather it is then only the semblance of an activity, only a forced activity, imposed upon me only by external and accidental necessity and not by an internal and determined necessity.'

The model here is almost an artistic one: man fashions the world as a sculptor would and work should be made coextensive with life as one could imagine — probably quite wrongly — the work of an artist's to be. The main point is that in this picture there is no distinction between work time and leisure time.

The 1844 description of unalienated man was written *before* Marx's working out of historical materialism in *The German Ideology*. But in the late 1840s the emphasis on the nefariousness of the division of labour and the necessity of its abolition is still present in Marx. Indeed, in the historical perspective of *The German Ideology,* the division of labour is viewed (along with its correlative private property) as *the* original tare in the social wheatfield that produced the weeds of class struggle, state power and so on. Marx is so keen on its abolition that he sometimes rather confusingly talks of labour itself being abolished. 'The proletarians,' he wrote, 'if they are going to assert themselves as individuals, will have to abolish the very condition of their existence hitherto, namely labour . . . it is not a matter of freeing labour but abolishing it.' This leads on to the question of whether the abolition of the division of labour under communism aims at liberating forces already present in human nature or of moulding that human nature itself. Here Marx distinguished between constant desires 'which exist under all circumstances, only their form and direction being changed by different social circumstances', and relative desires 'which owe their origin merely to a particular form of society, to particular conditions of production and exchange'. In a communist society, the former would merely be changed and given the opportunity to develop normally, whereas the latter would be destroyed by being deprived of the conditions of their existence. Marx continued: 'which desires would be merely altered under a communist organisation and which would be dissolved, can only be decided in a practical way, through the changing of real, practical desires, and not through historical comparisons with earlier historical circumstances'. He goes on to mention several desires (among them the desire to eat) as examples of fixed desires, and continues: 'neither do the communists envisage abolishing the fixity of desires and needs . . . they only aim to organise production and exchange in such a way as to make possible the normal satisfaction of all desires, that is, a satisfaction limited only by the desires themselves'. Those changes in the social nature of man and the regulation of desires can be made possible, according to Marx, by man's recovery of what he, in his earlier writings, referred to as man's species being. Marx occasionally traces the origins of the division of labour present in the sexual act — though clearly the abolition of that division would involve a transformation of human nature even more radical than that envisaged by Marx. Probably Marx's best known description of communist society is given in the following passage from *The German Ideology:*

'In communist society, where nobody has one exclusive sphere of activity but each can become accomplished in any branch he wishes, society regulates the general production and thus makes it possible for me to do one thing today and another tomorrow, to hunt in the morning, fish in the afternoon, rear cattle in the evening, criticise after dinner, just as I have a mind, without ever becoming hunter, fisherman, shepherd or critic. This fixation of social activity, this

66

consolidation of what we ourselves produce into an objective power above us, growing out of our control, thwarting our expectations, bringing to naught our calculations, is one of the chief factors in historical development up till now.'

The obvious difficulty here is that Marx's description involves an agricultural society where it is much easier to envisage the abolition of the division of labour than it is with an industrial, technological society. And Marx's phrases are, in fact, a kind of pastiche on Fourier. Another example that Marx mentions is that of painting:

'Stirner imagines that the so-called organisers of labour wanted to organise the entire activity of each individual, and yet it is precisely among them that a difference is drawn between directly productive labour, which has to be organised, and labour which is not directly productive. In regard to the latter, however, it was not their view, as he imagines, that each should do the work of Raphael, but that anyone in whom there is a potential Raphael should be able to develop without hindrance ... The exclusive concentration of artistic talent in particular individuals, and its suppression in the broad mass which is bound up with this, is a consequence of division of labour. If, even in certain social conditions, everyone was an excellent painter, that would not at all exclude the possibility of each of them being also an original painter, so that here too the difference between "human" and "unique" labour amounts to sheer nonsense. In any case, with a communist organisation of society, there disappears the subordination of the artist to local and national narrowness, which arises entirely from division of labour, and also the subordination of the artist to some definite art, thanks to which he is exclusively a painter, sculptor, etc., the very name of his activity adequately expressing the narrowness of his professional development and his dependence on division of labour. In a communist society there are no painters but at most people who engage in painting among other activities.'

Marx was clear that such a society was impossible under present conditions: capitalism was a necessary precondition, but so also was its transformation in a communist revolution.

We now come to the *Grundrisse* written in 1857-8 and to a radical change of position — a position which is, in my view, more representative of Marx's thought than the earlier. (Obviously this depends, in part at least, on a view of the *Grundrisse* as representative of the maturity of Marx's thought.) Here Marx approaches the question of will very explicitly by contrasting the views of Adam Smith and Fourier.

According to Marx, Smith conceives of labour as an imposition, some-thing to be avoided if at all possible. Against this, Marx speaks of labour as being potentially 'attractive labour and individual self-realisation'. 'This does not mean', he continues, 'that labour can be made merely a joke, or amusement, as Fourier naively expressed it in shopgirl terms. Really free labour, the composing of music for example, is at the same time damned serious and demands the greatest effort. The labour concerned with material production can only have this character if (1) it is of a social nature, (2) it has a scientific character and at the same time is general work, i.e., if it ceases to be human effort as a definite, trained natural force, gives up its purely natural, primitive aspects and becomes the activity of a subject controlling all the forces of nature in the production process.' But the main point about the *Grundrisse* is the way in which Marx's conception of the problem of work and the abolition of the division of labour is conditioned by his thinking on machinery and automation. Marx has a truly extraordinary vision of a fully automated society:

> 'This historical vocation of capital is fulfilled as soon as, on the one hand, demand has developed to the point where there is a general need for surplus labour beyond what is necessary, and surplus labour itself arises from individual needs; and on the other, general industriousness has developed (under the strict discipline of capital) and has been passed on to succeeding generations, until it has become the property of the new generation; and finally when the productive forces of labour, which capital spurs on in its unrestricted desire for wealth and the conditions in which alone capital can achieve this, have developed to the point where the possession and maintenance of general wealth requires, on the one hand, shorter working hours for the whole of society, and working society conducts itself scientifically towards the progressive reproduction of wealth, its reproduction in ever greater profusion; so that the sort of labour in which the activities of men can be replaced by those of machines will have ceased.'

Of course, this line of thought is important for Marx because, for him, it entails the downfall of the capitalist system since the capacity of that system to extract surplus value will diminish and involve a falling rate of profit in that surplus value is directly proportionate to time worked. But the corollary that interests us here is that there are enormous implications for the growth of leisure time. Marx remarks concerning this leisure time that it will afford time 'for the complete development of the individual'. And he says that this free time includes both 'leisure and time for higher activities'. He describes these higher activities as artistic, scientific, intellectual. This has two immediately obvious consequences: firstly, the problem of the division of labour as originally outlined in the earlier writings no longer exists in that people will only be working four, three, two or even fewer hours per day and could not be said to be impoverished even if they were doing the same job during those few hours. Secondly, the emphasis has shifted away from work as collective impact on and transformation of nature, towards activities that may well still be communal, but are much more exclusively intellectual.

Although this view is most clearly expressed in the *Grundrisse* it survives also in subsequent writings. In the third volume of the *Theories of Surplus Value,* Marx writes: 'Free time, the time one has at one's disposal, that is the true wealth; and this time is not, like labour, regulated by an external aim whose realisation is either a natural necessity or a social duty.' Marx returns to the same theme in the third volume of *Capital* where he contrasts the reign of liberty with that of freedom and declares the reduction of the working day to be the fundamental prerequisite of communism.

I would not want to maintain that this emphasis on the increase in leisure time is Marx's definitive solution to the problem of the division of labour. For he does speak – again in *Capital* – of heavy industry compelling society to replace the individual who does just one job the whole time by a much more diversified and responsible individual. But I think the main emphasis still remains on free time.

How, then, about the politics of the whole man? There is of course the description of the political organisation of the future communist society given by Marx in *The Civil War in France.* Marx welcomed the Commune's proposals to have all officials, including judges, elected by universal suffrage, responsible to their electors and revocable at any time; to pay officials the same wages as workmen; to replace the standing army by the armed people; and to divest the police and clergy of their political influence. Marx also thought that the Commune, if it had proved successful, could have paved the way for a decentralised, federal political structure and an economy based on cooperatives united by a common plan. Exceptionally interesting in this connection are Marx's marginal notes on Bakunin's *Statism and Anarchy* where it appears that socialist man will not be self-regulating as an individual but rather as a community. The following dialogue is excerpted from Bakunin's text and Marx's notes:

Marx: Under collective property, the so-called will of the people disappears in order to make way for the real will of the cooperative.
Bakunin: Result: rule of the great majority of the people by a privileged minority. But, the Marxists say, this minority will consist

of workers. Yes, indeed, but of ex-workers, who, once they become only representatives or rulers of the people, cease to be workers.

Marx: No more than a manufacturer today ceases to be a capitalist when he becomes a member of the municipal council.

Bakunin: There are about forty million Germans. Will, for example, all the forty million be members of the government?

Marx: Certainly! For the thing begins with the self-government of the Commune.

Bakunin: The whole people will govern and there will be no one to be governed.

Marx: According to this principle, when a man rules himself, he does rule himself; since he is only himself and no one else.

Bakunin: Then there will be no government, no State, but if there is a State in existence there will also be governors and slaves.

Marx: This merely means: when class rule has disappeared, there will no longer be any state in the present political sense of the word.

Not all of these ideas seem as capable of realisation in the second half of the twentieth century as they did to Marx. Two problems spring immediately to mind. Firstly, the evolution of the working class has not rendered the preconditions for the emergence of socialist man more likely. Of course, Marx himself was more familiar with artisans than with factory workers — a fact which tended to give some of his preconditions an unrealistic air. Nor do contemporary sociologists of work confirm the more optimistic passages of the *Grundrisse.* According to Riesman, in those sections of society where there has been an increase in leisure time it has tended to be stultifying rather than liberating, and the pressure for shortening actual working hours has decreased: improved working conditions are sought particularly by men who do not relish the prospect of spending more time at home with their families. Indeed, according to Wilensky, free time has not grown at all over the last hundred or so years. And sociologists such as Friedman have pointed out that automation also has its limits.[1] (But see further the essay by Tom Bottomore in the present collection).

The second lack in the Marxian theory is a developed theory of the individual. This is highlighted by the evident difficulty that socialism has experienced in coming to terms with Freud and the whole psycho-analytical school. Until recently it seemed that Reich was the only Marxist to have taken Freud seriously.

Nevertheless, socialist man is the richest conception so far produced by our civilization. The idea of a boundless and almost infinitely varied creative potential inherent in each individual the full development of which can be harmonious both individually and socially is indeed something we need. The question, of course, is whether alienated man will sufficiently want what he needs and become sufficiently conscious of where his true interest lies.

NOTE

1. See D. Riesman, *The Lonely Crowd,* Yale, 1950; H. Wilensky, 'The Uneven Distribution of Leisure: The Impact of Economic Growth on "Free Time,"' *Work and Leisre,* ed. E. Smigel, New Haven, 1963; G. Friedmann, *Industrial Society,* Glencoe, 1955.

4 SOCIALIST MAN: WILLIAM MORRIS AND BERNARD SHAW

Steven Ingle

Man, it seems, is hardly a suitable base on which to build 'progressive' political theories. Conservative theorists have been content to use him and have been willing to explain away the misfortunes of some men in terms of 'human nature': men are by nature selfish and unequal, and society, as a consequence, can never become much 'fairer' than it happens to be. But progressive theorists (by which I mean not only those who are normally referred to as utopians but also Marxist and, more broadly, socialist theorists, who write about a society fundamentally different from that which exists) have given up man, as we know him, as a bad lot. But human nature, they tell us, is not immutable. What we call man is simply the product of a particular set of social and economic relationships: change those and you will change him. Human nature is not a constant. 'What human nature?' asked William Morris. 'The human nature of paupers, of slaves, of slave-holders, or the human nature of wealthy freemen? Come, which?'[1] So man as he is (or seems to be) is discarded for man as he might become. As goes without saying, the variety of 'new' men is endless. All that unifies them is that none much resembles man as we know him.

In late Victorian England many of the prominent intellectuals of the day were drawn towards socialism. There was a multitude of socialist organisations, divided by doctrinal differences and personality clashes. Underlying the endless quarrels there existed fundamental differences of opinion, one of which concerned the degree of central control necessary to establish and maintain socialism. At one extreme were the anarchists (who wanted very little) and at the other, sections of the Fabian Society, (the so-called state socialists) and each separate group — perhaps each individual — could be found jealously guarding a little niche somewhere between, representing a unique mixture of the two theories.

It is my intention to explore certain aspects of this debate in detail by concentrating on the works of two of the major protagonists, William Morris and Bernard Shaw. Morris was no anarchist but he was a fundamental egalitarian, by which I mean he believed that in an unstratified society all men would be equally capable of controlling their own destinies and ought to be given the opportunity to do so. Shaw was a hierarchical egalitarian, by which I mean that he believed only in *economic and not political* equality. An economically equal society would allow the most talented to govern, thus permitting a 'social order aiming at the greatest available welfare for the whole population'.[2] This 'social order' was to be rigidly hierarchical. Morris's fundamental egalitarian theories were rooted in his idea of the nature of socialist man, just as were Shaw's, and I propose to examine and compare the theories of each in some depth and to show the relevance of both to socialist thought.

1

'Forsooth, too many rich men there are in this realm; and yet if there be but one, there would be one too many.'

Dream of John Ball

William Morris was born in 1834 at Walthamstow. His family's estate lay close to Epping Forest and the young Morris grew up in an idealised environment. He read all the Waverley novels while still a child and persuaded his father to buy him a pony and a suit of armour so that he could live out his fantasies. At the age of nine he was writing poems about '. . . the shivered spire once so tall, so tall'. As one critic remarked, Morris 'lived in his imagination a wild and clear dream of great and good and chivalrous activity, and in his mind he constructed a Utopia . . . blended from art, poetry, religion and romance'.[3] At the age of fourteen Morris was sent to the newly-founded Marlborough school where he was more or less allowed to follow his own bent. He became particularly interested in history, archaeology, church music and architecture. In 1852 he went up to Oxford, around the time of the Anglo-Catholic movement. Morris and his close friend Burne-Jones, whose paths seemed bound inevitably for the church at this stage, became increasingly interested in art. Burne-Jones introduced Morris to Rosetti whose influence was fairly decisive in persuading Morris to devote his energies not to religion but to art, despite great opposition from home. Financial security afforded Morris the opportunity to experiment unsuccessfully in various art forms. Having moved to London, his life took on a bohemian aspect, sustained by contact with many intellectual figures. Ruskin, 'our hero' as Morris called him, was a frequent visitor to the studio which he shared with Burne-Jones.

Morris then, before ever he became a socialist, was steeped in an intellectual tradition which encompassed writers like Ruskin and, to a lesser extent Carlyle and Arnold, whose inspiration was frequently drawn from medieval civilisation.[4] It was a tradition which despised the cultural and artistic achievements of its own age and which sought to revitalise and to 'purify' what is considered to be a decadent civilisation. A second ingredient of Morris's intellectual background was his great interest in Norse civilisation, an interest which he sustained by a visit to Iceland, and which was always important to him. His interest in medieval culture led Morris to found a Society for the Protection of Ancient Buildings, the operations of which enabled him gradually to appreciate that the state of the arts and the well-being of a society were inextricably linked. This was not a conclusion he reached with any joy, for it implied that the would-be reformer of artistic standards must interest himself in political reform. As he himself said; 'Both my historical studies and my practical conflict with the philistinism of modern society have *forced* on me the conviction that art cannot have a real life and growth under the present system of commercialism and profit-mongering.'[5]

Morris's political interest led him first to the Liberals, with whom he rapidly became disenchanted, and eventually, via Henry George, to Hyndman. Like Bernard Shaw, he was encouraged by Hyndman to read Marx as an antidote to George, and, also like Bernard Shaw, he experienced a 'conversion' of almost religious dimensions. Morris joined Hyndman's Social Democrat Federation and his life became increasingly taken up with politics. But he found Hyndman domineering and opposed the SDFs attempt to secure parliamentary representation — allegedly with the support of Tory money.[6] He left the SDF, along with men like Aveling and Bax, and formed the Socialist League. But Morris found life equally uncongenial in the League, for its structure had been infiltrated by anarchists and its journal *Common Weal* came to act increasingly as a vehicle for anarchism. By 1889 Morris had lost control of the SL and, once more, resigned to found the Hammersmith Socialist Society in 1890. Although he later played an important part in the unsuccessful attempt to unite the various socialist factions, Morris's political activities would scarcely have guaranteed him much of a place in the history of British socialism. His writings, however, were much more successful and one is drawn to conclude that he found socialist man in *Nowhere* more to his taste than the socialist men with whom he had to deal in the rough and tumble of everyday political life!

As we have seen, Morris was forced, to use his own word, into political thought and action and the principal impulse was artistic. It is of fundamental importance to appreciate that Morris was first and foremost an artist. Morris scholars like Page Arnot[7] and Thompson[8] have justly sought to emphasise Morris's passion for communism and his belief in revolution. Those who stress Morris's artistic interest or achievement are, to their minds, seeking merely to bring him under the penumbra of bourgeois respectability. That is certainly not my intention. But I believe it imperative to grasp that Morris himself was an artist, because Morris's socialist man is also an artist: his basic instinct is creative. For Morris man was *not* a political animal but a creative one. Morris himself resorted to politics, even to the point of accepting the prospect of violence, chiefly because he believed that bourgeois society was structured in such a way as to restrain man's creative instincts and thus prevent him from becoming a complete man. Morris then was persuaded to become a socialist because the men he saw about him were stunted and incomplete and in no way compared to his vision.

Morris's 'new' man, then, was an artist first and last. 'In the times when art was abundant and healthy, all men were more or less artists; that is to say, the instinct for beauty *which is inborn in every complete man* had such force that the whole body of craftsmen habitually and without conscious effort made beautiful things . . . and the audience was nothing short of the whole people.'[9] It is of great importance to attach a precise meaning to the word art for us to understand Morris, but before we attempt this task let us note the words in italics. Morris was firmly committed to the notion that every individual possessed creative ability and, despite the impact of capitalism, was still capable of making himself a complete man by using that creativity usefully. 'Three hundred years, a day in the lapse of ages, has not changed man's nature thus utterly, be sure of that: one day we shall win back art, that is to say the pleasure of life; win back art again to our daily labour.'[10] Now that we come to examine Morris's theory of art and to relate it to his socialist theories, let us be quite clear as to this one thing: potentially at least, we are all artists.

'Art,' says Morris, echoing Ruskin, 'is man's expression of his joy in labour.'[11] The implications of the statement are that Morris identified art not so much as a category of human activity but rather as a frame of mind in which activities may be undertaken, so that most activities are susceptible to artistic performance. Because one takes pleasure in doing a particular task, cooking a meal, sowing a crop or whatever, it becomes an art form. Some tasks, he conceded, are inherently distasteful and are therefore not to be performed artistically; these tasks must be shared around as much as possible, so as not to burden any particular individual or group, and wherever it can be managed they are to be performed by machines. If art is joy in labour, the question now posed by Morris is: how is joy to be restored to man's labours? His answer is to give man once again 'the pleasure of working soundly and without haste at *making* goods that we could be proud of . . . such a pleasure as, I think, the world has none like it.'[12] Now most of these art forms open to the labourer are, actually or potentially, to some extent decorative[13] and for Morris the decorative arts have two specific functions. The first is to give pleasure to men in the things 'they must perforce *use*' and the other to give men pleasure in the things 'they must perforce *make*'.

So man's pleasure, drawn from art, should be two-fold: pleasure in the making and pleasure in the using. Yet certain important preconditions inhere to this pleasure. First, for man to take pleasure from making an object he must know that its use is beneficial to society and second he must be able to make the object under agreeable conditions. Let us take the first point. Morris wrote: 'It would be an instructive day's work for any one of us who is strong enough to walk through two or three of the principal streets of London on a week-day, and take accurate note of everything in the shop windows which is embarrassing or superfluous to the daily life of a serious man. Nay, the most of these things no one, serious or unserious, wants at all.'[14] The reason for this state of affairs we shall see later but at the moment it is important only to observe that for Morris man could not be happy making such goods; in his ideal society there is no place for luxury. Secondly, Morris was opposed to the mass manufacture of 'shoddy' goods, and the existence in capitalist society of a large underprivileged class seemed to necessitate the production of such goods. Men can take no pleasure from making shoddy goods. So for men to take pleasure in making goods they must live in an egalitarian society in which only the apparent needs of a people living a simplified existence are met. 'No one would make plush breeches.' Morris argued, 'when there were no flunkies to wear them.'[15]

Let us move on to the second precondition: that men must work under agreeable conditions. Morris was keenly aware of the significance of the relationship between dingy homes, dingy factories and dingy lives. He believed that if such factories as would continue to operate – the majority, being currently given over to the production of either shoddy or luxury goods, would be found to be unnecessary in a just society – should become physically uplifting and 'centres of intellectual activity' providing a wide range of social and recreational facilities. But the working day must be a short one for 'when class robbery is abolished, every man will reap the fruits of his labour, every man will have due rest'.[16] Finally, Morris argued for variety of work. Under the capitalist system men are 'educated' to play a certain role in the system. But this is not 'due' education which should enable young people to become proficient in a variety of handicrafts, thus allowing them, in the first instance, to take up a task for which they are suited and later to turn their hand to something else should they wish. In Morris's just society these conditions would be fulfilled, so that it would be possible to envisage labour's becoming 'a real tangible blessing in itself to the working man, a pleasure even as sleep and strong drink are to him now'.[17] We begin to understand, then, that much is necessary in the way of new political arrangements if Morris's new man is contentedly to indulge his creative instinct in work.

It is now appropriate to explore more fully Morris's criticisms of capitalist society in order to discover why he rejected it totally both in existing and reformed guise as a possible framework for the development of the new life-style. Capitalism was guilty of the most heinous crime, said Morris: it had destroyed art. The capitalist, or 'commercial' system, had become so unfairly divided that the contrast between rich and poor has been fearfully intensified, so that in 'all countries, but most of all in England, the terrible spectacle is exhibited of two people, living street by street, and door by door – people of the same blood, the same tongue, and at least nominally living under the same laws – but yet one civilised and the other uncivilised'.[18] The result of this division was that art had been 'trampled down' and commerce 'exalted' into a sacred religion. The growth of commercialism, Morris went on, had destroyed the craft system of labour, in which the unit of labour had been the intelligent artisan, and had supplanted it with the 'work-shop' system 'wherein . . . division of labour in handiwork is carried to the highest point possible, and the unit of manufacture is no longer a man but a group of men, each member of which is dependent upon his fellows'.[19] The aim of capitalist production was increasing profit, not the usefulness of the commodity, and as a result there was no necessary limit to labour. That was the 'superstition of commerce': that man was made for commerce rather than commerce being made for man, and its implications for the life of the individual were clear enough. The economic system produced social stratification, with a small class of wealthy owners of capital (i.e. 'dead men's labour') who 'consume a great deal while they produce nothing'. So they had to be kept at the expense of those who did work. As to the middle class, the bulk of them worked but did not produce. Even where they did produce – usually wastefully – they consumed far more than they produced. 'It is their ambition and the end of their whole lives to gain, if not for themselves yet at least for their children, the proud position of being obvious burdens on the community.'[20] Next came the working class, employed in making 'all those articles of folly and luxury, the demand for which is the outcome of the existence of the rich non-producing classes; things which people leading a manly and uncorrupted life would not ask for or dream of[21]. Morris said of the working class that they were forced to produce either luxuries for the wealthy or shoddy goods for themselves, and hence by his definition were unhappy. On all counts the demand which the capitalist supplied was a false demand. 'The market in which he sells is "rigged" by the miserable inequalities produced by the robbery of the system of Capital and Wages.'[22] Every social class then was a slave to luxury, that 'invention of competitive commerce', and in such a system, the natural consequences of which were effeminacy and brutality, art, as defined by Morris was impossible, thus unhappiness – alienation – was inevitable.

But Morris had yet more to say on the evils of capitalism. It was not only preventing all men from fulfilling themselves, it was destroying their very physical environment: like some modern Midas it turned everything it touched to filth. 'Blacken rivers, hide the sun and poison the air with smoke and worse, and it's nobody's business to see it or mend it: that is all that modern commerce, the counting-house forgetful of the workshop, will do for us herein.'[23] Morris concluded his attacks against capitalism as follows: 'Was it all to end in a counting-house on the top of a cinder heap, with Podsnap's drawing room in the offing, and a Whig committee dealing out champagne to the rich and margarine to the poor in such convenient proportions as would make all men contented together . . .?'[24]

No, it was not! Capitalist society was to be overthrown and replaced by a socialist society of the fundamental-egalitarian type. Morris was unquestionably committed to revolutionary change and although at various times in his life he seemed hopeful that the change might come about peacefully as a consequence of widespread education of the working class to a state of true consciousness, he never ruled out the possibility of violent revolution.[25] Indeed in *News from Nowhere* Morris set out in some detail the course he thought such a revolution might take.[26] The purpose of the revolution was to seek to re-establish a simplified life-style, a return to Whitman's 'primal sanities', and the framework for this life-style was to be socialist:

'A condition of society in which there should be neither rich nor poor, neither master nor master's man, neither idle nor overworked, neither brain-sick brain workers, nor heart-sick hand workers, in a word, a world in which all men would be living in equality of condition, and would manage their affairs unwastefully, and with the full consciousness that harm to one would mean harm to all — the realisation at last of the word COMMONWEALTH.'[27]

Knowing Morris as we do we can be sure that his socialist society will not be of an entirely new variety. It will resemble medieval society in certain aspects. Morris's passion for medieval life, for chivalric codes of behaviour, and his sympathy for the Norse egalitarian robustness were, as we have seen, significant influences in his early upbringing. And they were nurtured by events and experiences throughout his life, never more significantly than by his contacts with Ruskin.

True, he admitted, medieval society was scarcely egalitarian, but divisions between men were 'arbitrary rather than real', by which he meant that there existed no gulf in language, manners and ideas. The historical accuracy of this assertion must remain highly dubious, but that is not relevant: what is relevant is that Morris believed it. For him medieval men were equal in the most important sense: they were all practising artists. 'The mental qualities necessary to an artist . . . had not then to go through the mill of the competitive market.'[28] Implicit within Morris's socialism is the attempt to regain lost dignity and simplicity, a 'backward glance' which typified the writing of a number of earlier socialist thinkers. It caused H.G. Wells, who attended many of the meetings of the Hammersmith Socialist Society, to say later that it had been absurd to imagine 'that we were being led anywhere but backward by this fine old scholar',[29] and caused Nordau to claim that Morris tended to see himself as 'a wandering minstrel of the thirteenth or fourteenth century'.[30] There is about Morris's writing, especially when taken as a whole, much which is highly romantic and of little political value. Yet it would be palpably absurd for any writer to refrain from drawing strength and inspiration from a particular set of social relationships because they had existed in the distant past! In the light of recent pronouncements concerning the desirability or inevitability of 'zero-growth' economies, Morris's futurist picture of a simplified pattern of life may become highly relevant, even though it is firmly rooted in medieval ideas.

Equality in all matters − fundamental equality − was to be the cornerstone of Morris's socialist society. We will do well to realise that this belief in equality stemmed not only, as Nordau suggested, from 'love and pity for his fellow men'[31] but from a belief that true art could only emerge from the spirit of a whole people. Free initiative and free creation in the everyday work of the world would bring to humanity 'a sense of growth and fulfilment − of spiritual, mental and physical expansion − which would enhance the beauty of life internally as well as externally.'[32] Equality in all matters was seen to be essential for Morris's socialist society for this very reason. 'I do not want art for a few, any more than education for a few, or freedom for a few.'[33]

Morris built a socialist society on the basis of his theory of man in a state of fundamental equality. It is necessary to examine the nature of this society and this can be most conveniently managed by focusing our attention chiefly, though not exclusively, on *News From Nowhere.*[34]

Nowhere comprises a federation of independent communities, an arrangement set out in some detail in *Dawn of a New Epoch* and, though Morris tells us little about it, the use of the word federation implies the existence of some central agency. In fact Morris was so vague on the matter that it seems likely that he included it in his scheme somewhat reluctantly, to avoid a charge of anarchism! He described this agency as 'some kind of centre whose function it would be to protect the principles whose practice the communities should carry out.'[35] In the early post-revolutionary days the central agency had important functions, though even then, with its decisions invariably based on 'the measure of the common wealth' its control was minimal. In establishing the clear expression of the majority will, the central agency would have been greatly assisted by what Morris called the 'reflex' of the terror of starvation. Once the majority will was established, the central agency could be disbanded. We can assume that since the Houses of Parliament in Nowhere have become the Dung Market and since society has obviously advanced considerably since the revolution, the central agency is no more. What is left to Nowhere is the independent communities made up of people who have 'no consciousness of being governed'.[36] In these communities each individual has a share in decision making, so that the whole notion of 'masters' has disappeared and all men are *fellows* working in the harmony of association for the common good'. In such a society man has come to realise that there is no real distinction between his own interests and those of the community. Moreover, in order that small communities may live a simple, self-sufficient existence, large-scale manufacturing has ceased; industrial towns have been de-urbanised (in fact this was supposed to have taken place in 1955!); the division between town and country, townsman and countryman has disappeared.[37] These small post-urban communities govern themselves through the Neighbourhood Mote in which all participate and in which majority decisions carry the day. Almost universally, Old Hammond explains to the traveller, minorities 'yield in a friendly manner'.[38]

In fact Nowhere's socialist society is post-political. 'We are very well off as to politics,' says old Hammond, the sage, 'because we have none.' What Hammond means is made clear somewhat later. Differences of opinion occur among the citizens but these 'do not crystallise into parties permanently hostile to one another'. How are decisions taken then? First it must be remembered that the people are equal in all respects and therefore they have no use for political or administrative elites. 'A man no more needs an elaborate system of government, with its army, navy or police, to force him to give way to the will of the majority of his *equals,* than he wants a similar machinery to make him understand that his head and a stone wall cannot occupy the same space at the same moment',[39] explains Hammond. In short, the whole paraphernalia of government has been found unnecessary. Transgressions occur, but society feels no compunction to punish the transgressors. The people recognise these transgressions for what they are: ' . . . the errors of friends, not the habitual actions of persons driven into enmity against society.'[40] There are no criminal classes in Nowhere simply because no wealthy class exists which uses the state unjustly to preserve its privileges, thus breeding enemies of the state. The transgressors, then, will be punished only by their own remorse, which will be certain, since there is no punishment to evade, no law to triumph over.[41] So Morris's fundamental-egalitarianism demands that 'political society as we know

80

it will have come to an end: the relationship between man and man will no longer be that of status or of property.'[42]

With no masters, the workers own the means of production. But here, as we have seen, Morris departed fundamentally from orthodox Marxism, in that this ownership becomes a preliminary to the breaking up of the industrial system. In Nowhere as much manufacture as possible has been taken from the factory and given back to the craftsmen. This becomes possible because fewer goods are needed. 'When the workers are society,' said Morris, 'they will regulate their labour, so that the supply and demand shall be genuine.'[43] So at last man can be truly happy because the requirements for contented, creative labour have been met: 'it is done, that is, by artists'.[44] Morris goes on to paint in detail not only the social arrangements of his socialist society, the child-directed, craft-centred education, the sexual equality, but also to provide a sense of the atmosphere of life. Nowhere is full of buxom girls and broad-shouldered youths, beautiful, strong and healthy. 'I demand a free and unfettered animal life for man first of all,' said Morris.[45] The consolations of life for the citizens of Nowhere are: freedom, happiness, energy, beauty of body and artistic environment. No mean aspirations these, but it is surely a major criticism that the life of the spirit has no place in Nowhere. 'Books, books! always books, grandfather! When will you understand that after all it is the world we live in which interests us; the world of which we are a part and can never love too much?' asks Ellen.[46] Looked at from a spiritual point of view, life in Nowhere is not so remarkably different from Huxley's Brave New World. As Maurice Hewlett commented: 'A race of fleshy perfection, worshipping phenomena, relying on appearance, arguing from sensation; a nation of strong men and fair women, conscious of their own growth and of their country's, owning an art which springs from and is directed to Nature, Simplicity, Truth, which yet sees no significance, no shadow behind these comely forms, dreams no future, owns no standard, accepts no explanation, needs no justifying.'[47] Morris seems unaware of this shortcoming, claiming only for the people of Nowhere that they pass their lives 'in reasonable strife with nature, exercising not one side of [themselves] only, but all sides, taking the keenest pleasure in all the life of the world'.[48]

Nowhere is open to another criticism which, though it may be stated briefly, is important; for a socialist society it seems to be highly individualist. Although its citizens call each other 'neighbour', share all things in common and have no private property, they seem to be remarkably untouched by any community spirit. That is to say, the community as such contributes little to their way of life beyond providing the most effective environment for each to explore the limits of his individuality and creativity. Yet, allowing for the gay colour of their clothes, there is a noticeable drabness and lack of individuality about the people of Nowhere.

Linking these two criticisms together we find in Nowhere a people who are individuals only at a superficial level, forming part of communities which appear in no sense to be anything more than the sum of the individuals composing them. Possibly this represents an artistic failure on Morris's part but it is also possible that he misunderstood the nature of community. Does there exist, in the entire span of human − or indeed animal − experience, an example of a community of complete equals? Does not community imply division of function and perhaps of status? In any event, Morris's communities appear to be mere shells and their members disappointingly superficial. The beautiful Ellen, when pointing out to her grandfather how much better things are in Nowhere than they were in nineteenth-century Britain, offers her beauty as an example; how quickly it would have deteriorated in the 'bad days'! Maurice Hewlett comments: 'It is as if a pheasant were endowed with sensibility and lamented the moulting season.'[49]

Finally perhaps the reader is left with a lingering doubt about how seriously Morris had considered the virtues of a simple life. When the traveller spends the day with Dick, Clara and Old Hammond, Morris writes: 'When we had done eating, and were sitting a little while, with a bottle of very good Bordeaux wine before us . . . '[50] Old Hammond's wine implies a sophisticated system of exchange at an international level; and the wine's being called 'very good' implies that some other neighbours had to make do with wine which was not so good! It is worth pointing out that if Morris's communities produced only their own apparent needs, then their lives would become rude rather than simple. If, on the other hand, Morris allows a system of exchange, especially at an international level, then communities may well have to produce goods for which they have no use themselves and which, indeed, may be regarded as luxuries.

When all is said and done, however, Morris's socialist society has much to commend it, and Morris's socialist man, though he is not a spiritual being, seems to live a full and enjoyable life at the physical level. He cares for his environment; above all he takes pleasure from his work and he owns no master. Morris's socialist man combines the two traditions which played such a large part in his own heritage: a belief in the instinctive creativity of man, as evidenced in the work of medieval craftsmen and an affinity with the Norse passion for equality, as evidenced in contemporary Icelandic society. Finally Morris's socialist man leaves us with a question of the utmost consequence; a question which he answers dramatically:

What shall ye lack when ye lack masters?
Ye shall not lack for the fields ye have
tilled, nor the houses ye have built, nor
the cloth ye have woven; all these things
shall be yours, and whatso ye will of all
that the earth beareth.

Dream of John Ball

2

'If you ask me "Why should not the people make their own laws?"
I can only ask you "Why should not the people write their own
plays?" '

Preface to the Apple Cart

Bernard Shaw was born in Dublin in 1856, and was thus almost twenty
years younger than Morris and a young man when the latter was in his
prime. Moreover there was between them a social gulf of greater
proportion and probably of greater significance. Shaw did not share
Morris's accustomed ease of life. Although born into a Protestant family
in a city where Protestantism was synonymous with social and political
eminence, little of that eminence attached to the Shaws. They were
poor and teetered on the brink of real poverty.

At the age of twenty-three Shaw left Dublin to join his family in
London, determined upon a literary career. With his family in considerable economic difficulties Shaw's intention ruled out the possibility of
his making any worthwhile contribution to the family income. As he
said later: 'I did not throw myself into the struggle for life, I threw my
mother into it.'[51] At all events Shaw wrote three novels, each of which
was unsuccessful, and one of which was acclaimed by the Macmillan's
reader as being the work of a young man who knew nothing about life.

In the year 1883 two events occurred of the greatest moment for
Shaw's future. First Shaw discovered socialism and second he discovered
the theatre. Shaw's and Morris's paths to socialism were strangely
similar. Both had been most impressed by public meetings held by
Henry George; both were later advised by Hyndman to read Marx, and
both were converted on the spot, as it were. But in the same year Shaw
also met William Archer, who introduced him to the work of Ibsen and
encouraged him to write not novels but plays. The result of these two
circumstances history well knows. Like Morris, Shaw entered red
socialist politics and worked socialist themes into his art. But unlike
Morris he was successful in both enterprises.

Let us consider briefly Shaw as an active socialist. As is
well known Shaw joined the Fabian Society and later became one

of its pillars. What is not so well known is that, with Webb, Shaw was largely instrumental in directing Fabian energies away from non (and even anti) constitutional activities towards the parliamentary and 'permeative' tactics with which the Fabian is more commonly associated today. Fabius Conctator had a reputation not only for biding his time but also for decisive action when the time was ripe: there is evidence to show the Fabians, when Shaw and Sidney Webb joined them, to be more interested in striking hard than in waiting for the right moment. Shaw wrote that the Fabians in the 1880s were caught up in a 'sort of influenza of anarchism',[52] and that during these years they were 'just as anarchistic as the Socialist League and just as insurrectionary as the [Social Democratic] Federation'.[53] There was, he says, a genuine belief that their campaign to 'educate, agitate and organise' would bring about a 'tremendous smash up of existing society'.[54]

But if revolution was to be organised by an elite it had to be manned by the proletariat, and Shaw was perfectly well aware that the capacity of the British proletariat for revolution was not without limits. 'You can buy any revolution off for 30 bob a week,' he once claimed.[55] It was a fact that the industrial slump which the country had been experiencing had begun to ease off and industrial relations had improved at least for the time being. So although not in theory opposed to revolution we can conclude that Shaw saw general obstacles to the British revolution.[56] Shaw's experience of the failure of the demonstration in 1887 and his conspicuous part in that failure inspired him to lend his full weight to Webb's theoretical justification of gradualism. Together they helped to purge the Fabian of insurrectionism and anarchism and made of it a group wholly committed to parliamentary socialism. This was to have a considerable effect on the development of British socialism, though Shaw himself later entertained doubts as to its ultimate wisdom. Certainly it was this policy which, in practical immediate terms, set the Fabian apart from the Socialist League, and Shaw apart from Morris.

For twelve years Shaw spoke on average three times weekly wherever he could get a hearing, and he was one of the best public speakers of his day. At the same time he was an energetic councillor for St Pancras. He was, that is to say, active in politics. Most important was Shaw's work behind the scenes in keeping Fabians together, and keeping them apart from the SDF and Morris's Socialist League. Shaw helped to hold the Fabian together for twenty-seven years by dint of skilful concili- atory moves. As a result, of the four socialist groups of the early days — the Fabian, the Social Democratic Federation, the Socialist League and Headlam's Guild of St Matthew, only the Fabian outlived its founders. And it was the Fabian which was the permanent influence on the development of British Socialism.

Without doubt, Shaw was a far more successful political activist than Morris. He was more realistic and, perhaps, more devious. But Shaw's socialism stemmed from a pattern of belief based upon the nature of socialist man and makes sense only within the context of that pattern. And Shaw's socialist man was very different from Morris's conception. It is appropriate at this point then to consider the overall pattern of Shaw's political thought.

Shaw began with a criticism of capitalist society which in many respects was similar to Morris's; in fact was common to most socialists. He was appalled by capitalism's apparent waste and inefficiency and detested the consequences of this for the mass of mankind. But it must be understood that Shaw rejected absolutely the notion of the class war. True he was more impressed by Marx's indictment of capitalist society than by his economic theories but he always remained totally out of sympathy with the working class and its aspirations.

His hatred of poverty was simply part of a more general hatred of the poor and in this we find a complete break with the normal socialist tradition. For Shaw socialism was not about giving power to the people, it was not about taking up cudgels on behalf of one class against another. As he wrote on behalf of himself and his Fabian colleagues: 'We have never advanced the smallest pretention to represent the working classes of this country.'[57] He came to reject out of hand any possibility of the working class's forming a base for revolutionary or evolutionary change.

It is not difficult to discover the reasons why Shaw was prepared to reject the notions fairly common among intellectuals of the left that the industrial proletariat possessed certain enviable qualities. In Dublin the Shaw family had never been far from toppling into the ranks of the poor, a state of affairs which was to leave its mark on Shaw just as it did, though to an even greater extent, upon H.G. Wells. For Shaw poverty was a great crime. As we see clearly from *Major Barbara,* it was better in his eyes to make money selling guns than to be poor; a greater sin to be exploited than to exploit. (We shall have to return to this theme later in more detail.) When we remember that Shaw also believed the workers to possess little potential for revolution or even for sustained militancy, we begin to realise that when Shaw spoke of abolishing the working class he was not being profoundly humane and far-sighted; he was callously dismissing a range of problems with which he would prefer not to deal. One cannot escape the conclusion that at heart Shaw believed that nobody was poor who did not deserve to be.

Shaw's socialism envisaged three stages in the development of society. The first and most crucial stage was that of the economically equal society, run by an elite in the interests of all. The second stage was that of the society of supermen and the final stage that of men like gods who lived a life so spiritual that material considerations came to be of no consequence. We see immediately from this pattern that Shaw had not one socialist man but three and although we must begin at, and concentrate chiefly upon, the first stage, we must nevertheless work our way towards the final stage in order to understand Shaw's socialism in its entirety. Let us then begin at the beginning.

Shaw was described earlier as a hierarchical egalitarian. He believed that economic equality — more precisely equality of income — was a prerequisite to socialist society stage one. Income, he argued, is the *only thing* about human beings that you can equalise,[58] and there is really very little difficulty about managing it. Against arguments that with equal pay nobody would do the unpleasant jobs nor the most taxing, Shaw pointed out that the most unpleasant jobs were usually the worst paid anyway, and that the most taxing were always the most rewarding, irrespective of financial gain. It has to be admitted, however, that Shaw withdrew from this position towards the end of his life, accepting that the masses should be given only half of their share, the remainder to be distributed among the 'top 10 per cent', society's natural leaders, so that they might cultivate the arts. All the same, in his most fervently socialist days, Shaw was for strict equality of income.

In an economically equal society there would be no bar to prevent the emergence of natural leaders. Here Shaw's first socialist man makes his appearance: the natural leader. 'Now I'm for any Napoleon or Mussolini or Lenin . . . that has the stuff in him to take both the people and the spoilers and oppressors by the scruff of their silly necks and just sling them into the way they should go', says the trade union leader Hipney, in *On the Rocks.* Although written much later this speech captures clearly the spirit which moved Shaw from the first. It is not difficult to understand why Shaw was later to call himself a totalitarian democrat, neither is it difficult to prove false the notion that his totalitarianism came on with advancing senility. When he claimed: 'I was a national socialist before Hitler was born' he was stating an approximate truth. He had always believed in the ability of natural leadership to assert itself in a socialist society and to run that society in such a way as to maximise welfare for the whole population. He showed boundless faith in their ability to create a 'social order aiming at the greatest available welfare for the whole population'. Shaw's writing on this point is often redolent of the kind of phraseology of writers like Ruskin and Carlyle, arguing for an 'aristocracy' of talent and intellect. But Shaw's leaders would only be able to emerge and achieve 'self expression' in an economically equitable society. The theme of *Major Barbara,* of *Man and Superman,* even of *Pygmalion* is of people who were exceptionally talented and who possessed or discovered the capacity to dominate others, usually to the others' advantage. Indeed in *The Millionairess* the heroine gave up one fortune only to accumulate another immediately, by virtue of sheer ability, heaping benefits upon those with whom she came into contact in the process. The activities of these people ought not to be limited by society for they work naturally to the advantage of mankind, Shaw argued. These were the 'realists' of politics, uncluttered by the delusions shared by many of Shaw's contemporaries, such as that of 'an ideal proletariat, forced by the brutalitities of the capitalist system into an unwilling acquiescence in war, penal codes and other cruelties of civilisation. [His contemporaries] still see the social problem not sanely and objectively, but imaginatively, as the plot of melodrama, with its villain and its heroine, its innocent beginning, troubled middle and happy ending. They are still the children and romancers of politics.'[59] The realists, then, by, permeating the structures of the major parties and, more broadly, by using the accepted parliamentary techniques, establish a society of equal incomes. From this much more economically equal society more of the natural leaders will emerge – between five and ten per cent of the population in all. It would then become their task to eradicate poverty.

For their own good the people were to be 'dominated' by this 'rational and well-informed superpower'[60] and led out of their poverty, like it or not. The task of abolishing poverty would not be easy, but all shoulders would be at the wheel. 'For my part,' Shaw tells us, 'I cannot understand how anyone who has the most elementary comprehension of socialism can doubt that compulsory labour and the treatment of parasitic idleness as the sin against the Holy Ghost must be fundamental in socialist law and religion.'[61] This elemental puritanism was always part of Shaw's socialist belief, though he tended to argue the case more flamboyantly as he got older. 'Compulsory labour with death as the final penalty is the keystone of socialism.'[62] In the late 1950s a series of laws known as the Anti-Parasitism Laws appeared on the statute book in the Soviet Union, with harsh prison sentences for offenders. Indeed Fidel Castro produced a law in Cuba in 1970 against the *predelictivo de vagancia,* arguing in a public speech in September of that year: 'In a collective society, where man works for society, laziness must become a crime – a crime similar to stealing.' Shaw would have applauded loudly; Morris would have been mortified!

Shaw believed passionately in the regimentation of life, enslaving people, as he said, in order to secure the utmost freedom for them. The spiritual advancement of mankind, as we shall see, was Shaw's *prime* consideration, but as he makes equally clear, in, for example, the Gospel according to St Andrew Undershaft, man's material welfare is the *first* consideration. It was man's job to better himself in the capitalist system;

in the socialist system it was the state's job to eliminate poverty altogether, and thus to provide men with the necessary foundation of the spiritual life. Undershaft convinced his daughter, a major in the Salvation Army, that he was doing more for men by giving them decent working conditions, good salaries, and by providing the kind of amenities that Morris was disposed to claim as of right, than she was in trying to save souls at her soup kitchen in the East End of London. For Shaw the only truly socialist government, then, is the one that got things done. 'The notion . . . that government is a tyranny to be minimised at all costs in the name of liberty will have to be eradicated by genuine scientific education of the children.'[63]

Society's leaders would operate in a nominally democratic manner through a system of panels of ascending importance. Periodically the voters might select their leaders at various levels from among the relevant panels. But not on a party basis, for Shaw loathed party politics. What is more, to vote at all one had to pass an ingelligence test. The system would operate as follows. At the local level, the panel system would provide for election by those sufficiently 'intelligent' to be enfranchised to local government panels. These would be responsible for the administration of local affairs (a gesture to the Webbs' municipal socialism) and for electing area panels. This process would repeat itself upwards until a national panel was provided.

Now Shaw was well aware that many good socialists would have good socialist reasons for opposing his scheme. But he was at pains to point out that although it was designed to produce efficient totalitarian government, it was also designed to operate in an economically egalitarian society. Thus the elite would be representative of the people if not directly responsible to them. The keystone of Shaw's system, then, was equality of income. It seems strange, however, that although Shaw expected that the mass of people might be given to idleness — a very antisocial state of mind — they would not be given over to rebelliousness. How could they be, Shaw exlaimed, when the sole criterion for the decisions made by the leaders would be wisdom! How could the people demur in the face of truly scientific politics? As Shaw argued: 'When a railway porter directs me to No. 10 platform I do not strike him to the earth with a shout of "Down with Tyranny" and rush violently to No. 1 platform.'[64] This analogy, which after all is representative of Shaw's thinking, might well merit a repeat of the comment from Macmillan's reader; Shaw is legislating for people when he knows nothing about people. Perhaps not all people would accept the leaders' primacy in deciding what is wisdom in the same way they might a railway porter's in deciding which was the best train for them. In the second case the criteria upon which the porter's decision is reached are very likely to be accepted by the passengers. But we can hardly take this common ground for granted so far as social and political decisions are concerned! Ultimately we cannot be satisfied that Shaw's utopia is sufficiently clearly thought out even to pose, leave alone answer, the most important questions.

There remains one final criticism of the equal society run by the naturally dominant. If the leaders, like Plato's, are to receive a special kind of education to fit them for their tasks then quite obviously the system has a basic inbuilt inegalitarianism. It assumes, quite incorrectly, that the naturally dominant will produce naturally dominant children. It would obviously be very difficult for children who receive standardised education to break into the guardian class, since Shaw envisaged separate systems of education for the two groups. Social stratification would probably be only two generations away, closely followed, if history is any guide, by inefficient government.

But let us assume that Shaw's socialist man — stage one — has managed to eradicate poverty and rid the country of idleness. What then follows? Here the contrast with Morris is at its most pronounced. For Shaw, far from an indulgent life of craftsmanship and 'reasonable stride' with nature, socialist society stage one simply makes possible a more dynamic social movement; that of evolution to the society of the supermen.

The idea of the superman is something of a paradox. It is we who recognise superman; we, therefore, who decide precisely which set of criteria shall be employed in adjudicating his supremacy; to this extent he is, although something more than a mere man, at the same time something less. Yet the concept of superman, the true socialist man, enabled Shaw to dispense altogether with the limitations of 'bourgeois' man. Bourgeois man has been socialised 'to be unsocial at every point', said Shaw. 'You need a new human being.'[65] Thus by dint, largely, of selective breeding, a new kind of man was to be evolved. Shaw said that: 'The only fundamental and possible socialism is the socialisation of the selective breeding of men; in other terms, of human evolution.'[66] We shall examine this theory in a moment, but let us not overlook a point of great importance. I have said that Shaw was not fundamentally an egalitarian but it could be said, in his defence, that his belief in equality was in fact more fundamental than that even of Morris, for Shaw believed in equality so fervently that he was prepared to sacrifice man in its name! Against Morris, Shaw claimed that man is *not* by nature equal, not in creative potential, not in anything; therefore we ought to change the nature of man. Not tinker with his environment; not make him stronger and more beautiful, but make him a species as distinguishable from bourgeois man as the latter is from Neanderthal man! 'Why not?' asked Shaw. If a weightlifter can 'put up a muscle', cannot a philosopher 'put up a brain?[67]

Shaw's evolutionary theories were neoLamarkian. Briefly, he believed that a species changed because it wanted to and that although Darwin's principle of natural selection tells us how a species evolves it does not tell us why. Shaw argued that 'everything almost that exists is created by the mere desire that it should exist',[68] and that behind the will to exist lay the Life Force. Shaw's theories were not without confusion, especially where he equated the Life Force with 'our old friend the soul or spirit of man'; and anyway most of what he had to say had been said more clearly by Samuel Butler and more consistently by Bergson. But basic to the second and third stages of the Shavian socialist society was the idea that by individual thought and collective planning man could evolve to a higher species, so long as natural ability and leadership were allowed to emerge, as they would only do in an economically equal society.

The Life Force, in matters of breeding at least, operated through the female sex, and in Shaw's *Man and Superman* we see it in action. In many senses this play is a model of the Shavian technique of expressing ideas which to him were of great moment in a manner such as to make it almost impossible to take them seriously. Studies of animal behaviour over the last thirty to forty years seem to suggest that the female role is indeed paramount in selecting the best partner for breeding and thus if the so-called Life Force can be equated with the innate capacity which species seem to possess for survival, Shaw's picture of the Life Force operating through Anne Whitefield is by no means fanciful. She saw herself as the vehicle of the Life Force and set out, mercilessly, to ensnare Tanner, a socialist man, duly realistic, unsentimental, who on stage dressed remarkably like Hynman. Eventually the two marry and, we may assume, set out to make superchildren.

When a society of supermen has been attained it becomes possible at last to discard the restrictions of 'the human condition' altogether, passing through a phase in human development when pleasure taken in intellectual and spiritual tasks would 'intensify to a chronic ecstacy surpassing that now induced momentarily by the sexual orgasm', to a time when matter itself will be of no consequence. At this stage Shaw's socialist society has, like a space rocket, discarded its second stage and is headed, in every sense, for the stars; we might be forgiven for leaving it to its journey.

Shaw's ideas concerning the ultimate development of socialism may be thought of as fanciful in the extreme. Indeed, it is hardly necessary to criticise the two later stages of development in any detail, since they seem barely to relate to the problems of socialism. But to ignore these stages is to do Shaw an injustice. Shaw's socialist man is constantly aiming at massive progress. Unlike the citizen of Nowhere the Shavian socialist is not content to while away the hours in hay making or drinking bottles of Bordeaux. When, in *Man and Superman,* Don Juan leaves the pleasures of Hell for the ardours of Heaven, he says to the Devil: 'But at least I shall not be bored. The service of the Life Force has that advantage, at all events.' Don Juan would have been equally miserable in Nowhere, for the idea of struggle which Shaw believed to be essential to the well-being of the species is quite artificial there, as it is in Hell. Who knows but the good citizens of Nowhere, in a few more centuries, might not become like the Eloi in Wells's *Time Machine* – as contented as cattle! But in addition to this important consideration, Shaw also felt that socialism needed a 'religion' and that in evolutionary socialism he was providing one; an expectation of the distant future for which men would be prepared to make sacrifices. It remains only to say that, worthy though these ends may have been, Shaw failed. Generally speaking he is not remembered either for his society of equal supermen or for his men like gods; neither did they ever have great impact.

Surely the most momentous feature of Shaw's socialist man is his insatiable desire for 'progress'. Not only was he discontented with a society of waste and inequality, but with human sloth and negligence – indeed with the human condition itself. Yet one feels that concern for superman must lead to – or indeed from – lack of concern for man, and it is this fundamental lack of charity which, I believe, makes us draw back from Shaw's socialist man. What he had to say about the working class can be seen as a general indictment of man because of his incapacity to progress along Shavian socialist lines:

'As to the working classes I believe neither in their virtues nor their intelligence, on the contrary my objection to the existing order is precisely that it inevitably produces this wretched, idolatrous, sentimental, servile, anti-socialist mass of spoiled humanity which we call the proletariat and which neither understands, believes in us nor likes us. I am no friend of the working class. I am its enemy to the extent of ardently desiring its extermination.'

Speech given on March 26th 1914

3

When we compare the socialist men and the socialist societies of William Morris and Bernard Shaw we become aware more of the gulf that divided the two men and their theories than of what they believed in common. Their systems of thought are unique of course, but many of their theories were shared by other socialists and, when compared, bring into sharp focus the disputes which divided socialist thinkers of the time. Morris argued for revolution, for the overthrow of the industrial system, for a simplified and hedonistic life-style, and above all, for the rediscovery of the impulse of artistic creativity in all men which the capitalist system, by virtue of its structure and demands, had all but destroyed. The essential ingredient in Morris's socialism was its fundamental equality.

For Shaw, on the other hand, socialist man sought his objectives through state activity; he sought to maximise the power of the state, not to minimise it. He sought to improve the lot of his fellow men, not to listen to their opinions. He sought to abolish poverty and idleness and to attempt consciously to move human life onto a higher spiritual plane. Shaw's socialist man was not an individual but part of society, part of the species. He saw what he took to be the necessity of struggle, whereas Morris's man had a life of ease and material sufficiency. As for the bulk of mankind, poverty had made them less than human; Shaw's enforced welfare would give them the opportunity to become complete men. Those who did not take it would be eliminated. If Shaw's position seemed extreme it is well to remember that many of his 'totalitarian' views were shared by numbers of the influential Fabian, including, of course, the Webbs.

Morris's socialist man finds fulfilment through his creativity; he is quintessentially an individual. He takes little from society — in the sense that it fulfils few of his needs — and he contributes little to it beyond making its buildings more beautiful. Shaw's socialist man, on the other hand, is a highly differentiated creature. He achieves fulfilment only by virtue of his acting out a specific social function; his main criterion for action must be 'the good of society as a whole'. It is precisely this different conception of the nature of socialist man which makes the hierarchical socialism of Bernard Shaw so different from the egalitarian socialism of William Morris.

Socialist critiques of capitalist society are considerably enriched when seen as part of a coherent view of 'the good life', an elementary point but often overlooked. Many would find Morris's view romantic and idealistic, Shaw's lacking in humanity — he believed, for example, that the citizens of Stalin's Russia were the freest in the world.[69] Yet in their separate ways they raise the same fundamental point; if, by their very different methods, Morris and Shaw managed to create their socialist men, what would be the object of life of these men? Would the men of Nowhere really be contented playing at working? Is Shaw's evolutionary efficiency a sufficient goal for the socialist man or the socialist superman?

Finally it is worth pointing out that idealised societies or utopias are usually constructed in such a way that their creator might feel perfectly at home in them; so the socialist men of Morris and Shaw are in fact none other than Morris and Shaw themselves living the kind of life which they feel bourgeois society prevented them from leading:

Morris the neighbourly craftsman, untroubled by politicians; Shaw the true political scientist, running society for its own good and rid at last of the spectre of poverty that had always haunted him.

NOTES

1. Old Hammond in *News from Nowhere,* Collected Works of William Morris, vol. XVI, London, Longman Green and Company, 1912, p.87.
2. *Time and Tide,* 10 February 1945.
3. L.W. Grey, *William Morris,* London, Cassell and Company, 1949, p.21.
4. See R. Furneux Jordan, *The Medieval Vision of William Morris,* London, William Morris Society, 1960.
5. Quoted Grey, *op. cit.,* p.138. Emphasis in the original.
6. It was alleged that in 1885 the Conservative party had given financial assistance to the SDF in two seats in London, in the hope of their defeating the Liberals.
7. R. Page Arnot, *The Man and the Myth,* London, Lawrence and Wishart, 1964.
8. Edward Thompson, *William Morris: Romantic to Revolutionary,* London, Lawrence and Wishart, 1955.
9. See *Art Under Plutocracy.* My italics. It is worth pointing out that Morris's political tracts are available in several collections, most notably in the *Complete Works of William Morris,* published by Longman Green and Company. A number of the more important tracts have been issued in *Political Writings of William Morris,* edited and with an introduction by A.L. Morton, London, Lawrence and Wishart, 1973. Throughout, where I refer to a tract, I have simply given its title.
10. *Art and Socialism.*
11. *Art Under Plutocracy.*
12. *The Lesser Arts .* Emphasis in the original.
13. 'Art by means of which men have at all times more or less striven to beautify the familiar matters of everyday life.' *(The Lesser Arts)*
14. *Art and Socialism.*
15. *Useful Work versus Useless Toil.*
16. *Useful Work versus Useless Toil.*
17. *Art and Socialism.*
18. *Art and Socialism.*
19. *Art Under Plutocracy.*
20. *Useful Work Versus Useless Toil.*
21. *ibid.*
22. *ibid.*
23. *The Lesser Arts.*
24. *How I Became a Socialist.*
25. See *How We Live and How We Might Live.*
26. Chapter XVII.
27. *How I Became A Socialist.*
28. *ibid.*
29. *Saturday Review,* October 1896.
30. *Degeneration,* London, 1896, pp.98-9.
31. Nordau, *loc. cit.*

32. Grey, *op. cit.,* p.146.

33. *The Lesser Arts.*

34. I have used the version contained in vol. XVI of *The Collected Works of William Morris,* London, Longman Green and Company, 1912.

35. *Dawn of a New Epoch.*

36. *The Society of the Future.*

37. The descriptions of socialist London are captivating: 'The wholesomeness of architecture which we had come upon so suddenly from amidst the pleasant fields was not only exquisitely beautiful in itself, but it bore upon the expression of such generosity and abundance of life that I was exhilarated to a pitch that I had never yet reached' (*News From Nowhere,* p.24).

38. *ibid,* p.89.

39. *ibid,* pp. 75, 76.

40. *ibid,* p.80.

41. *ibid,* p.83.

42. *The Society of the Future.*

43. *How We Live and How We Might Live.*

44. *News From Nowhere,* p.92.

45. *The Society of the Future.*

46. *Nowhere,* p.150.

47. *National Review,* August 1891.

48. *News from Nowhere,* p.58.

49. *loc. cit.*

50. *News From Nowhere,* p.101.

51. Hesketh Pearson, *Bernard Shaw – His Life and Personality,* London, Methuen & Co., 1961, p.18.

52. *Essays in Fabian Socialism,* London, Constable, 1932, p.131.

53. *The Fabian Society, What It has Done and How It has Done It.* See J.W. Hulse, *Revolutionists in London,* Oxford, Clarendon Press, 1970, pp. 113-17.

54. *Essays in Fabian Socialism, loc. cit.*

55. Quoted H. Pearson, *op. cit.,* p.73.

56. On Sunday, 7 November 1887, Bloody Sunday, Shaw, who was leading a column of marchers into Trafalgar Square, had beaten a hasty retreat when fighting broke out, earning Cunningham Graham's jibe he had been 'the first man to run away from the square on Bloody Sunday'.

57. *Essays in Fabian Socialism, op. cit.,* p.158.

58. See Frank Harris, *Bernard Shaw – An Unauthorized Biography based on First-hand Information,* London, Gollancz, 1931, p.53.

59. *Cosmopolis* iii, London, September 1896, p.659.

60. *Intelligent Woman's Guide to Socialism, Capitalism, Sovietism and Fascism,* London, Constable, 1929, p.452.

61. *Collected Works,* vol. 29, London, Constable, pp.146-7.

62. In *Labour Monthly,* October 1921.

63. Chappelow, *op. cit.,* p.195.

64. *Intelligent Woman's Guide,* p.376.

65. Frank Harris, *op. cit.,* p.61.

66. *ibid.,* p.160.

67. Preface to *Back to Methuselah.*

68. A.C. Ward, *Bernard Shaw,* London, Longman, Green, 1957, p.122.

69. *Tribune,* 25 April 1943.

5 THE UNDIVIDED SELF*

Robert Eccleshall

> I am not yet born; O fill me
> With strength against those who would freeze my
>   humanity, would dragoon me into a lethal automaton,
>   would make me a cog in a machine, a thing with
>   one face, a thing, and against all those
>   who would dissipate my entirety, would
>   blow me like thistledown hither and
>   thither or hither and thither
>   like water held in the
>   hands would spill me.   Louis MacNeice,
> *Prayer before Birth.*

A central and persistent theme in radical literature is that man as
collective subject has built a world which in the process of construction
has somehow eluded his control, burning back on its creator and
precluding him from that inward response by which life is suffused with
richness and diversity. Thrust into a hostile environment, the agent of
the historical process is a mere caricature of what he might or ought to
be, because determined by alien life-experiences and governed by a
set of regulations bearing no resemblance to his human needs, he
embodies within himself all the contradictions of that system of social
constraints which conspires to diminish him. Crushed and routinised,
the human self disintegrates into a series of disconnected functions and
antagonistic attributes in which thought is dissociated from action and
duty is opposed to feeling. As compensation for this gloomy picture
radicals affirm the possible negation of the existing social order and,
with its transcendence, the emergence of a dynamic self responsible to
life in all its forms. My intention is to outline the connection which
radicals trace between the human being divided within himself and the
determinate set of socioeconomic conditions to which he is subject.
Once this has been done, I shall examine their various images of
authentic existence. In particular, a critical stance will be taken towards
certain twentieth-century radicals who, adopting some form of

---

*Thanks are due to Robert Benewick, Andrew Collier and Graham Day
   for their comments on the original draft.

instinctual monism, imagine that in a humanised environment the whole man will be one who lives in the unbridled fullness of his liberated passions.[1]

Human fragmentation was a major preoccupation of Enlightenment thinkers half a century and more before its solution was perceived in terms of a drastic reshaping of the social structure.[2] In *An Essay on the History of Civil Society* (1767), Adam Ferguson's attitude to increasing occupational specialisation was ambivalent. Though an inevitable aspect of social progress, the division of labour developed in the individual only those faculties which equipped him for his particular social function. Ferguson's work was especially influential in Germany where, immersed in the Greek ideal of the all-round individual and confronted by a politically and culturally divided nation, Herder, Humboldt and Schiller protested against a narrow professionalism which repressed so many facets of a potentially rich human nature. And a good case can be made for taking the search for a solution to the problem of human fragmentation as providing the unifying theme of Hegel's thinking.[3] Schiller's impassioned outburst against a social system which destroyed the harmonious interplay of the intellect, senses and imagination, thereby producing stunted and partial human beings, equals in intensity anything to be written by Marx:

> 'Everlastingly chained to a single little fragment of the Whole, man himself develops into nothing but a fragment; everlastingly in his ear the monotonous sound of the wheel that he turns, he never develops the harmony of his being, and instead of putting the stamp of his humanity upon his own nature, he becomes nothing more than the imprint of his occupation or of his specialized knowledge. But even that meagre, fragmentary participation, by which individual members of the State are still linked to the Whole, does not depend upon forms which they spontaneously prescribe for themselves . . . it is dictated to them with meticulous exactitude by means of a formulary which inhibits all freedom of thought. The dead letter takes the place of living understanding, and a good memory is a safer guide than imagination and feeling.'[4]

Contained here are all the main ingredients of the radical charge against the established order. Yet German writers were on the whole content with expressing moral outrage, or with advocating a solution whereby human wholeness was to be recovered either through aesthetic experience (Schiller) or by individual integration into a revitalised political culture, neither of which demanded transformative political action on a grand scale.

It was Feuerbach who, in focusing philosophical attention on multidimensional natural man, supplied the theoretical impetus required for radicalism to emerge. Fragmentation in his view occurred whenever men lost touch with any of the various facets of their sociosensuous nature. 'Man, the complete and true man, is only he who possesses a sense that is aesthetic or artistic, religious or moral, philosophic or scientific; in general, only he who excludes nothing essentially human is man.'[5] The idealist philosopher was the epitome of fragmented man because his selection of reason from a totality of attributes as denoting the human essence was indicative of the fact that he had severed all links with sensory experience. Rejecting that which might confound his categories by relegating the human sensorium to the realm of appearance, the philosopher became a prey to self-deception.[6] Yet he merely high-lighted, albeit acutely, the disease with which all who ignored the sensuous were afflicted, for his illusions had their analogue in the efforts of ordinary men to overcome their finitude through a fantastic pro-jection of frustrated desires. God was the creation of an imagination run amok, a creation with unfortunate practical implications because the man who debased himself before an idol of his own making became amenable to manipulation by all those oppressive forces which main-tained their hegemony by perpetuating the errors of the mind.[7]

Human dignity was restored when men realised that their particular limitations were transcended in the infinity of the species. The complete man, possessing a complex sensory equipment, was a participant in the culminated achievements of the species. None of the attributes of generic man were conceivable as belonging to an isolated being. It was through contact with others that the individual established his human identify, so that love was expressive of the fact that men confirm themselves in a relational context. Similarly, it was by means of speech that the rational faculty was developed and the species was the repository of all knowledge acquired by sensory perception. Feuerbach thought it sufficient for men to recognise their indebtedness to the species in order to make their existence accord with their essence. Nature was not for him an unruly mass awaiting pacification through activity which reshapes it to suit human needs, but a static whole requiring adaptation through adequate comprehension. Indeed, he viewed with suspicion the imagination, that faculty which might be instrumental in recreating the object world, as being the major source of self-deception. As an onlooker, confronted by an unmediated and independent object yielding data which his senses had to learn to accept, man was reconciled to the world by perception which 'enlightens the mind'. Enlightenment, therefore, was considered sufficient to banish from the earth those forces of oppression which were nourished by servility. Unable to comprehend that the objects apprehended by the senses had already been mediated by human practice, Feuerbach failed to grasp that the illusions fostered by the mind might adequately reflect a distorted reality. Hence the paradox that, having retrieved the notion of the whole man from its dissolution and submergence in idealism, Feuerbach's solution to the problem of fragmentation itself had an idealist flavour. The fault was cognitive and mind was to be the liberating agent whereby mastery of the world was to be attained. Offering no satisfactory explanation as to why men found themselves adrift in a hostile world, Feuerbach's validation of the sensuous and social degenerated into the sentimental plea that each should seek self-realisation through love of others.

'But from the abstract man of Feuerbach one arrives at real living men only when one considers them as participants in history.'[8] Replacing natural but passive Feuerbachian man with the conception of a being who actually shapes extra-human reality, Marx made fragmentation an historical problem to be resolved by human activity. Hegel had been the first to give systematic expression to the notion of man as an active being because his claim that the Idea transformed the world through human activity led him to identify labour as a central onto-logical category, the medium whereby men both modify themselves and recreate their environment in the process of satisfying needs. It was through his demystification of Hegel, a purification that entailed the retention of the active conception of man, that Marx was able to demonstrate how a practical mastery of the world might be attained in such a way that, contrary to Hegel's view, mankind would not lose itself in the process of objectification. The dehumanised world awaited destruction by its creator and radical thought emerged as a demand for radical transformative action. As Marx wrote in one of the *Theses on Feuerbach:* 'All social life is essentially *practical.* All systems which lead theory to mysticism find their rational solution in human practice and in the comprehension of this practice.' Actively inclined towards the world around him by the necessity of satisfying wants, man creates his own human nature because in the process of working up nature, his inorganic body, into embodiments of subjective intent he continually develops new possibilities for the actualisation of human potentialities, scope for the expression of his hitherto latent powers. A 'coming-to-be of nature for man' by virtue of the fact that human activity mediates between subject and object, history is also a coming-to-be of man for himself.

The implication is that human wholeness is a confirmation of the active humanisation of nature. 'Universally developed individuals . . . are the product not of nature but of history.'[9] As a conscious being the individual participates in the historical achievements of the species, not merely sharing in its accumulated knowledge, but satisfying the various aspects of his sensuous nature because he inhabits an environment which objectification has made into a fitting medium for the expression of his powers. So the whole man is the product of an environment humanised throughout, a world which has been recreated by human activity to the extent that no part of a potentially rich sensorium has been left unrefined.[10] He is the man who feels inwardly compelled to seek fulfilment in multiple directions and does so because external reality assumes the form, not of a series of limiting factors, but as so many objects of human need which present an infinity of possibilities for self-determination. 'The *rich* human being is simultaneously the human being *in need of* a totality of human life-activities — the man in whom his own realisation exists as an inner necessity, as need.'[11] Appropriating 'his total essence in a total manner', every activity of the whole man is integrated into an harmonious pattern of self-affirmation. Thus his capacity to love a woman, considered by Marx to be the clearest indication of the degree to which the human essence had been appropriated by man, issued from more than a refinement of the urge to sexual gratification but called into operation every facet of his *human* nature, a kaleidoscope of faculties, attributes and powers which in the total man combined into an interwoven tapestry of self-expression. Man, then, is whole when his every experience, activity, relationship and associative form constitutes an enrichment and extension of his personality, an entity constantly unfolding in search of modes through which to express the inner need for objectification.

In practice actual individuals represent the antithesis of this conception because interposing itself between men and their mastery of the natural world is the struggle between men themselves. The result is a system of exchange propelled by its own dynamic which, in the horrifying climax of commodity production, combines to an unprecedented degree the conquest of nature with the fragmentation of men. Here, compelled to produce commodities in exchange for money, the individual performs physically and mentally debilitating tasks and so diminishes himself in an activity which is quintessentially human. Work having been debased into a means of satisfying the biological need of remaining alive, it becomes a 'forced activity, imposed upon men only by external and accidental necessity and not by an internal and determined necessity'.[12] The effects of this ontological catastrophe are manifold because, objectification being achieved in the performance of a circumscribed function that entails self-loss rather than self-affirmation, other outlets for the expression of the self are closed to the individual. For the 'division of labour seizes upon, not only the economic, but every other sphere of society, and everywhere lays the foundation of that all engrossing system of specializing and sorting men, that development in a man of one single faculty at the expense of all the other faculties.'[13] Shackled to an exclusive sphere of activity the individual assumes the characteristics of his social role so that, instead of a dynamic self of cultivated sensibilities able to adapt to any mode, there is only a passive receptacle into which has been poured skills sufficient to equip him for a task calculated to serve productive requirements.[14]

What the externally conditioned individual cannot do through his lack of creative powers he can achieve through his pocket. Money is the universal mediator between men whose potentially diverse sensibilities are distilled into the single sense of having, the subhuman need of possession. Money, however, quantifies all relationships, dissolving them into exchange values which obscure personal idiosyncracies, so that each appears to the other as a possible source of that metal for which the whole world can be bought. The consequence is the transformation of society into an arena of indifferent individuals, accepting the illusion of self-sufficiency, yet interlocked in a system of mutual hostility by the necessity of having to exchange for the sake of private gratification. Such individuals embody within themselves all the contradictions inhering in the system of domination. Imprisoned, on the one hand, in a sphere of particularity and egoism where all relationships degenerate into instrumentalities, they are confronted on the other with moral and political injunctions persuading them to be virtuous in pursuit of a common well-being. Since privatisation is presupposed by both morality and politics, the demands of the former appear as prohibitions which descend from on high rather than as confirmations of the self's urge to objectification, while the State assumes the shape of a 'supernaturalist abortion' which preserves in illusory form that universality which men are denied in their actual relations. 'It stems from the very nature of estrangement that each sphere applies to me a different and opposite yardstick — ethics one and political economy another; for each is a specific estrangement of man and focuses attention on a particular round of estranged essential activity.'[15] With this bifurcation and compartmentalisation of life the individual becomes an abstraction, torn asunder by demands which stand in sharp contrast to his estranged experience.

That fragmentation is an historical problem creates the possibility of resolving the contradiction between productive wealth and inner poverty through the transition to a communal form in which 'self-activity (will) coincides with material life, which corresponds to the development of individuals into complete individuals and the casting-off of all natural limitations'.[16] As the social group most annihilated by the existing system of domination, the proletariat is conceived as the agent of the impending transition to an historical formation in which the rational control of productive forces will permit the human essence to be appropriated in a total manner, replacing the 'detail-worker of today, crippled by life-long repetition of one and the same trivial operation, and thus reduced to the mere fragment of a man, by the fully developed individual, fit for a variety of labours, ready to face any change of production, and to whom the different social functions he performs, are but so many modes of giving free scope to his own natural and acquired powers'.[17]

Radicals since Marx have been more or less content to reiterate themes already explored by him. There is the same belief in the unrealised but historically realisable potentiality for self-determination, the same compelling urgency to negate a socioeconomic structure which thwarts the expression of the self in an infinity of modes by reducing it to a set of anonymous and conflicting roles. The Port Huron Statement, formulated in 1962 by the Students for a Democratic Society, is perhaps the best of many documents recently inspired by the desire to recreate social reality so as to stimulate individuals to engage in an infinite range of creative life-experiences:

'We regard *men* as infinitely precious and possessed of unfulfilled capacities for reason, freedom, and love . . . We oppose the depersonalization that reduces human beings to the status of things . . . Men have unrealized potential for self-cultivation, self-direction, self-understanding, and creativity. It is this potential that we regard as crucial and to which we appeal, not to the human potentiality for violence, unreason, and submission to authority. The goal of man and society should be human independence: concern not with the image of popularity but with finding a meaning that is personally authentic; a quality of mind not compulsively driven by a sense of powerlessness, nor one which unthinkingly adopts status values, nor one which represses all threats to its habits, but one which has full, spontaneous access to present and past; one which openly faces problems which are troubling and unresolved; one with an intuitive awareness of possibilities, an active sense of curiosity, and ability and willingness to learn . . . Personal links between man and man are needed, especially to go beyond the partial and fragmentary bonds of function that bind men only as worker to worker, employer to employee, teacher to student, American to Russian . . . As a *social system* we seek the establishment of a democracy of individual participation, governed by two central aims: that the individual share in those social decisions determining the quality and direction of his life; that society be organized to encourage independence in men and provide the media for their common participation.'[18]

Where radicalism of the post-Freudian era is significant, however, is in the attempt to describe the psychological process of disintegration suffered by the self in an alien environment:[19] an attempt sometimes accompanied by a loss of faith in the logic of history to solve the human predicament or, at least, a novel focus on marginal social groups in contradistinction to the pacified proletariat as providing possible catalysts of historical development.

Take, for instance, Wilhelm Reich's claim that a repressive social system reproduces itself in a repressed psyche, 'a limitation of the total ability to live'.[20] Reich's point of departure is Freud's suggestion that the ego became differentiated from the id in order to mediate between it and the environment. Steering the instincts towards gratification in ways which do not conflict with the external world, the conscious self facilitates a reconciliation of the claims of the pleasure principle with those of the reality principle. Whereas instinctual renunciation and sublimation was in Freud's view an essential concomitant of civilization, Reich took the inhibition of libidinal energy to be indicative of a distinct type of culture, a class dominated society whose members were rendered submissive by the influence of the patriarchal family as the major agency of socialisation. As armour by which to protect the id, the ego introjects in the form of conscience the repressive demands of the parental representatives of the social order. The consequence is a personal rigidity that is exemplified in the closed, predictable responses of stereotyped characters – the worker, the official, etc. – as they act out their role requirements. 'The character structure,' wrote Reich in a sentence expressing the fusion of Marxian and Freudian analyses, 'is the crystallization of the sociological process of a given epoch.'[21] Rejecting Freud's hypothesis of the death instinct by explaining the destructive tendencies of the organism as manifestations of a socially induced neurosis, Reich foresaw the possibility of a nonrepressive society in which externally imposed imperatives in the form of moral injunctions would be rendered redundant. This was so because the organism which derived instinctual gratification (equated by Reich with genital satisfaction) was equipped with an internal mechanism for avoiding conflicts, engaging in experiences which were both sensuous and social.

A more sophisticated adaptation of Freudian categories to the radical cause is Marcuse's analysis of advanced industrial society as one which has managed to contain those contradictions which for Marx spelt its imminent collapse by creating artificial needs that facilitate individual acquiescence to oppression, at the same time as providing a temporary solution to crises of overproduction. In this 'totalitarian' society the dichotomy between private and public spheres has been transcended by the dissolution of leisure time activities into patterns of consumption which ensure a passive surrender to productive requirements. Even the desublimation of sexuality into permissiveness is a repressive device for maintaining that high rate of consumption which induces a socially cohesive sense of comfortable affluence. Here socially repressive demands are more than introjected by the ego in its striving to guard the id but are actually incorporated into the instinctual structure, creating a biologically specific individual who adequately reproduces the needs demanded by the ongoing requirements of the system of domination.

The critical philosopher cannot prompt the members of this society into transformative action by confronting them with the spectacle of their fragmented selves for, strictly speaking, there is no self suffering disintegration. The responsibility of taming the instincts has been transferred from the ego to the superego, replacing a guilt-ridden conscience by the 'happy consciousness' of one who discovers his soul in his commodities. Subject to heteronomous needs, the whole of experience is distorted for this selfless creature and he has no critical faculties which might generate revulsion against a system that, dispensing with the aid of the family, acts directly through its image-makers and advertisers.

'The conscious processes of confrontation are replaced to an increasing degree by immediate, almost physical reactions in which comprehending consciousness, thought, and even one's own feelings play a very small role. It is as though the free space which the individual has at his disposal for his psychic processes has been greatly narrowed down; it is no longer possible for something like an individual psyche with its own demands and decisions to develop; the space is occupied by public, social forces. This reduction of the relatively autonomous ego is empirically observable in people's frozen gestures, and in the growing passivity of leisure-time activities, which become more and more inescapably de-privatized, centralized, universalized in the bad sense, and as such controlled.'[22]

Such beings respond to their environment not inwardly and affirmatively but automatically, responses wholly conditioned by the social roles they have been so seductively manipulated into performing. Marcuse's conception of human wholeness will be taken up later and it suffices here to say that it is predicated on the possible pacification of the struggle for existence in a manner permitting libido to seek non-repressive outlets.

What emerges from our exposition so far is that radicalism traces the internally related components of fragmentation — blunted sensibilities, the inability of the individual to discover adequate modes of self-expression, his severance from others in quantified relationships that divide his personality by compelling him to adopt patterns of conduct appropriate to the social role he happens to be playing at a particular moment — to a single determinant, a constraining environment.

Radicalism is heir to the Enlightenment in wishing to translate apparent natural limitations to self-determination (original sin, etc.) into the effects of social control. The dialectical tension by which the subject-object relationship is characterised provides men with the opportunity of contriving the conditions necessary for their sensuous participation in the world. Their inevitable contact with external reality confronts them with the stark alternative of moulding it into an adequate medium for the expression of their powers or, by either insufficiently reshaping raw nature or else constructing a social form that develops according to its own laws, allowing it to subjugate and diminish them. Radicalism thus rejects the suggestion that men are subject to the constraints of an immutable human nature for the image of a self-mediating being who creates the possibilities of human realisation through participation in the historical process. In demanding the negation of the present socio-economic system to allow the the realisable possibilities of human fulfilment, the validity of radicalism is dependent upon the acceptability of two propositions: that present reality precludes the actualisation of certain human potentialities and that in a different environment the human being is capable of becoming self-determining and inwardly responsive to life in its multiple forms, that is, a whole man. Most of the remainder of the discussion will be concerned with examining the different conceptions of wholeness offered by radicals. But the general claim, that the existing structure stands condemned as inhibiting a potentially rich response to life, can be dealt with briefly because it is not difficult to substantiate.

We are all familiar with the stereotyped reactions of those who over-identify with their roles, and with the agencies of social control, especially educational institutions, that are largely heedless of the latent potentialities of individuals as they sort them into occupational categories designed to meet productive requirements. And there is ample empirical evidence, much of it adduced from the work situation, to illustrate that, given the opportunities to associate with others in a sensuous participation in their environment, people do develop new capacities for self-expression. To cite only one example. In 1972 a group of female workers, faced with the closure of the shoe factory where they were employed, staged a work-in and used their ingenuity to make handbags, watch-straps, skirts and other articles from the scraps of leather that remained. One of the women spoke of the euphoria that accompanied the completion of the first product. 'We were all whooping and laughing, we were that excited. After years of doing nothing but shoe tops, specification work, this felt so . . . *creative* if you know what I mean.' Another, referring to the collective effort entailed in making the enterprise viable, said: 'It's been astonishing in the *human* sense. We were all just faces with names attached before. Now we've become so close. We've lived and worked together, and we've learned to love each other. Yes — love. I'm not ashamed to say it.'[23] At the very least, such examples ought to warn us against complacent acceptance of those existing social forms which provide inadequate modes of self-affirmation.

They ought also to make us critical of any ideology which, ignoring the dialectical relationship of the human subject with its object, lends support to a social system which suppresses the potentialities of its members. Take the state of current moral theory. Well known are the criticisms levelled at the traditional liberal conception of man for preserving a measure of dignity for the human self only by detaching it from the prevailing system of social constraints: the image of the moral agent retreating to the inner citadel in order to promulgate universal rules which he is compelled to contradict in his actual relationships. The radical conception of wholeness is an evident indictment of such a bifurcation of human existence. In recent years writers such as Hart and Emmet have reacted against Kantian formalism by focusing attention on the social content of morality.[24] A simplified version of the theory suggests that many activities with a moral flavour presuppose a context of socially regulated behaviour. An obligation, for instance, is typically incurred by the obligee making use of a conventional procedure whereby he brings into existence a special tie between himself and the person to whom the obligation is owed. A person's duty consists of tasks deemed necessary to satisfy the requirements of a given social position or role. The agent who fails to fulfil his obligation or perform his duty lays himself open to censure from his peers, so that the standardised behaviour and predictable responses facilitated by role playing and the existence of conventional devices such as the practice of promising lays the foundation of human cooperation. Thus, on the basis of observable behaviour patterns, we are offered a justification of moral rules as being socially integrative, serving to 'correlate our feelings and behaviour in such a way as to make the fulfilment of everyone's aims and desires as far as possible compatible'.[25]

Leaving aside the question of whether social living analytically implies rule-governed behaviour, the assumptions made by theorists in discussing the institutional aspect of morality betrays an attachment to the bourgeois way of life, and an acceptance of the individual fragmentation which it entails. For presupposing their approach is the assumption of an inevitable clash between particular interests (thus of the ineradicability of economic scarcity), a conflict that demands mediation through the individual internalisation of socially desirable tasks, that is, conformity to moral rules. Social relationships are thereby envisaged as arrangements of convenience, mutually beneficial arrangements of a contractual nature between parties not intrinsically connected. The good man in this conception is he of limited sympathies and enlightened self-interest who diligently conforms to his role requirements in the awareness that a mutual satisfaction of needs demands uniformity of behaviour. He is the man for whom supererogatory activity is optional; indeed, the prerogative of exceptional individuals, of saints and heroes, for ordinary mortals are not naturally altruistic. In this way theory reduces men to the status of private entities who must receive a social content in order to regularise their behaviour and so promote social cohesion, passive recipients of predetermined values and behaviour patterns which enable a hypostatised system to function smoothly. Individuality is thus relegated to the margins of communal life, the residue of what remains once roles have been performed, for of social significance is not how the individual plays his role but that he does in fact perform it. Significantly, those theorists who wish to salvage something of the self by describing the unique manner in which roles are enacted not infrequently resort to Sartre's notion of bad faith — the undesirable attitude of one who completely identifies with his role. So we end with an image of the individual divided between, on the one hand, his private conscience and personal interests and, on the other, his social functions dictated by rules that stand, not as the outward manifestation of an inner compulsion to be affirmative, but as imperatives imposed for the sake of social stability. The shift in liberal theory from Kantian formalism to a recognition of the social aspect of morality is not, therefore, an attempt to transcend the bourgeois outlook but a sign that members of the academic establishment have been bewitched by the measure of social control and manipulation that corporate capitalism has achieved. The radical attack on human fragmentation provides a necessary antidote to such theorising, as well as a castigation of the social matrix of which it is the superstructural reflection.

We come now to an assessment of twentieth-century radicalism for where it is open to criticism is in regard to its notion of the self-directed being who will supposedly emerge with the negation of the network of social constraints which presently divides the human self into a series of dislocated functions. Here contemporary radicals betray a naive faith in the capacity of preconscious mechanisms to direct the human organism to fulfilment in a manner that fuses every activity into an integral pattern, precluding any dissociation of human attributes. The fault lies in a shift from the surely valid assumption that a humanisation of the environment will be registered at the biological level, i.e. that the organism which does not have to repress needs in order to cope with a hostile world will be less inclined to act aggressively, to the invalid inference that nonrepressed libido is automatically self-regulating without the aid of conscious reflection. Abbie Hoffman, who apparently believes that he has anticipated the experience of a liberated environment by adopting an alternative life-style within the confines of present society ('reality is a subjective experience. It exists in my head. I am the Revolution'), is representative of this attitude. Embodying microcosmically, so it seems, what has yet to be attained for everyone through the abolition of scarcity and thus of the routine, toil and self-discipline now entailed by work, Hoffman admits that he likes 'being crazy. Letting go. Losing control. Just doing what pops into my mind. I trust my impulses. I find the less I try to think through a situation, the better it comes off.'[26] Given this anti-rationalist bias, a high premium is attributed to immediate, instinctual gratification in contrast to rationally mediated and postponed satisfaction. Thus Hoffman suggest that we need to alter our perspective regarding 'postponement of pleasure vs. instant gratification'.[27] The projected society, according to Jerry Rubin, is a world where 'feeling and emotion will be unsuppressed'.[28]

Associated with this emphasis on the spontaneous, unreflective aspects of behaviour is the affirmation of life as a joyful celebration that excludes seriousness, an attitude which informs the conviction of many young radicals that one should be totally involved in that activity to which one is inclined at a given moment, transferring to something else at the first sign of boredom. It finds expression in Rubin's updated version of the romantic suggestion of *The German Ideology* that total man is he who in the course of one day is involved in a diversity of activities. 'Communist society will usher in Universal Man. The economy will be a game of musical chairs. Everybody will drive a cab, sell shoes, grow food on a farm, work on a newspaper. The expert-specialist will be a museum piece.'[29] The picture is made more delectable by Rubin's hope that such activities will be liberally interspersed with those of a sexual nature.[30] Leaving aside the fact that all but the young might well discover such an existence too strenuous to be long enjoyable, there is an element of triviality in the conception of life as an endless merry-go-round of frolics and unrestrained spontaneity (though to be fair, recent flirtations with the esoteric and transcendental implies that the youth movement is much more than a hedonistic revolt against delayed gratification but an attempt, however misguided, to recover the lost self through genuinely subjective experiences).

The distrust of a conscious control of the libido that would entail instinctual delay of sublimation is not entirely misplaced for technological rationality does provide the basis of that system of domination which invades and distorts the instinctual structure; a form of social repression that derives theoretical justification from the way in which most systems have conceived reason as standing in a hierarchical, combative relation to the instincts, providing injunctions that descend from on high, not as a means of directing impulses into adequate modes of expression, but in order to intimidate the sensuous or lower nature into submission so that the higher or true self might emerge as victor. Freud himself was none too complimentary to the ego because as a mediator facilitating the sublimation of libido into socially acceptable channels it was tempted 'to become sycophantic, opportunist and false, like a politician who sees the truth but wants to keep his place in popular favour'.[31] And it was Freud who admitted that 'the feeling of happiness derived from the satisfaction of a wild instinctual impulse untamed by the ego is incomparably more intense than that derived from sating an instinct that has been tamed.'[32] It is not surprising, therefore, to find someone like Reich hostile to the conscious self, claiming that a rational control of the instincts is rendered superfluous with the eradication of conflicts between the id and external reality. Destructive drives are not, as for Freud, the manifestation of an ineradicable generic disposition which must be contained by the processes of civilisation but a feature of the pathological organism. Unrepressed instincts are conducive to individual well-being in a manner which is socially beneficial. Like Reich, Shulamith Firestone identifies ego control of the id as renunciation designed to perpetuate social repression which must be historically transcended through a cultural revolution that will integrate the male response to the environment (the technological mode corresponding to the objective, logical realistic, practical, conscious, rational) with the female response (the aesthetic mode corresponding to the subjective, intuitive, fantastic, subconscious, emotional) in a dialectical synthesis of cultural categories. But it appears that the dialectical transcendence which she projects amounts to the predominance of the female moment of present reality, the whole of reality being experienced aesthetically in the transformed society.

> 'With the full achievement of the conceivable in the actual, the surrogate of culture will no longer be necessary. The sublimation process, a detour to wish fulfilment, will give way to direct satisfaction in experience, as felt now only (sometimes) by children, or adults on drugs. (Though normal adults "play" to varying degrees, a more immediate example — zero on a scale of accomplishment ("nothing to show for it") but nevertheless worth your while — is lovemaking.) Control and delay of *id* satisfaction by the *ego* will be unnecessary; the id can live free. Enjoyment will spring directly from living itself, the process of experience, rather than from the quality of achievement. When the male technological mode can at last produce in actuality what the female aesthetic mode had envisioned, we shall have eliminated the need for either.'[33]

This cult of immediacy in which instinctual sublimation is minimal is a natural outcome of radicalising Freud's description of the self as subject to an interminable struggle between libido and cultural requirements. If instinctual renunciation is *merely* a device for reproducing the prevailing system of domination, then it cannot be otherwise conceived than a negative element of the present which will of necessity be transcended in a nonrepressive communal form.

There is the additional fact that previous revolutionary movements are felt to have fallen short of their liberating intentions because they failed to break through the repressive controls and authority structures characteristic of the societies which they were seeking to replace. Inspired by the conviction that the potentialities latent within capitalism, given what Marx termed its 'civilizing mission', would inevitably be released if there existed a working class sufficiently organised to precipitate change, such movements tended to reproduce the elitism and self-discipline of the system which they were attempting to overthrow, the vanguard supplying 'rational' direction to the 'spontaneous' mass. The consequence was a society more centralised and bureaucratised, hence in some ways more dismal and inhuman than its predecessor. Contemporary radicals have responded by asserting that the recreation of the self is inseparable from the revolutionary process itself, not something to be shelved until the control of productive forces has been snatched from the hands of the bourgeoisie. Hence the stress on the act of revolt as a surrealistic event, a festive occasion entailing a massive upsurge of libidinal energies in which established patterns of social control suddenly and dramatically disintegrate. A revolutionary transformation, on this view, can be initiated only by those who have already refused to accept the instinctual constraints of existing society. Hoffman, for example, distinguishes himself from the New Left by affirming that revolutionary activity is fun. 'I think fun and leisure are great. I don't like the concept of a movement built on sacrifice, dedication, responsibility, anger, frustration and guilt . . . Stop trying to organize everybody but yourself. Begin to live your vision.'[34] Even Cohn-Bendit, whose revolutionary credentials are less questionable, proclaims that 'the revolution must be born of joy and not of sacrifice'.[35] We must 'rid ourselves, in practice, of the Judaeo-Christian ethic, with its call for renunciation and sacrifice. There is only one reason for being a revolutionary — because it is the best way to live.'[36] Spontaneity and self-expression, in contrast to self-denial and rigorous organisation, offer the key to revolutionary success.

While understandable, for instinctual conflicts are surely partially induced by societal contradictions and because primacy must be attributed to the sensuous in that sensory experience of the world determines the possibilities of human fulfilment, this antipathy towards a rational mediation of the instincts is a mistaken view suggesting a partial liberation in which nonintellective attributes are confused with the whole man who is consequently assimilated to his biological functions. No matter how refined the senses may become in virtue of a transformed and hospitable environment, without rational guidance, even domestication, of the instincts it is difficult to imagine how the self could avoid being swept hither and thither by competing impulses and feelings, a poor substitute for the potentially rich human being whose activities coalesce into a unity unfolding through the flux of circumstance.

Two major objections may be levelled at the radical's devaluation of a rational mediation of the instincts. The first is connected with the claim, deriving from a postulated preconscious synthesis of the liberated senses, that tensions are either absent from the unrepressed libido or else are resolved by nonreflective processes. Even supposing that all conflicts experienced by individuals could be resolved by removing those societal contradictions which now reproduce themselves in fragmented beings, a dubious proposition, a state of affairs in which tension did not penetrate to the level of consciousness would be nevertheless undesirable. For something distinctively human is involved in the rendering of competing drives into an unfolding pattern of development, in the pursuit of self-appointed goals which entail a rational direction of the instincts. The contrary claim preserves human wholeness by precipitating man into a hypothetical condition of stasis where, deprived of the inner compulsion to self-determination, he engages in an endless series of trivial activities which are conceived, not as a temporary release from tension nor as a preparation for truly human experiences, but as an adequate substitute for a richly complex existence.

It is no coincidence that this type of attitude is associated with the drug cult, the assumption that liberation is somehow equivalent to detachment from the world which can be induced through smoking pot and the use of hallucinatory drugs.

> I smoke marijuana every chance I get.
> I sit in my house for days on end and stare at the roses in the closet.

So writes Allen Ginsberg in his poem *America*, implying that an extended period of repose is a desirable state of affairs. Timothy Leary, apparently rejecting any form of sublimation on the grounds that it is a means of adapting the instincts to a repressive social structure, contrasts 'Painful duty versus what comes naturally'.[37] Getting high, the suspension of socially conditioned reflexes, is a means of restoring the natural condition of polymorphous-perverse pleasure. Leary in effect is advocating a retreat from the world whereby the self no longer finds it necessary to interact with its environment in order to contrive the conditions of its own realisation. 'Turning on is an ominous threat to any social system. It leads to the smiling dropout. *You no longer bother to fight the old system.* You just start living in the old society – a new, smiling, conspiratorial style.'[38] Yet a self which ignores the world, preferring introspection and contemplation to an active mastery of its surroundings, is an abstraction consisting of unactualised potentialities. To lose contact with the world is to forgo the opportunity of appropriating reality through the subjective recreation of the object. And that amounts to a loss of self because a worldless self cannot affirm itself. Affirmation is the reward of a subject which seeks a rational control of reality, simultaneously modifying itself and the world through its own mediating activity.

This is not to decry those fleeting periods of repose from which striving is excluded when all parts of the organism form a temporary equilibrium, moments which correspond to Schiller's notion of aesthetic determinability, a condition in which man achieves a respite from the constraints of his sensuous-rational nature and which Schiller believed had been immortalised by the Greeks in their art for

'they banished from the brow of the blessed gods all the earnestness and effort which furrow the cheeks of mortals, no less than the empty pleasures which preserve the smoothness of a vacuous face; freed those ever contented beings from the bonds inseparable from every purpose, every duty, every care, and made idleness and indifferency the enviable partner of divinity – merely a more human name for the freest, most sublime state of being.'[39]

Such a condition, captured but briefly and rarely in pure form, was not for Schiller an escape from, but a means to, a potentially full life, an opportunity to restore one's humanity and emerge to tackle any determinate activity or condition with faculties that had been refined and renewed.[40] Whereas for Schiller the aesthetic experience was worldly orientated, active though without specific determination, contemporary radicals tend to equate tranquillity and repose with life itself. Yet a world in which human beings were robbed of the satisfaction contingent upon a struggle to overcome tension through a rational mediation of the instincts would be an inhuman abode where Eros had succumbed to Thanatos and men had been seduced into passive submission by the Nirvana Principle.

The second objection is that the devaluation of a conscious mediation of the instincts unwittingly provides theoretical underpinning for a system of domination hardly less oppressive than that which radicals wish to see destroyed. The antiprimitivism of radicalism implies that unhindered instinctual gratification is contingent upon a rational organisation of the realm of necessity. But once having deprived the rational mediation of the instincts of human significance, radicals cannot level any serious complaint against the division of society into two camps, a minority who happen to derive satisfaction from a rational oversight of this realm and who thereby provide the facilities whereby the majority may indulge themselves in an orgy of unsublimated desires. One is reminded of Fourier's design for a pastoral utopia in which unarrested passions will discover adequate outlets through a multiplicity of social activities. Such a life of frivolity is, however, dependent upon the existence of an elaborate organisation capable of channelling the oddest impulse in a socially constructive direction: the vision, for instance, of children who enjoy playing with dirt being grouped into squads for the removal of sewage. Fourier was able to conceive the possibility of unhindered instinctual gratification for the mass of men only by making reason a property of the communal whole rather than of its individual members, an attribute that was to be exercised on behalf of the community by administrators 'who have made the greatest contribution in terms of capital and industrial or scientific knowledge'.[41] In Fourier's projected society the majority were able to enjoy a plenitude of passionate experiences precisely because a complex set of communal arrangements had been devised, and was maintained, by rational guardians. The paradox of his vision is that libidinal energies may flow unstemmed only for individuals who are subject to a high degree of institutional manipulation.

The unpalatable implications which these criticisms are intended to highlight are illustrated through the contradictory strands of Marcuse's thought. In his more sober moments Marcuse specifically links human autonomy with the continuing effort of the subject to create a sensuous environment, an effort which is creative and rewarding because beset with tension. Thus Marcuse writes in his critique of Norman O. Brown:

> 'Tension can be made non aggressive, non destructive, but it can never be eliminated, because (Freud knew it well) its elimination would be death − not in symbolism but in a very real sense. And we still want to live, within our boundaries and divisions, which we want to make our own instead of leaving their determination to our fathers and leaders and representatives . . . Eros lives in the division and boundary between subject and object, man and nature, and precisely in its polymorphous-perverse manifestations, in its liberation from the "despotism of genital organization," the sexual instincts transform the object and the environment − without ever annihilating the object and the environment together with the subject.'[42]

On this basis Marcuse explores in a most exciting fashion, which owes much to the inspiration of Schiller, the possibility of a new subject for whom erotic energy would integrate all faculties into a unified pattern of self-affirmation. Here the imagination would mediate between reason and the senses, resulting in the aesthetic transformation of reality through the activities of associated individuals. In this environment tension and sublimation would be individually satisfying and culturally creative.

There is, however, another thread in Marcuse's thought which betrays a yearning to escape from the tension which he elsewhere equates with life itself. The desirability of pacifying the struggle for existence, and the possibility of peace and quiet, are recurrent themes of his thought. But the continuing presence of the realm of necessity constitutes a problem because, necessitating at least a minimum of discipline and routine and thus of instinctual arrest or diversion, it would appear that it can never be made wholly attractive. Marcuse's solution is to suppose that a rational recreation of the object world through the conscious application of technology will lead to a full-scale automation that permits libidinal energy to be expended outside the work sphere. The qualitative transformation of the realm of freedom consequent upon its quantitative expansion will, it is claimed, not leave the realm of necessity unaffected so that the small amount of work which remains will be experienced as play rather than toil.

The trouble here is that, being somewhat less concerned with transforming work into a medium of self-expression than with reducing it to the barest minimum through the abolition of scarcity, Marcuse allows his attention to be diverted from considering exactly how it might become a mode through which associated individuals express their creative powers. It is conceded, for instance, that the most efficient appropriation of nature might require a centralised control of the productive apparatus, in addition to a division of labour in which technical functions are performed by experts. 'However, the executive and supervisory functions would no longer carry the privilege of ruling the life of others in some particular interest.'[43] This bald statement is rather lame, perhaps a piece of wishful thinking, because Marcuse does not provide a convincing account of the institutional arrangements and participatory processes that are required to prevent those who, occupying authoritative positions on the basis of their acknowledged expertise, might seek to form themselves into an elite group. He appears to accept the indispensability of technical expertise and occupational specialisation in order to create the material basis of human freedom (equated here with tranquillity) without facing the possible consequences of what he is advocating. The two aims, the most efficient appropriation of extrahuman reality in order to reduce the amount of time spent in necessary labour and the transformation of work into a truly human activity for all, might well conflict. If they do it would appear that Marcuse is prepared to attach priority to the former even should that entail a failure to erect adequate safeguards to rule by a technocracy, for such an arrangement might prove to be a convenient device for eliminating tension from the lives of the majority.[44] Marcuse is perhaps closer to Fourier, for whom he has a high regard, than he would care to recognise.

It might be thought that we have become involved in an academic quibble by stressing the ontological and practical implications of denying to reason a mediating role between the instincts. A respectable case can be made that the intellectual with a radical bent ought to concern himself with exploring the dialectical possibilities of contemporary capitalism because of overriding importance is the necessity of the surgeon's knife for eliminating those structurally generated conflicts presently reflected in the fragmented lives of men and women. To speculate about self-activity in a society which has yet to be created lays one open to the charge of utopianism. Yet is is well to be aware of what is historically possible and desirable, not merely to safeguard against the inevitable disillusionment that would occur should revolutionary activity be inspired by a critical theory which had degenerated into a fairy tale picture of pure delight and carefree existence, but as a means of persuading sceptics that socialism is the only human alternative to capitalism. As it is, the conception of human wholeness projected by many contemporary radicals is likely to appeal only to an incurable romantic. To say this is not to dismiss the positive features of twentieth-century radicalism. Radicals have transcended the characteristically bourgeois outlook, the supposedly ineradicable dualism of feeling and duty, reason and instinct, by revealing the crippling socioeconomic factors of capitalism as the source of this dichotomy. And, using as their model or ideal the spontaneous affection, intensity of feeling, and abandonment of young lovers, they have envisaged a community of human beings who, freed from the necessity of having to survive in a competitive world, are instinctively generous and mutually responsive.

The flaw implied by the devaluation of a conscious direction of the instincts is the inability to conceive that life can be experienced as at once enjoyable and effortful, fulfilling because it is enveloped in tension. Take the remarks of Brecht in his *Short Organum for the Theatre:*

'Sexual pleasure with us turns into marital obligations, the pleasures of art subserve general culture, and by learning we mean not an enjoyable process of finding out but the forcible shoving of our nose into something. Our activity has none of the pleasure of exploration, and if we want to make an impression we do not say how much fun we have got out of something but how much effort it has cost us.'[45]

Brecht is rightly exposing the absurdity of a social system which turns every activity into a matter of duty and it is perhaps a little unfair to lift these remarks out of context as providing an example of the radical fallacy. Yet his juxtaposition of the terms 'fun' and 'effort', as if they were mutually exclusive descriptions of how an activity could be experienced, reveals the trap into which many radicals have fallen. It is the failure to recognise that in a humanised environment the fundamental drive to be human, the openness to life in its multiple forms, might entail accepting challenges that call for the sublimation of immediate desires, that the curiosity of the subject sensitive to his surroundings might lead him to explore in a manner both demanding and pleasurable. What radicals have forgotten is that human wholeness is not a fully ripened fruit to be plucked from the laps of the gods once the surgeon has performed his operation but is something which comes to the subject who, actively orientated to life, is not afraid to take decisions which might in retrospect be mistaken nor to experiment with activities and form relationships aware that they may prove to be ultimately unsatisfactory.

The current notion of wholeness marks a retreat, a willingness to settle for an equilibrated, tension-free existence when life could be so much more. To make sense of the notion we need to preserve something intimated by Schiller, and more particularly by Marx, the conception of life as a process in which faculties and sensibilities are continually expanded and refined because, inhabiting a world in which it is good to be, the human subject is for ever seeking outlets for his multifaceted nature.

Schiller was aware of the dialectical connection of the self with its world. Brought into contact with its environment through sensory experience, the human self could appropriate the world by subjecting it to the unity of its own rational activity.[46] The aesthetic condition provided for the control and recreation of, not the flight from, reality, permitting self-growth because of the infinite possibilities for shaping the object.

Marx's use of the dialectic as a means of comprehending the transitory nature of preceding historical formations signified his greatest debt to Hegel. In his projection of a social form in which productive forces were rationally controlled by associated individuals this idealist residue, the concept of process, was retained, not as a tool of historical analysis, but in order to characterise the existence of liberated individuals in terms of a continual unfolding and expansion. For Marx

115

the ultimate nonidentity of subject and object supplied the framework within which human wholeness was a conceivable possibility.[47] Criticising the suggestion that autonomy was possible only beyond the realm of necessity, he wrote:

'It seems to be far from A. Smith's thoughts that the individual "in his normal state of health, strength, activity, skill and efficiency", might also require a normal portion of work, and of cessation from rest. It is true that the quantity of labour to be provided seems to be conditioned by external circumstances, by the purpose to be achieved, and the obstacles to its achievement that have to be overcome by labour. But neither does it occur to A. Smith that the overcoming of such obstacles may itself constitute an exercise in liberty, and that these external purposes lose their character of mere natural necessities and are established as purposes which the individual himself fixes. The result is the self-realisation and objectification of the subject, therefore real freedom, whose activity is precisely labour . . . Really free labour, the composing of music for example, is at the same time damned serious and demands the greatest effort. The labour concerned with material production can only have this character if (1) it is of a social nature, (2) it has a scientific character and at the same time is general work, i.e. if it ceases to be human effort as a definite, trained natural force, gives up its purely natural, primitive aspects and becomes the activity of a subject controlling all the forces of nature in the production process.'[48]

Sympathetic to activity which was creative because demanding, Marx was able to perceive the human significance of instinctual sublimation. And, rejecting the notion that work is intrinsically oppressive, he did not succumb to the temptation of demanding its abolition in a manner which permitted rule by a technical elite. It was because the appropriation of the object world was an ongoing achievement that there would always be problems to be tackled by human ingenuity, obstacles to be encountered and overcome through skill and endurance, projects to be set that required a rational mediation of the instincts. So that while an expansion of the time spent outside the realm of necessary labour would provide the individual with opportunities for a plenitude of rewarding experiences, experiences which would better equip him in his capacity as a producer, the abolition of the realm of necessary was undesirable. In a real sense labour was the prototypical human activity, evoking all the creative powers of man as a socio-sensuous, rational-purposive being. As with Schiller, it is for Marx man's aesthetic capacity that allows him to formulate projects and so subject the world to rational control through self-activity. William Morris expressed the point aptly when he wrote that 'Art is man's expression of his joy in labour'. Or, as the dialectical interchange of the human subject with its world was more generally stated by Hegel in his *Phenomenology of Mind*, 'mediating is nothing but self-identity working itself out through an active self-directed process'.

So we find in Marx that which is absent from contemporary radicalism, a conception of life which is purposive, because directed outwards to the continual transformation of the object world through subjective activity, yet without the abstract *telos* which idealists and others would impose upon it, a constant going beyond in which human powers are for ever seeking new modes of expression, a process described as 'the absolute movement of becoming'.[49] In this way, he was able to envisage a community where the constraining effects of socioeconomic factors had been annulled without projecting a utopia of superficial pleasure or tranquillity in which all that is human is obliterated in an orgy of instinctual gratification. Revolutionary praxis is no automatic guarantee of human wholeness because this remains a problem to be faced anew by each individual. What can be achieved now is the transformation of the social world so that each is stimulated to begin the process of integrating all his activities into a complex pattern of lifelong self-determination.

NOTES

1. Though most of the thinkers discussed would describe themselves as socialists, I prefer to use throughout the broader concept of radicalism as denoting a specific attitude to social change, an acceptance of the world's historicity and a belief that men can and ought to create the conditions of human fulfilment through their collective production and reproduction of reality. The reason is partly that no attempt is made to cover any major socialist thinker – there is, for instance, no consideration of Lukacs in whose writings the problem of human wholeness was a dominant theme – but largely because the latter part of the article contains a criticism of a certain mode of thinking, prevalent in the United States and historically linked with the manifest failure there of the proletariat to be an agent of revolutionary change, from what I take to be a Marxian standpoint. It seems desirable, therefore, to use the more inclusive term radicalism, though hastening to disclaim any intention, polemical or otherwise, of wishing to underplay the socialist elements in the writings of the thinkers discussed.
2. See Roy Pascal, ' "Bildung" and the Division of Labour', in *German Studies Presented to Walter Horace Bruford* London, 1962, pp.14-28.
3. As does Raymond Plant in *Hegel* London, 1972.
4. *On the Aesthetic Education of Man,* ed. E.M. Wilkinson and L.A. Willoughby Oxford, 1967, VI.7.

5. *Principles of the Philosophy of the Future,* trans. Manfred H. Vogel New York, 1966, sec. 55.

6. Marx made a similar point against Hegel in the *Economic and Philosophical Manuscripts of 1844,* trans. M. Milligan Moscow, 1959, p.155: 'The man estranged from himself is also the thinker estranged from his essence – that is, from the natural and human essence. His thoughts are therefore fixed mental shapes and ghosts dwelling outside nature and man.'

7. Thus he explained his preoccupation with religion as a desire 'to illumine the obscure essence of religion with the torch of reason, in order that man may at least cease to be the victim, the plaything, of all those hostile powers which from time immemorial have employed the darkness of religion for the oppression of mankind'. *Lectures on the Essence of Religion,* trans. Ralph Manheim New York, 1966, p.22.

8. Engels, 'Ludwig Feuerbach and the End of Classical German Philosophy', in Marx and Engels, *Selected Works* London, 1968, p.617.

9. *Grundrisse,* ed. David McLellan London, 1971, pp.70-1.

10. *Manuscripts, op. cit.,* p.101: 'Only through the objectively unfolded richness of man's essential being is the richness of subjective *human* sensibility (a musical ear, an eye for beauty of form – in short, *senses* capable of human gratifications, senses confirming themselves as essential human powers of *man*) either cultivated or brought into being. For not only the five senses but also the so-called mental senses – the practical senses (will, love, etc.) – in a word, *human* sense – the humanness of the senses – comes to be by virtue of its object, by virtue of humanized nature. The forming of the five senses is a labour of the entire history of the world down to the present.'

11. *ibid.,* p.104.

12. 'Excerpt-Notes of 1844', in *Writings of the young Marx on Philosophy and Society,* ed. L.D. Easton and K.H. Guddat New York, 1967, p.281.

13. *Capital* Moscow, 1961, I, p. 354.

14. *The Poverty of Philosophy* New York, 1963, p. 129: ' In principle, a porter differs less from a philosopher than a mastiff from a greyhound. It is the division of labour which has set a gulf between them.' The same work reveals the extent to which Marx, along with other German thinkers, was influenced by the Greek ideal of the all-round individual. Thus on p.144: ' "We are struck with admiration," says Lemontey, "when we see among the Ancients the same person distinguishing himself to a high degree as philosopher, poet, orator, historian, priest, administrator, general of an army. Our souls are appalled at the sight of so vast a domain. Each one of us plants his hedge and shuts himself up in his enclosure. I do not know whether by this parcellation the field is enlarged, but I do know that man is belittled".'

15. *Manuscripts, op. cit.,* p.112.

16. *The German Ideology* London, 1965, p.85.

17. *Capital, op. cit.,* I, p. 488.

18. In Paul Jacobs and Saul Landau (ed.), *The New Radicals* London, 1967, pp. 158-60.

19. Freud's significance for the radical is stated by R.D. Laing, *The Politics of Experience* London, 1967, p.22: 'The relevance of Freud to our time is largely his insight and, to a very considerable extent, his *demonstration* that the *ordinary person* is a shrivelled, desiccated fragment of what a person can be.'

20. *The Sexual Revolution* London, 1972, p.4.

21. *Character Analysis,* trans. T.P. Wolfe 3rd ed., London, 1950 p. xxv.

22. *Five Lectures* London, 1971, p. 14.

23. Reported in the *Sunday Times,* 23 July 1972, p. 35.

24. The literature is vast but see, H.L.A. Hart, 'Legal and Moral Obligation', in

A.I. Melden (ed.), *Essays in Moral Philosophy* Seattle, 1958, pp. 82-107, and *The Concept of Law* Oxford, 1961; Dorothy Emmet, *Function, Purpose and Powers* London, 1958, and *Rules, Roles and Relations* London, 1966; R.S. Downie, 'Social Roles and Moral Responsibility', *Philosophy,* XXXIX 1964, pp. 29-36. The ideological framework of the perspective is made explicit by Hart in *The Concept of Law,* pp. 190-4, where he outlines the 'natural facts' which explain why social rules, legal and moral, must contain a specific content. For among the so-called facts of human nature and universal features of social life are included limited altruism and economic scarcity; an inclusion which reveals the error at the basis of the whole approach, the invalid assumption that the observation of human behaviour under determinate socioeconomic conditions is sufficient evidence of an immutable human nature.

25. S.E. Toulmin, *The Place of Reason in Ethics* Cambridge, 1958, p. 137.
26. *Revolution for the Hell of it* New York, 1968, pp. 62-3.
27. *ibid.,* p. 218.
28. *Do It!* London, 1970, p. 251.
29. *ibid.,* p. 128.
30. *ibid.,* p. 256: 'People will farm in the morning, make music in the afternoon and fuck wherever and whenever they want to.'
31. *The Ego and the Id* London, 1942, pp. 82-3.
32. *Civilization and its Discontents* London, 1973, p. 16.
33. *The Dialectic of Sex* London, 1972, p. 182.
34. *op. cit.,* p. 61.
35. Gabriel and Daniel Cohn-Bendit, *Obsolete Communism: The Left-Wing Alternative* London, 1969, p.112.
36. *ibid.,* p. 255.
37. 'Episode and Postcript', in *Getting Busted,* ed. Ross Firestone London, 1972, p. 215.
38. *ibid.,* p. 233, my italics
39. *op. cit.,* XV. 9.
40. cf. XXI and XXII.
41. J. Beecher and R. Benvenue (eds.), *The Utopian Vision of Charles Fourier* London, 1972, p. 249.
42. *Negations* London, 1968, pp. 236-8.
43. *One Dimensional Man* London, 1968, p. 49.
44. Paradoxically, Marcuse's concern with the most efficient appropriation of reality appears to stem, in part at least, from a residual primitivism, a desire to deal with productive requirements as swiftly as possible in order to increase the opportunities for unmediated natural experiences. He sometimes refers, for example, to the restoration rather than the conquest of nature (cf. *The Responsibility of Power* London, 1968), p. 443 and of recapturing such natural experiences as that of lovemaking in a meadow. A septuagenarian may be allowed his dreams but this feature of Marcuse's thought confirms our suspicion that contemporary radicalism contains an element of the absurd.
45. *Brecht on Theatre,* trans. John Willett London, 1964, p. 204.
46. *op. cit.,* XIII.
47. To which due emphasis is given by Alfred Schmidt, *The Concept of Nature in Marx,* trans. Ben Fowkes London, 1971.
48. *Grundrisse, op. cit.,* p. 124.
49. *Pre-Capitalist Economic Formations,* ed. E.J. Hobsbawn London, 1964, p.85.

Irving Louis Horowitz

By all reports, the socialist legacy is ambiguous; in addition, the problem
of knowledge is ubiquitous. The implausible task in one brief paper is
to transcend ambiguity and dissolve ubiquity. Clearly, these remarks will
fall far short of such a self-imposed task. About the most we can hope
for in this brief excursion is to render an orderly account of the
socialist tradition and its treatment of the problem of knowledge. For
the most part, we shall concentrate on the major expression of that
tradition − Marxism, and leave for others the task of sorting out
arguments between the varieties and strands within socialism. Indeed,
there is enough puzzlement to resolve even by confining our tasks in
the aforementioned manner. For the main thesis which I shall put forth,
and one for which there appears to be more than ample evidence, is that
what is set forth by Marx in stages, is presented by latter day socialism
as options; or at the least, different ways of viewing the relationship of
socialism to the accumulation and uses of knowledge.

What emerged over time in Marx represents three clearly defined
options for a socialist vision of scientific knowledge and the process of
human liberation. It is no accident that 'mechanistic' versus 'dialectical'
visions of exact knowledge competed for preeminence in the formative
period of Soviet socialism. It is no accident that 'metaphysical' versus
'positivist' interpretations of knowledge have continually vied for
attention in Western socialism. And it is no accident that a huge struggle
between 'early', 'middle' and 'late' varieties of Marxian analysis have
found representatives at one time or another in different movements of
the struggle on behalf of socialism.

To some degree, this is the inevitable fate of any encyclopedic
thinker. Socialism had such a towering figure in Marx that the impulse
to justify any given course of action by doctrinal references becomes
overpowering. Unlike the philosophical preeminence of Thomas
Aquinas within the Roman Catholic Church, which was established
centuries later by Papal *fiat,* the preeminence of Karl Marx emerged out
of the special circumstances of nineteenth-century Europe. The struggle
for socialism at that time inevitably required legitimation and
justification in Marx. Since then, while there can be no satisfactory

answer concerning 'periodicity' in Marx, or even which aspect of Marxism is specifically suited to what form of socialist vision, we can at least show how each of the major expressions within contemporary socialism (social democracy, Old-Left Bolshevism, New-Left Revisionism) reflects the peculiar historical antecedents that are to be found in Marx's thought. The socialist vision of knowledge concerns less the matter of knowledge and more that of democratic horizons. The socialist movement has cleaved not nearly as much over the doctrinal contents of Marxism as over the right to access to certain forms of knowledge. This right is either guaranteed or blocked off by how one evaluates the relationships of Marxism itself as a body of knowledge to the general accumulated knowledge of the sciences and social sciences.

Marx's attitude toward the problem of knowledge exhibits three basic stages — corresponding to his philosophic, economic and political concerns. It would be futile to enter into a discussion of 'periodisation' in Marx; I will attempt to show how in Marx these three stages correspond to three strategic responses by socialism as a system to the problem of knowledge. The first 'philosophic' stage covers Marx's attitudes between 1840 and 1848, highlighted by his writings in the *Economic and Philosophic Manuscripts of 1844-45.* The second 'economic' stage, comes after the production of *The Communist Manifesto,* and is largely contained in the *Foundations for a Critique of Political Economy.* The final 'political' stage corresponds to Marx's growing movement away from an economic determinism to a political determinism, or better, to an increasing awareness that the political variable of State power cannot simply be spoken of in 'long-run' terms, but as the essential pivot in the immediate practical struggle of people for socialism; that the political arena is the arena of class struggle, just as the economic arena is the essential area of class contradictions. For Marx the *class contradictions* manifested in the economic realm resolve themselves in the *class struggles* that take place in the political realm. How Marx viewed knowledge profoundly affects how socialism generally reacted to the question of the positive fruits of science and technology.

Althusser's four-fold classification represents an improvement over earlier formulations of the 'young Marx' and the 'mature Marx'. He gives us the following period table: '1840-44: the Early Works; 1845: The Works of the Break; 1845-57: the Transitional Works; 1857-83: the Mature Works' (Althusser, 1969: 35-39). But he too has considerable trouble with these formal categories. Phrases like 'the works of the break' and 'transitional works' express a sentiment more than a temporal reality. I will concentrate on three distinct and distinctive views of the relationship of knowledge to society and of science to socialism.

Hyppolite (1969:17) sees in Hegel's philosophy 'a remarkably creative attempt to give a philosophical account of spiritual relations and to describe the human situation, in the course of which we believe we have found the source of Hegel's dialectical thought. To Hegel what is fundamental in experience is the experience of spiritual relations and their development: the relation between man and man, between the individual and society, God and man, between master and slave.' That is an apt description of the tasks laid out by Hegel in *The Phenomenology of Mind*. And while a certain formal continuity does exist between Hegel and Marx, it is hard to confront the evidence and deny that Marx was motivated by a total reversal of philosophical priorities: the materialisation of the spirit which he derived from Feuerbach; the relationship between man and man as an uneven contest of superordinate and subordinate classes which he derived from classical economics from Smith to Ricardo; and the study of how to break and not simply comprehend relationships between master and slave, derived pragmatically from the French Revolution and theoretically from the European Enlightenment. The rupture between Hegel and Marx is real enough, whatever the methodological linkages through dialectic. What must be established is how Marx viewed the process of exact knowledge as a function of socioeconomic conditioning and political liberation.

In his remarkably synthetic study of Marxism, Rudolf Schlesinger (1950:429) concludes with a clear cut economic interpretation of Marxist doctrine, as if it were consistent from start to finish. His interpretation corresponds with the second phase in Marx, and the second type of socialist vision. 'Marxism is a theory of social dynamics, and nothing else. It is impossible to prove its basic tenets except by proving the advantages of choosing the development of productive resources as the independent variable amongst the various interdependent factors in social evolution.' But what if the seizure of State power by one class from the clutches of another proves to be the key independent variable? This transition from a political economy to a political sociology is precisely the characteristic of Marxism in its later stages; and one that is far less addressed than the earlier transition from a philosophic to an economic perspective in Marxian socialism.

For Marx and for the socialist tradition generally, there could be no theory of knowledge without a theory of action; the sources of knowledge are connected to the act. The nature of that act may change over time, located first in the minds of labouring individuals; then in the character of economic class struggles; and finally in the competition for domination and control of State authority. But whatever the modality, true knowledge is derived from exact practice, not as an arbitrary slogan, but as an article of faith within the Marxist-socialist tradition.

In this sense, Marx was taking on the history of philosophical theory, especially the Platonic-Aristotelian world, in which a series of great dualisms were not only sanctioned but encouraged: the gap between mind and matter; man and nature; and theory and practice. For Marx, this series of dualism is the substance of alienation in history. What appears as a series of fundamental distinctions in the history of philosophy, represented to Marx nothing more than the inability of all class society to resolve the differences between true knowledge and false consciousness. Avineri (1970:131) understood this point well in noting the distance between theory and practice in the world of Aristotle:

'The traditional confrontation of theory and practice goes back to Aristotle's *metaphysics*. According to Aristotle, *theoria,* the general view, seeks to know the world and understand it with the sole aim of knowledge itself. The opposite of *theoria* in this sense is *praxis,* or practical knowledge, which does not strive for the ultimate, universal truth, but contents itself with instrumental applicable knowledge. Theoretical knowledge is thus more comprehensive and more true: the more any particular knowledge is related to principles and general rules, the more it is theoretical, i.e. aiming at a general truth and having knowledge itself as its sole aim. Practical knowledge on the other hand, because of its applicability, is by definition less universal and more particular. While theoretical knowledge is permanent and eternal, practical knowledge is momentary and ephemeral. The main point is that both *theoria* and *praxis* are different modes of knowledge.'

Avineri's point would have to be qualified to the extent that Aristotle was modifying Platonic dualism. Aristotle located both theoretical and practical expressions of knowledge within a naturalistic and not a transcendental realm of theoretical knowledge. Marx himself appreciated the materialist character of Aristotle's thought, and expressed this in his rejection of the 'vulgar' materialism of Lange and Buchner (Marx, 1875:80). The larger position Avineri takes is sound. The classical conservative view does hinge on an unresolved dualism between theory and practice — with the former elevated to new heights.

Our concern is how a periodic tabulation within Marx led to a differential view of the role of knowledge in the life of man and society. At first, Marx saw knowledge as related to history rather than action: 'history is a true natural history of man' (Marx, 1844:182); and at the same time that history is located in societal consciousness, it is brought down from its Hegelian pedestal. Marx did this by naturalising the world of knower and known. During this first period, he favours naturalism rather than materialism: 'Consistent naturalism or humanism distinguishes itself from both idealism and materialism, constituting at the same time the unifying truth of both. We see also how only naturalism is capable of comprehending the act of world history' (Marx, 1844:181). The problem of knowledge becomes a relational problem; an experientially determined and defined event: 'The way in which consciousness is, and in which something is for it, is *knowing*. Knowing is its sole act. Something therefore comes to be for consciousness in so far as the latter knows this *something*. Knowing is its sole objective relation' (Marx, 1844:183).

Marx often referred to the one-sidedness and limitations in Hegel — usually with reference to the *Phenomenology*. During this period the problems that Marx dealt with in terms of knowledge, derived precisely from what Hegel referred to as absolute knowledge, or the way in which the individual transcends his alienation through the act of knowing an external environment. Exact knowledge becomes the basic modality for liberation. What Marx does deal with and Hegel was unable to get at, is the role of labour and work in the process of learning. Hegel had a concept of knowledge but no concept of learning. Marx accepted the Hegelian framework, but through the labour process understood the role of the learning process.

'Let us provisionally say just this much in advance: Hegel's standpoint is that of modern political economy. He grasps *labour* as the essence of man — as man's essence in the act of proving itself: he sees only the positive, not the negative side of labour. Labour is man's coming-to-be for himself within alienation, or as alienated man. The only labour which Hegel knows and recognises is abstractly mental labour. Therefore, that which constitutes the essence of philosophy — the alienation of man in his knowing or himself, or alienated science thinking itself — Hegel grasps as its essence; and he is therefore able to gather together the separate elements and phases of previous philosophy, and to present his philosophy as the philosophy. What the other philosophers did — that they grasped separate phases of nature and of human life as phases of self-consciousness — is *known* to Hegel from the *doings* of philosophy. Hence his science is absolute [Marx, 1844:131-132].

What we have in this first stage is what might be called the educative path to human liberation: knowledge as a liberating device, and work as the basic learning instrument for the realisation of such liberation. Hegel gave Marx his first deep commitment to the idea of communism as the society of total labour dedication. This is not just a naive stage in Marxist development, but the Enlightenment ideal in its Germanic form, in its specifically naturalised version of the Hegelian vision of coming to truth through coming to grips with the problem of knowledge. Socialism (or communism in this sense) is not much different from Hegel's vision of absolute knowledge — a society in which every person is realised in the free pursuit of self-understanding through social labour.

By the time of *The Communist Manifesto,* Marx had broken away from the German philosophic tradition and even the German socialist tradition Hegel had spawned. In one of the most biting paragraphs in the *Manifesto,* Marx and Engels announced their liberation from the idealist vision of knowledge as well as the capitalist vision of society. 'The robe of speculative cobwebs, embroidered with flowers of rhetoric, steeped in the dew of sickly sentiment, this transcendental robe in which the German socialists wrapped their sorry "eternal truths", all skin and bone, served to wonderfully increase the sale of their goods among such a public. And on its part, German socialism recognised more and more its own calling as the bombastic representative of the petty-bourgeois Philistine' (Marx, 1848:35).

It remained for Marx to move beyond his criticism of Philistinism, Chauvinism and 'the meanness of this model man', into a more economic view of the source of both knowledge and its distortion.

The second stage in Marxian thought was far less sanguine about the realisation of knowledge through labour and the overcoming of alienation through self-understanding. By the late 1850s, or what might be called the *Das Kapital* period, Marx had grown weary of the possibility of individual self-realisation — or for that matter, the philosophical character of the process of knowing. He had also grown weary of labour as a sheer learning experience; rather he saw the problem of knowledge in terms of the problem of social systems.

Knowledge under capitalism is purely instrumental. It is a source of alienation because of its one-sided demystification of experience. Capitalism gives a scientific character to production, but does not give a scientific character to the relationships of human beings within the production process. The process of labour, which in the earlier phase was to be the source of knowledge and liberation, is thereby reduced within capitalism to an element of technology and little else.

'The development of the means of labour into machinery is not fortuitous for capital; it is the historical transformation of the traditional means into means adequate for capitalism. The accumulation of knowledge and skill, of the general productive power of society's intelligence, is thus absorbed into capital in opposition to labour and appears as the property of capital, or more exactly of fixed capital, to the extent that it enters into the production process as an actual means of production. The tendency of

125

capital is thus to give a scientific character to production, reducing direct labour to a simple element in this process' [Marx, 1857:134-135].

When Marx turns to the question of knowledge under communism in this middle period or economic stage, leisure and labour become factors. In a mood almost reminiscent of Aristotle, he sees the need and the possibility of 'leisure time' for the 'higher activities'. In the realm of communist freedom both leisure and labour define and determine the character of what we know. And in this world of communism, practice becomes equated with experimental science on the one hand, and historical science on the other. The latter being the accumulated wisdom of society as a whole:

'Free time — which includes leisure time as well as time for higher activities — naturally transforms anyone who enjoys it into a different person, and it is this different person who then enters the direct process of production. The man who is being formed finds discipline in this process, while for the man who is already formed, it is practice, experimental science, materially creative and self-objectifying knowledge, and he contains within his own head the accumulated wisdom of society. Both of them find exercise in it, to the extent that labour requires practical manipulation and free movement, as in agriculture'. [Marx, 1857:148-149].

In this second stage of the Marxian vision of knowledge there is a liberating power of the economy *per se*. The way in which economic transformations permit exact human knowledge is no longer a matter of individual effort, no longer a matter of knowledge searching its true opposite; but rather the way in which economic evolution, first one-sidedly through the capitalist expansion of natural science, and then multidimensionally through the socialist concept of the human sciences, permits a knowledge without distortion. False consciousness dissolves in practice rather than in introspective or even experiential reflections.

Although Engels in particular sought intellectual confirmation, in *Dialectics of Nature* and parts of *Anti-Duhring,* of socialism through the natural sciences, basically Marx and most other socialists — pre- and post-utopian — considered the natural sciences as a common human property, rather than the special property of those in possession of dialectical reasoning. Since the physical sciences are in the 'interests' of all contending social classes, such sciences are said to be in the general domain, largely undistorted by ideological considerations. It is the social sciences, specifically the science of political economy, that represents the specifically socialist contribution to the march of science

For it is in the transformation of 'classical' or 'bourgeois' political economy as a study in the propertied sources of inequality, into a socialist political economy that starts with the class struggle itself (rather than with property) and concludes with the elimination of such struggles through the termination of antagonistic classes as such, that one locates the knowledge input of socialist doctrine into the general scientific corpus.

But at this second stage in the evolution of Marxian socialism, there was an assumption of automaticity, or spontaneity as the Russian Marxists were to call the economic vision of the transformation of capitalism into socialism. It remained a task for the third and final stage in the evolution of Marxist thought to develop a framework for showing how these inexorable economic properties were in fact, or in future values, linked to the political mission of an industrial working class. As Marxism became more linked to 'free will' and less to a 'determinism', so too did the tasks for bringing about socialism move increasingly to the political realm and decreasingly to the production realm. Much, if not all, of Marx's late writings were taken up with the careful analysis of civil warfare in the United States, revolutionary conditions in Spain, national liberation in Poland and Russia, etc. The processes by which classes come to power, rather than the process of class competition in the economic marketplace became paramount. As a result, the concept of knowledge became saturated with that of history; no longer economic history alone, but the relationships between political change and economic exploitation. Engels summed up this classical position in his essay on 'Socialism: Utopian and Scientific':

'The materialist conception of history starts from the proposition that the production of the means to support human life — and, next to production, the exchange of things produced — is the basis of all social structure; that in every society that has appeared in history, the manner in which wealth is distributed and society divided into classes or orders is dependent upon what is produced, how it is produced, and how the products are exchanged. From this point of view the final causes of all social changes and political revolutions are to be sought not in men's brains, not in man's better insight into eternal truth and justice, but in changes in the modes of production and exchange. They are to be sought not in the *philosophy*, but in the *economics* of each particular epoch. The growing perception that existing social institutions are unreasonable and unjust, that reason has become unreason and right wrong, is only proof that in the modes of production and exchange changes have silently taken place with which the social order, adapted to earlier economic conditions, is no longer in keeping. From this it also follows that the means of getting rid of the incongruities that have been brought to light must also be present, in a more or less developed condition, within the changed modes of production themselves. These means are not to be invented by deduction from fundamental principles, but are to be discovered in the stubborn facts of the existing system of production.' [Engels, 1880:90].

Engels' point of view still represented a somewhat earlier vision; and it was Marx who uniquely took the question of knowledge one step further in his biting and cynical response to the Gotha Programme. It was here that he confronted not only revisionist socialism, but his own earlier vision of the emancipatory properties of knowledge. Inequality, in its very existence, makes a society based on true knowledge impossible:

'This equal right is an unequal right for unequal labour. It recognises no class differences, because everyone is only a worker like everyone else; but it tacitly recognises unequal individual endowment and thus productive capacity as natural privileges. *It is therefore a right of inequality in its content, like every right.* Right by its very nature can only consist in the application of an equal standard; but unequal individuals (and they would not be different individuals if they were not unequal) are only measurable by an equal standard in so far as they are brought under an equal point of view, are taken from one *definite* side only, e.g., in the present case are regarded only as workers, and nothing more seen in them, everything else being ignored.' [Marx, 1875:9].

One can easily understand how delighted Lenin and the latter-day revolutionaries were with Marx's *Critique of the Gotha Programme* because it was a confrontation of socialism with liberalism. Liberalism, which had made the most over its concern with the free exercise of knowledge and had been most forthright in championing equal rights and the rights of the free spirit, became a fundamental protagonist in the Marxist vision of knowledge. The ultimate cut was the equation of a Prussian constitution and its emphasis on the freedom of science with the liberalist catchwords and their emphasis on freedom of conscience:

' *"Freedom of science"* says a paragraph of the Prussian Constitution. Why then here?
"Freedom of conscience"? If one desires at this time of the *Kulturkampf* to remind liberalism of its old catchwords, then it surely could have been done in the following form: Everyone should be able to attend to his religious as well as his bodily needs without

the police sticking their noses in. But the Workers' Party ought at any rate in this connection to have expressed its consciousness of the fact that bourgeois "freedom of conscience" is nothing but the toleration of all possible kinds of *religious freedom of conscience* and that for its part it endeavours rather to liberate the conscience from the spectre of religion. But there is a desire not to transgress the "bourgeois" level.'[Marx, 1875:21].

There is a slow, but by no means uncertain evolution in Marx's thinking from individualistic and philosophic reasons for why we can accumulate exact knowledge, to a final stage in his thinking of why, as a result of political, social and economic conditioning, we cannot achieve such knowledge, short of a political revolution. Knowledge which leads away from the making of a revolution, from the theory and practice of social change, is no longer knowledge — but false consciousness.

At this point a major ambiguity in the socialist legacy rears itself. One view of the Marxian approach to knowledge is that of a continuum: from magic, rites, rituals at the primitive end, to theology and ideology at the middle range, to science and technology at the most sophisticated end. For Engels (1885, 1886) in particular, there was no doubt that ideology, the most troublesome of forms to express something more than mysticism and something less than pure science, comes into existence to express class interests and not personality defects. History distinguishes between ideological systems and conscious deceptions. There is furthermore a clear correlation of types of social systems and forms of ideological expression. And while ideologies are conditioned by the stages reached in scientific development no less than national peculiarities, they exist and persist primarily to defend class interests. Hence, the root condition for the elimination of ideology is the end to class exploitation (cf. Horowitz, 1961: 127-28).

But increasingly this view of ideology was displaced by the activist camp, particularly theorists of the Soviet socialist revolution. Lenin (1908) for example, considers ideology as a simple quantitative distinction in ideas. Ideology is said to contain a range of ideas from false notions of the ruling class to the true notions of the revolutionary class. On Lenin's premises, ideology is reduced to a heuristic principle for regulating theory. He thus finds no difficulty in employing terms like 'scientific ideology' and 'religious ideology'. With Lenin, ideology no longer was a special relation of ideas to material institutions as it was in Marx. Political alliance replaces class affiliation as the touchstone for estimating ideologies. Admittedly, Lenin was dealing with a political context requiring immediate ideological choices. He was confronted with a situation demanding a wholesale commitment to certain policies on the part of an elite and its following. In this context, Lenin contributed to a wide realisation that oppressed and oppressor cannot automatically transcend ideological boundaries; that ideology is indeed a barrier to be passed. Thus a revolutionary conflict, in so far as it engages the mental energies of the combatants, is no intellectual idyll, but rather a hard fought struggle between ideologies. What Lenin did not understand, and what was already apparent to the psychological school of Michels, Sorel and Pareto, is that ideology first and foremost functions symbolically to galvanise men into action. Ideology contains an irrational element without which it could serve no moral or political end, and this end exists quite apart from the intrinsic needs of a scientific sociology.

With this double legacy of perceiving ideology both as something less than science (i.e. a secularised theology) and contrariwise as something more than science (i.e. the source of revolutionary energy), the socialist vision of knowledge as a liberating force becomes considerably muddied — not to say muddled. It is scarcely any wonder therefore that under socialism, or at least under the Soviet system, social science has been considered as everything from a manifestation of bourgeois false consciousness to the embodiment of the highest principles of precise knowledge. In this sense, the very sophistication of the socialist theoretical tradition to that ubiquitous concept of ideology has been a source of profound confusion and discontent — permitting and even encouraging a struggle not only over ideas but whether it is fitting and proper to even express certain ideas. In this way, the nature of the socialist approach to knowledge is intimately bound up with the basic political questions of freedom of expression and the rights of criticism and self-criticism without the necessity of punishment for being declared wrong or in error.

Quite apart from the personal evolution in Marx's thinking; and apart too from the fact that each of these three types of approaches have developed adherents within the socialist camp, is the question of whether socialism is a system. This constitutes the next stage beyond bourgeois consciousness in a social science of liberation, or is in fact simply the next stage in the evolution of those social sciences. This becomes an extremely touchy and fundamental point throughout the twentieth century. What we constantly confront is not simply the Marxian or socialist vision of society, but just as definitely the socio-logical vision of the Marxist theories or socialist theories for the promulgation of change and consciousness.

Whether Marxism is part of social science knowledge, or is itself the generalised expression of social science in a 'post-bourgeois' context, divides many socialist scholars, who on other grounds might line up on the same side. Even within one collection of papers, in tribute to Lukac's *History and Class Consciousness,* one finds sharp disagreement on this issue.

Tom Bottomore (1971: 61-62) writing on class structure and social conscioussness, notes:

> The intellectual uncertainties of the present time, to which Lukacs alludes, are revealed in the disarray which prevails within some established ideologies (notably Marxism itself), and in the emergence of a confusing variety of new doctrines, or new styles of thought (for example, in the student movements) which seem to be only loosely connected with social classes, or indeed with any identifiable social group which could be seen as a potentially effective agent of social change. It has become increasingly difficult to be sure of having understood the influences which form political consciousness, and thus to be able to discern the main direction of events . . . We have long since passed out of the era in which the real consciousness of social groups, expressed in their beliefs and actions, could be discussed as mere "psychological false" consciousness, and be contrasted with the "rational consciousness" enshrined in the ideology of a Communist party.' [Bottomore, 1971:62].

It is evident that for Bottomore, the Party does not embody Marxism as a body of authentic knowledge, while in turn (and perhaps the more serious admission) Marxism by no means embodies the entire range of scientific truths. In contrast, Istvan Meszaros (1971:116), a most able interpreter of twentieth-century socialism, has no doubt whatsoever that contemporary events confirm rather than refute the general propositions of Marxism. Beyond that, in quite orthodox fashion, he entertains the view that whatever analytic problems arise, do so within a Marxian context, and hence must be resolved within such a context.

> 'Marx's general analysis remains as valid as ever, since it does not concern the "developed" countries, nor the "underdeveloped" ones, taken separately, but the capitalist world system as *whole,* with all its inherent structural contradictions, whatever particular forms of "exception" they may – indeed must – assume at different times and in different socioeconomic settings characterized by varying degrees of industrialization. In an object dialectical framework of reference, working "exceptions" constitute the general "rules" which, in an unending interchange, are made into new "exceptions" and new "rules," thus both modifying (concretizing) and confirming the general conception itself.' [Meszaros, 1971:116].

What we have in Meszaros is a variation on a standard theme that history may be imperfect, but doctrine remains always perfect. The difficulty in this position is the inability to counterfactualise, the inability to ever show at what point one doctrine can be legitimately replaced by another; or knowledge in its abstract form can be overthrown by another system or another paradigm. At what point does modification of an old system yield to its overthrow? One can, for example, still manufacture an Aristotelian epicyclic theory of planetary revolution, but it is far simpler to change the system and make the sun the centre and the earth a rotating periphery.

The question of knowledge and liberation must lead not simply to Mannheim's relativity of systems, but beyond that, to the yielding of Marxism itself as a system to a larger set of truths about the nature of the world — and the nature of socialism in that world.

REFERENCES

Althusser, Louis
1969   *For Marx*. New York: Pantheon Books/Random House.
Avineri, Shlomo
1970   *The Social and Political Thought of Karl Marx*. Cambridge: Cambridge University Press.
Bottomore, Tom
1971   'Class Structure and Social Consciousness', *Aspects of History and Class Consciousness* (edited by Istvan Meszaros). London: Routledge & Kegan Paul.
Engels, Friedrich
1880   'Socialism: Utopian and Scientific'. *In Basic Writings on Politics and Philosophy — Karl Marx and Friedrich Engels* (edited by Lewis S. Feuer). Garden City, New York: Doubleday & Co., 1959.
Engels, Friedrich1
1885   *Herr Eugen Duhring's Revolution in Science (Anti-Duhring)*. New York: International Publishers, 1939.
Engels, Friedrich
1886   *Ludwig Feuerbach and the Outcome of Classical German Philosophy*. New York: International Publishers, 1941.
Horowitz, Irving Louis
1961   *Philosophy, Science and the Sociology of Knowledge*. Springfield, Ill.: Charles C. Thomas-Publishers.
Hyppolite, Jean
1969   *Studies on Marx and Hegel* (edited and translated by John O'Neill). New York and London: Basic Books.
Lenin,
1908   *Materialism and Empirico-Criticism: Critical Comments on a Reactionary Philosophy*. Moscow: Foreign Languages Publishing House, 1947.
Marx,
1844   'Critique of the Hegelian Dialectic and Philosophy as a Whole', *Economic and Philosophic Manuscripts of 1844* (translated by

	Martin Milligan). New York: International Publishers, 1964.
Marx,	Karl and Friedrich Engels
1848	'Manifesto of the Communist Party'. In *Basic Writings on Politics and Philosophy – Karl Marx and Friedrich Engels* (edited by Lewis S. Feuer). Garden City, New York: Doubleday & Co., 1959.
Marx,	Karl
1857	*Grundrisse der Kritik der politischen Okonomie* (edited and translated by David McLellan). London: Macmillan & Co., Ltd., 1971.
Marx,	Karl
1868	'Letters to Dr Kugelmann – December 5, 1868', *Letters to Dr Kugelmann.* New York: International Publishers, 1938.
Marx,	Karl
1875	*Critique of the Gotha Programme.* New York: International Publishers, 1938.
Meszaros,	Istvan
1971	'Contingent and Necessary Class Consciousness', *Aspects of History and Class Consciousness* (edited by Istvan Meszaros).
Schlesinger,	Rudolf
1950	*Marx: His Time And Ours.* London: Routledge & Kegan Paul Ltd.

7 SOCIALISM AND THE IDEA OF SCIENCE

Anthony Arblaster

No socialist in the 'advanced' world in the third quarter of the twentieth century, whatever his affiliation, can avoid seeing that the actual condition, public reputation and future prospects of socialism are all overshadowed by its tragic twentieth-century history — by the comparative failure of its two major organised traditions, orthodox communism and social democracy — to realise the hopes and aims that were placed in them a hundred, or even fifty years ago. For many of us, indeed, that failure is so complete and decisive that we remain obstinately unattached to either of those two dominant traditions, suspended in the active but confused limbo of small groups, transient protest movements and multiplying 'tendencies'. Inevitably, the whole scene continues to be dominated, in part at least, by the effort to discover 'what went wrong'; and the confusion will continue so long as no widely agreed answers to that question have been arrived at. In this essay I want to suggest one direction in which I believe a part of the answer lies — in the generally damaging impact of nineteenth-century Positivism on socialist thought and action.

The general question 'what went wrong?', can, for our present purposes, be subdivided into two specific areas of enquiry. First there is the effort to get to the roots of what went wrong with the Soviet Union after Russia had experienced what was generally believed, by both its friends and enemies, to be the world's first socialist or proletarian revolution. This enterprise has by now gone far beyond its original starting-point, the critique of Stalin and Stalinism — a critique which began with writers like Trotsky and Victor Serge, but received a quite decisive impetus from Khrushchev's celebrated denunciation of Stalin in 1956.

Second, there is the failure of non-revolutionary socialism, or social democracy, to fulfil the hopes of its early pioneers and its latter-day socialist supporters, and its corresponding adjustment to far more modest aims. Some of the first Fabians, such as Bernard Shaw and Sidney Webb writing in the original *Fabian Essays* of 1889, argued that revolution was unnecessary because socialism was coming in any case: all that was required was a little gradualist agitation to accelerate the inevitable march of progress towards the Left. But contemporary social democrats have not generally shared that early confidence. Many of

134

them have come to social democracy because they have despaired of revolution, or because they have turned away in revulsion from the pattern offered by the Soviet Union and the other so-called 'socialist states' of Eastern Europe. They have preferred gradualism as being a more humane strategy, if not necessarily one more likely to produce a socialist society; although they have also argued that the revolutionary path, as exemplified by the Soviet Union, has involved immense cruelty and repression, yet produced in the end only commonplace results. This was essentially the case put forward, for example, in *The Strangled Cry* by John Strachey, the Marxist propagandist of the 1930s who by the 1950s was defending the British manufacture of nuclear weapons on behalf of the leadership of the Labour Party. The mood of the social democratic convert can be summed up in some lines of C. Day Lewis, another sympathiser with Communism in the 1930s, who ended up as Poet Laureate, rather like the ex-radical Robert Southey one hundred and fifty years earlier:

> It is the logic of our times,
> No subject for immortal verse —
> That we who lived by honest dreams
> Defend the bad against the worse.

But however acceptable such modest objectives may be to the disillusioned ex-radical, they offer no kind of solution to the problem of *socialist* effectiveness. So the disappointment of both revolutionary and reformist hopes has produced a crisis for socialism. In this crisis, as Peter Sedgwick has pointed out in an excellent essay,[1] it has unavoidably been the case that most of the necessary rethinking has had to take place *outside* the two great movements primarily identified with those disappointments — institutionalised communism and established social democracy. So, for sound historical reasons, the decades since 1956 — the year of the Hungarian revolt and the Suez invasion as well as of Khrushchev's secret speech — have seen a ferment of Socialist debate and activity in the capitalist West. The Vietnam war in particular has had a catalytic impact.

But this was not only because the war exposed the inherent brutality and ruthlessness of American imperialism to many people who, ten years before, would have been sceptical of the very existence of anything which could properly be called 'imperialism'. ('Imperialism', like 'capitalism', was well known to be a figment of the fevered imaginations of the surviving left-wing sectarians.) Nor was it only because the war imperatively demanded active opposition (above all in America itself) and solidarity with the brave and battered Vietnamese. It was also because the war radicalised people by compelling them to ask the most searching questions about the quality and nature of the society which was capable of such appalling crimes against a people and country so much less privileged than itself.

One question in particular concerns us here. It was raised most insistently and incisively by Noam Chomsky. It had to do with the nature of the 'rationality' with which the war was waged by the American government, and most specifically with the character of the political and social 'science' which was so extensively used to further the war effort.

I believe that the doubts which Chomsky voiced about the kind of rationality and science exemplified by America's war policies in Vietnam have a direct bearing on the problems which, I have suggested, are central to the present crisis of socialism. I believe that a thorough exploration of these problems — the tragedy of the Soviet Union, the failure of social democracy, together with the disappointment of all hopes of revolution in the capitalist West — must bring us to the point where we are forced to question the adequacy of the conceptions of rationality and science with which most socialists as well as liberals have hitherto been content to work. I want to query whether the notion of 'scientific' socialism is really a possible or desirable one, and I shall suggest that this is one of the ways in which socialist thought and action and organisation have in fact taken on some of the characteristics of the capitalist society they are supposed to challenge. In a word I believe that an essential element in socialist rethinking must be a critique of the effects of scientism and Positivism on socialism.

To attack Positivism is, of course, not novel. It is not even novel on the Left. It is a position which has been adopted repeatedly by theorists in what may be called the Hegelian stream of Marxism, such as Lukacs and Marcuse. It is particularly associated with the Frankfurt school and its leading figures such as Theodore Adorno, Max Horkheimer and Jürgen Habermas. The current growth of interest in the Frankfurt Marxists, evidence by Martin Jay's study, *The Dialectical Imagination,* and recent English translations of Adorno, Walter Benjamin and others, may, of course, be no more than the latest Leftish intellectual fad. But it could also be a sign of, or else lead to, a greater understanding of the socialist critique of Positivism. But it is not the sheer novelty of such a critique that matters, politically speaking. What matters is that it should make a significant impact on the main currents of socialist thought and action. So far as I can judge, such an impact has yet to be widely achieved. Repetition and popularisation of a case which for many people still lies concealed in impenetrable thickets of Hegelian terminology, is therefore necessary.

But first to return to the Vietnam war and Chomsky's opposition to it. Chomsky was not merely concerned with the *exploitation* of the social sciences to serve the American war effort and 'counter-insurgency' programmes in Southeast Asia. Nor was he concerned simply with the voluntary prostitution of intellectuals in the service of those policies. The perversion of intellectual life by war, and the collaboration of professors in that perversion are, after all, all too familiar occurrences. What particularly disturbed Chomsky, and what produced a major crisis among the social scientists themselves, was the striking *facility* with which American social science was adapted to the requirements of American war policies.

Consider the following passage by Professor Samuel Huntington of Harvard, which has subsequently become notorious as a result of the demonstration against Huntington at Sussex University in 1973:

> '. . . if the "direct application of mechanical and conventional power" takes place on such a massive scale as to produce a massive migration from countryside to city, the basic assumptions underlying the Maoist doctrine of revolutionary war no longer operate. The Maoist-inspired rural revolution is undercut by the American sponsored urban revolution.'[2]

This is what Huntington termed 'forced-draft urbanization'. It takes a moment or two to realise (in the precise sense of making real to oneself) what he is actually talking about. He is saying, in effect, that if you drop enough bombs and defoliant on the villages and fields, and drive enough tanks through them to destroy the village and its crops, and kill many of its inhabitants, the survivors will have no choice but to abandon what was once their home and make for the relative safety of the cities. This is a banal observation, which hardly needs to be dressed up in the pseudo-theoretical jargon of the social scientist. But what is worse is that this miserable abstract language serves — no doubt very effectively for many people — to conceal the human and inhuman realities of the war strategy Huntington is supposedly analysing in what he thinks of as a 'scholarly and objective fashion'.[3] What is objectionable is not only the use of euphemisms to mask cruelty and killing, nor even just what Orwell objected to in his essay on 'Politics and the English Language' — the way in which abstract jargon distances us from concrete reality. The crucial point is that such language is the *characteristic* language of the contemporary social sciences, and that it reflects, or rather embodies, the characteristic thinking of the contemporary social scientist.

It might be argued that thinking such as Huntington's represents essentially a perversion of social science, or that it is a misapplication of what in other contexts remains a perfectly sound and useful mode of analysis. I find this unconvincing. The whole project of developing a science of man and society has from the start been founded on the premise that it is both desirable and possible to apply the methods developed and used with such signal success in the natural sciences to the study of human nature and society. As Saint-Simon said, social theory was to use 'the same method that is employed in the other sciences of observation. In other words, reasoning must be based upon the facts observed and discussed, instead of following the method adopted by the speculative sciences, which refer all facts to reasoning'.[4] This was an argument for empiricism, as against reasoning not firmly founded on observed facts; but it was also an argument for treating man himself as an object, to be observed and analysed by the same dispassionate, impersonal method as scientists had applied to stars or rocks or the circulation of the blood. As Marcuse said, one purpose of 'positive philosophy' or 'positivism' was 'to teach men to view and study the phenomena of their world as neutral objects governed by universally valid laws'.[5]

For a long time the pioneers of the social sciences continued to believe that the development of such an approach would, in the end, yield results which would be as certain and conclusive as those of the natural sciences, but far more useful because they would be directly, and not merely instrumentally, connected with the social life of mankind. Thus John Stuart Mill opened his essay on *Utilitarianism* (published in 1861) by lamenting that a 'science of ethics' had not yet been developed, yet not doubting that eventually it would be. Sidney and Beatrice Webb were confident that in helping to set up the London School of Economics and Political Science they were automatically advancing the cause of socialism, for how could an enlarged understanding of society not form the basis for a more enlightened and rational administration of social life?

Such expectations now appear naive. And the Huntington instance may serve to point to a much grimmer conclusion: that it is only a short step from seeing man as an object to treating him as one. Just as the scientific observation of nature has been, since at least the time of Francis Bacon, the basis for the scientific manipulation of nature to serve human purposes, so the attempt to model the study of man and society on the same pattern now provides a basis for the technocratic manipulation of human beings. The fate of the people of Vietnam provides only one example — though one of the most terrible — of such manipulation.

But whereas in the past the 'scientific' or, to use Michael Oakeshott's term, 'rationalist' approach to politics has usually been associated with radicalism and socialism, what is significant about the Vietnam war is that it also was planned and administered by people who apparently endorsed that approach. The war was not directed by a bunch of Right-

138

wing anticommunist fanatics – it was Goldwater who *lost* the election in 1964. It was the work of two successive Democratic administrations, both of which plumed themselves on the intellectual calibre of those who worked for them in Washington. And over this intelligentsia presided the Defense Secretary, Robert McNamara, a man whose very name became a byword for undogmatic administrative rationality:

'As paradoxical as it may sound, the real threat to democracy comes, not from overmanagement, but from undermanagement. To undermanage reality is not to keep free. It is simply to let some force other than reason shape reality . . . '

'Vital decision-making, particularly in policy matters, must remain at the top . . . But rational decision-making depends on having a full range of rational options from which to choose, and successful management organizes the enterprise so that process can best take place. It is a mechanism whereby free men can most efficiently exercise their reason, initiative, creativity and personal responsibility.'[6]

It sounds obscene to suggest that the barbarities of Vietnam represent any kind of triumph for reason. Yet they *were* the end-product of a certain type of rationality, and it was, of course, not the architects but the active opponents of the war who were denounced, in Irving Kristol's words, as 'unreasonable, ideological types'[7], or by McGeorge Bundy as 'wild men'[8]. They were portrayed as the sentimentalists, the victims of irrational emotionalism, by contrast with the cool, calm, rational calculators in the Pentagon, the State Department and the White House. Clearly there was something radically wrong with a rationality which could issue such frightful policies, which didn't even have the *realpolitik* virtue of being successful. Stuart Hampshire has expressed it well:

'The break evidently came with the realization that professors and deans of great universities, with their panoply of educated reason, could dismiss the critics of the Vietnam war as adolescent sentimentalists. The relation between reason and sentiment in politics and the nature of adult judgment in modern politics had to be rethought, because it seemed that the official reasoning was the computation of strained and stunted men, who to their younger critics had the look of overgrown schoolboys in Machiavellian dress.'[9]

Hampshire went on to suggest that rationality which characterised the American administration of the war was a fraud: it carried the superficial trappings of reason without containing its essential substance:

'The academic and near-academic experts on foreign policy, who have advised the Kennedy, Johnson and Nixon governments, provide an interesting counterfeit model of rationality, with all the traditional external marks of reason, without the underlying substance; this same model of rationality was paraded by Mr McNamara and his defense advisers . . . '[10]

The student opponents of the war were wrongly labelled as irrationalist, or antirational, he argues, because they were right in judging that this 'counterfeit' ought not to have been awarded 'the honorific title of reason'. This is perceptive, and it is certainly true that the term 'reason' has often stood for something more than the mere ability to calculate or make deductions without regard to the ends such activities were intended to serve.

But I think it must also be recognised that the type of rationality exemplified here is not simply a fraud, or a distortion. It does correspond to a certain conception of reason and its role in relation to means and ends which has been a commonplace of Western thinking for over three hundred years. Hampshire goes some way towards acknowledging this when he characterises 'the established model of reason' as 'a coarse, quantitative, calculative Benthamism, refined by games theory'. Bentham was only one of a succession of thinkers — Hobbes and Hume were others — who did, roughly speaking, equate rationality with the ability to calculate. For this empiricist, utilitarian tradition it was axiomatic that reason was related only to means, not to the ends of human activity, whether collective or individual. These ends were determined by human desires or passions, and were thus essentially placed beyond rational criticism. For Hobbes, man's innate appetites were to be accepted as the basic natural fact upon which, or around which, all social and political arrangements must be constructed. These appetites could be controlled, but they could never be eliminated. For Bentham anything that a man wants is *ipso facto* good. There is no possibility of judging human desires by any independent and superior ethical criterion. There is no reason to think that one activity rather than another is intrinsically more likely to be a source of happiness, and therefore good. The role of reason is to work out how happiness can be maximised, which is to say, how human desires can be most completely and harmoniously gratified. Reason is, and can only be, in Hume's words, 'the slave of the passions'.

Rationality therefore can be applied to means, but not to ends. Ends are matters of ethics or of taste, and are therefore essentially subjective. Thus the separation of means from ends roughly corresponds to the distinction between the objective and the subjective, or even between the rational and the irrational or the emotional.[11] Then, by a further extension of this mode of thought, the objective or factual comes to be defined still more narrowly as only what can be actually observed, or only what can be proved, or even only what can be measured and quantified. The dismissal of fundamental criticism of the Vietnam war as 'emotional' or 'subjective', and of the critics themselves as 'unreasonable', was plausible rhetoric because it implicitly invoked these familiar and widely accepted distinctions. To confine 'rational' debate on the war to a discussion of the means to be employed and their effectiveness reflected the same assumptions: that rational argument about ends was hardly conceivable; the debate would inevitably end up in a mire of subjectivity and 'mere' emotion. Thus the pattern of applied rationality exemplified by Vietnam, from which issues of justice and humanity were naturally excluded as subjective and and non-measurable, with attention being concentrated solely on the effectiveness of particular military and political means to attain given, undebated ends, is a pattern fundamentally in conformity with one traditional conception of the scope and nature of reason in human affairs.

But the truth is that there are two major concepts of reason within Western thought, not one. Alongside the negative or neutral concept of rationality as no more than an instrument or faculty, an ability to calculate and think logically which can be used with equal effectiveness for good purposes and bad, there is the positive, 'honorific' conception of reason, or Reason, to which Hampshire referred. This conception is rightly associated with the eighteenth-century Enlightenment, for which Reason was not simply an instrument or means, but a norm and individual and social goal. Reason in this form has something to say about ends as well as means. It asserts, for example, that some political principles and policies are more rational than others, either because they are more in accordance with human dignity and progress, or because they conform to the limits of human knowledge and the possibilities of rational certainty. Thus tolerance is a more rational policy than intolerance, since it does not make claims to proof and certainty in areas, such as religion, where such things are in principle unattainable. Cruelty, brutality, and any infliction of suffering are likewise irrational, because they create misery, and it is an obvious and reasonable presumption that most people wish to avoid misery and increase happiness. (There is a clear link with utilitarianism here.) Thus Reason is not morally neutral: Reason and humanity, Reason and tolerance go together. Reason is not compatible with cruelty, or barbarism or superstition.

Both conceptions of reason retain some vitality. Obviously it is through our sense of the second positive conception that we are led to reject the suggestion that the atrocious conduct of the war in Vietnam had anything at all to do with human reason. Yet it is simultaneously clear that these horrors *were,* in part, the products of rationality, of a purely instrumental rationality divorced from any consideration of what might constitute morally and humanly acceptable purposes and methods. 'I am certain', wrote the physicist Max Born, 'that the human race is doomed, unless its instinctive detestation of atrocities gains the upper hand over the artificially constructed judgment of reason.' It is an extraordinary situation in which a leading scientist can openly express his mistrust of reason, and find nothing else to rely on except the fragile hope that some fundamental, prerational 'instinct' will assert itself against the appalling dangers into which instrumental rationality has brought us.

Must we fall back on putting our trust in 'instinct'? Or is it a renewal of the positive, Enlightenment concept of Reason that is needed? Or does the rationality of the Vietnam war indicate only how potentially progressive modes of thought can be perverted and misused by imperialism and capitalism? I think it is clear why this last conclusion ought to be rejected. There is no reason to accept the neutral, instrumental concept of rationality as being identical with human reason as such. It is a serious mistake for socialists to accept, either tacitly or explicitly, that reason can be applied only to means, and that ends lie beyond the sphere of rational debate. It is equally mistaken to accept the parallel conventional separation between the sphere of fact and the sphere of values, as if the choice of values was an essentially arbitrary affair, to which empirical considerations were wholly irrelevant. Such considerations point towards the positive concept of reason. But is a response in these terms adequate? And what is the bearing of this debate to the specific problems of socialism which I mentioned earlier?

In considering the question of what went wrong in the Soviet Union it ought to be clear by now that to load all the blame on to something labelled 'Stalinism' is to leave all the really central questions still unanswered. For although the addition of the suffix 'ism' avoids the crudity of attributing every crime and error to a single individual, the germ still conveniently suggests that the malady was essentially transitory, a difficult and unpleasant phase — bearing no close relation to what came before or after. Thus the reputations of Lenin, Trotsky and the Bolsheviks can remain essentially uncontaminated by any association with the dictatorship of the man who first succeeded, and. then destroyed (most of) them.

This is wholly unconvincing. We do not need to subscribe to the view that Stalin and his policies were the 'inevitable' outcome of the revolution to recognise that it is quite implausible to suggest, as the term 'Stalinism' so often implicitly does, that Stalin's tyranny and mass executions came like a bolt from the blue, a phenomenon without precedent or preparation.

There have been broadly two ways of explaining the emergence of 'Stalinism'. One holds that it was essentially due to the pressure of hostile circumstances taken together with the basically fortuitous advent to power of Stalin. Things would have been different, it is argued, if Lenin had lived, or Trotsky had won the struggle for the succession. The other type of explanation suggests that the transition from Leninism to Stalinism embodied the working out in practical terms of the authoritarian implications of the revolutionary ideology, which is variously named as Marxism of Marxism-Leninism. The interpretations of socialists and others who have been to some degree pro-Soviet in their sympathies, have naturally leaned towards the first, 'circumstantial' type of explanation. Such interpretations have emphasised the way in which harsh, and even regressive, policies were forced upon the new revolutionary regime in Russia by the unanimous and active hostility of the capitalist powers, which extended even to the promotion of civil war; by the failure of attempted revolutions elsewhere in Europe, and by the unwelcome, enforced isolation which the combination of these two massive setbacks produced. There can, indeed, be no doubt that these adverse external factors, lying quite beyond the power of the Russian regime itself, compelled the regime to abandon many of its earliest hopes and projects and to adopt policies which were essentially pragmatic responses to unforeseen and unwelcome emergencies. To interpret the development of Soviet policies through the 1920s and 1930s as if they were the working out of the implicit programme of revolutionary Marxism is fundamentally implausible because it posits the absolute sovereignty of ideology and disregards the impact of events and circumstances. Such an interpretation places the revolution and its development in an historical vacuum.

What is more it must overlook the fact that the Bolshevik leaders themselves did not regard the actual development of the Soviet state with equanimity. Even if Trotsky's bitterly hostile criticisms of Stalin were to be dismissed (wrongly, in my view) as inspired only by personal rancour and therefore not an intrinsic part of the development of Marxist thinking, we still have to recognise that Lenin himself was, in his last years, racked by anxiety and even guilt about the direction in which the Soviet state was evolving.[12] Nor did he ever claim that each change of policy, each response to each new emergency, necessarily represented a step forward for the revolutionary project itself. Unlike Stalin, he did not dress up every retreat as an advance, or every compromise as a victory.[13] We cannot possibly hold the view that the development of Soviet policy and the Soviet state in this period represented the fulfilment of the hopes or aims of the leaders of the revolution. It clearly did not.

However, having said this much, I do not think we can fall comfortably back upon any simple form of the 'circumstantial'explanation. Unless we are prepared to argue that the ideology of the Bolsheviks was of no account, or that Stalinism owes nothing to Bolshevism, we cannot evade the quite reasonable presumption that some of the responsibility for the crimes and horrors of Stalinism must lie with the tradition of revolutionary socialism in its Russian form. What, then, are the elements in that tradition which helped to make the crimes of Stalinism possible?

One of them can be identified quite promptly. It is what Trotsky, in 1904, described as 'substitutism'. This is the principle of representation applied to the proletariat. If it is, for one reason or another, 'unrealistic' to expect the proletariat as a whole to act as a revolutionary force on its own behalf, then we should look to the politically conscious 'vanguard' of the working class, which possesses the consciousness and the will to act that the proletariat as a whole would have if only it saw its own situation clearly, if it were not mystified and pacified by the myths and distortions of bourgeois ideology. The organised and effective political expression of that clear-sighted vanguard is the revolutionary party. The party, therefore, can reasonably claim to be acting on behalf of the working class, since it acts in its true interests — as that class could act if only it were not blinded and misled by the mythology of its class enemies.

But this substitution of the party for the class is the beginning, not the end, of the process. Trotsky argued in his 1904 pamphlet, *Our Political Tasks:* 'Lenin's methods lead to this: the party organisation at first substitutes itself for the party as a whole; then the Central Committee substitutes itself for the organisation; and finally a single "dictator" substitutes himself for the Central Committee . . .'[14] Trotsky at this time argued in the manner that Rosa Luxemburg was to adopt at the time of the revolution itself:

> 'The tasks of the new regime will be so complex that they cannot be solved otherwise than by way of a competition between various methods of economic and political construction . . . by way of long "disputes", by way of a systematic struggle . . . between many trends inside socialism . . . No strong, "domineering" organisation . . . will be able to suppress these trends and controversies . . . A proletariat capable of exercising its dictatorship over society will not tolerate any dictatorship over itself . . . this intricate task cannot be solved by placing above the proletariat a few well-picked people . . . or one person invested with the power to liquidate and degrade.'[15]

That Trotsky's attack on Lenin may have been unfair, as Deutscher suggests, and that Lenin had no intention of allowing the process of

144

substitutism to go so far, is not the point. What is important is that Trotsky, perhaps without really understanding what he was saying, had, in Deutscher's phrase, held up 'the faithful mirror of the future'. After the revolution it was Lenin, with his usual clear-sightedness, rather than Trotsky, who saw what was happening. As early as 1919 Lenin observed that

'the Soviets, which according to their program were organs of government *by the workers,* are in fact only organs of government *for the workers* by the most advanced section of the proletariat, but not by the working masses themselves.'[16]

'in fact "the forces of the working class" consist at present of the powerful advance guard of this class: the Russian Communist Party.'[17]

By March 1922, three years later, Lenin frankly admitted to the Central Committee that the process had gone further still:

'It must be recognized that the Party's proletarian policy is determined at present not by its rank and file, but by the immense and undivided authority of the tiny section that might be called the Party's Old Guard.'[18]

It can be argued that the process of substitutism was rendered inevitable by the unpropitious circumstances under which the revolution was made, and that the virtual destruction of the leading cadres of the proletariat in the civil war left the Party with no option but to concentrate power in its own hands if anything of the revolutionary project was to be salvaged. This is dubious. The Bolsheviks did not merely accept a power which was thrust upon them; they engaged in the active suppression of both working class agitations (as at Kronstadt) and competing or critical tendencies within the broad spectrum of supporters of the revolution. But I think it must in any case be accepted that the process of substitutism, whether necessary or not, was facilitated by the doctrine of the vanguard party set out in Lenin's *What is to be done?* The collective self-confidence of the Bolshevik party, that it did represent the real interests of the masses, made it easier for Stalin to claim to be the ultimate representative of those interests, and, no less important, for others to be willing to accept that fatal claim. For the success of Stalinism had to rest not merely on brute force and terror, but also on authority — that is, on a measure of positive and active respect and consent. This Stalin obtained by posing as the heir of Lenin, as the man who incarnated the will of the party which itself was the true representative of the masses.

145

There are thus, to say the least, obvious dangers in the principle of the 'vanguard' party as the representative of, and therefore substitute for, the class it is supposed to lead. The regrettable fact that these dangers are more keenly perceived by anti-socialists than by socialists is one reason why revolutionary socialism continues to inspire mistrust and misgivings, even among radicals and non-affiliated revolutionaries. But the crucial question for our present enquiry is in the roots of substit-utism itself. It is at this point that we encounter Positivism in its Marxist form. For the roots of the theory of substitutism lie in the basic contrast between the 'objective' needs and interests of a class (in this case, the working class), and the 'subjective' consciousness of that class, or rather, perhaps, its *lack* of consciousness of its needs and interests. In a different formulation this corresponds to the antithesis between true and false consciousness.

It is often suggested that such dichotomies are inherently elitist in that they imply that some person or group can know better than a whole class or mass of people what their interests are, and what they really want, as opposed to what they *think* they want, and what they *think* their interests are. But this criticism is facile. If we accept, for example, that a benevolent parent of guardian can know better than a child what a child wants or what is in his or her interests, simply because the child is ignorant of the dangerous properties of stinging nettles or large quantities of aspirin or running across busy roads, we have conceded the general principle. It is quite often the case that a specially well informed or well educated minority does know better than a majority what is in their best interests — as we all acknowledge daily by submitting to the advice and prescriptions of doctors, dentists, plumbers, builders, and other specialists — although the Chinese are demonstrating that specialisation does not have to be carried to the lengths it currently is in most, if not all, 'advanced' societies. It must be obvious, too, that we cannot dispense with such a basic antithesis as that between the 'subjective' and the 'objective'. Whatever the strengths of complete relativism may be at the theoretical level, in practice we do not and cannot accept that every interpretation of reality has equal validity. An illusion does not become reality simply because many people devoutly believe it to be true. We must allow that in principle a distinction can be made between true and false consciousness, whatever the problems of establishing such a distinction in practice and in detail.

The substantive question is not the general and theoretical one, but whether a presumption of superior and specialist knowledge ought to be so widely applied and accepted as it is, and in particular how far such a presumption can be made in the sphere of politics. The basis of the assumption that a revolutionary Socialist party could act in good faith as a proxy for the working class lies in the belief that it was

Marxism, rather than bourgeois political economy or sociology, which constituted that 'science of society' which nineteenth-century Positivism had set out to construct. If we are looking for an explanation of the particular self-confidence of political leaderships within the Marxist revolutionary tradition it lies here – in their conviction that in Marxism they held the key to the scientific understanding of society. The dream of science has operated, and continues to operate, strongly within the Marxist tradition. This can be seen, not only in the revival of the claim that Marxism constitutes a, or rather *the* science, by Althusser and his followers, but also by the general use among Marxists of terms like 'correct' and 'incorrect', as if the truth or falsity of a piece of social analysis, or even the appropriateness of a particular political tactic or policy, could be ascertained with the precision of a branch of mathematics.

Such claims, whether explicit or implicit, are both implausible and dangerous. The dangers have already been alluded to. The implausibility is apparent from the fact that no 'correct' analysis or strategy has ever been able to compel the assent of rational people in the way that a piece of reasoning in mathematics or one of the natural sciences can do. Rosa Luxemburg suggested that

'The tacit assumption underlying the Lenin-Trotsky theory of the dictatorship is this: that the socialist transformation is something for which a ready-made formula lies completed in the pocket of the revolutionary party, which needs only to be carried out energetically in practice.'[19]

She was perhaps caricaturing the attitudes of the Bolshevik leaders, but she was not wrong to champion, within the context of the revolutionary process, a more open, more democratic and less arrogant approach to the problems of constructing socialism. She rightly suspected that the means would determine the end, and that socialism could not be achieved by elitist political methods, but only through 'the active, untrammeled, energetic political life of the broadest masses of the people'.[20]

Attacks on the elitism of Bolshevism, or Marxism-Leninism, are not new and have come from libertarians on the Left as well as from conservatives, liberals and social democrats to the Right. Often such attacks have been associated with an attack on 'ideology' and its supposedly malign influence on politics. That is not, however, the position from which I have been arguing. On the interpretation offered here, the damaging influence is not that of ideology (defined in a highly tendentious way) as such, but of a particular ideological formation, that of Positivism and the cult of science. It would be ironic if it was among Marxists that the Victorian Positivists' confidence in the possibility of converting politics into a science lingered on after it had been repudiated not only by radicals but also by all the most sophisticated bourgeois theorists of politics and society.

Social democratic thought has also suffered from the impact of Positivism, in two contrasting ways. First there has been a social democratic counterpart of Bolshevik elitism — namely Fabianism. Even more than their predecessors on the interventionist wing of Utilitarianism, the Fabians were inspired by a belief in the possibility, and indeed the necessity, of rational and scientific reform and administration based on common-sense notions of human welfare and happiness which it seemed inconceivable that any humane and rational person could seriously challenge. It was just because the questions of ultimate political aims and values seemed to them so simple that they were confident that politics could be converted into a science. It was a matter of discovering the most efficient means of attaining certain obvious, generally agreed goals. The irrational partisanships of conventional politics could be replaced by competent and rational administration based upon accurate knowledge derived from the scientific study of society. Hence the Fabian strategy comprised two complementary campaigns: one to promote the social sciences, and the systematic investigation of social problems and social evils; the other to implement the practical policies which would be logically derived from such investigations and their conclusions. The latter programme involved purging the administrative machinery of the traditional evils of aristo-cratic dominance — nepotism, patronage, and the resulting incompetence and amateurism. These were to be replaced by trained, professional public servants, committed to sensible utilitarian ends. (Harold Wilson put forward a programme for the rationalisation and modernisation of British capitalism along these lines in the early 1960s, when he talked frequently about 'sweeping the dead wood out of the boardrooms' (their replacement by keen, young managers etc.)

The Fabians, like social democrats generally, rejected the Marxist dialectic of progress through class conflict, and rejected, too, the identification of the working class as the key agency of socialism. Social democrats, the Fabians again being no exception, have always preferred to define socialism in terms of certain abstract, ethical goals or principles:

'The true aim of the Labour Movement has always been not the dramatic capture of power by the working class, but the conversion of the nation to the socialist pattern of rights and values . . .'[21]

Consequently social democrats, despite the occurrence of terms like 'labour' in the names of many of their political parties, have not been troubled to the same extent as Marxists by the problems of the relationship of a socialist political party or organisation to the working class, and have not felt the same need to develop theories of 'vanguardism' or 'substitutism'. Elitism has been easily accommodated within the flexible and capacious embrace of conventional notions of what a representative, as opposed to direct, democracy allows. (It is noticeable that the adaptation of traditional democratic theory, as represented, say, by John Stuart Mill, to incorporate the highly dubious conclusions of the theorists of the twentieth-century elite went unchallenged by social democratic theorists, who were happy to invoke writers like Schumpeter and James Burnham as authorities. It was left to the New Left radicals of the 1960s to call a halt to this debasement of democratic thinking.)

If the identification of the working class as the indispensable agency of socialist transformation provides one theoretical brake on the development of elitism within Marxism, the Marxist theory of the state constitutes another. Since Marxism explicitly denies that the state can be regarded as lying beyond or above the class structure of society as a whole, but must be seen as an instrument of the interests of the dominant class, it is not open to Marxists to adopt a political strategy aimed at capturing state power within existing capitalist societies — although established communist parties have devised various unconvincing arguments designed to circumvent this prohibition. By contrast the capture of existing state power, and its use for socialist ends, is the central, and by now almost the only, strategy of all gradualist, parliamentarian social democratic parties, and, as Crosland pointed out: 'Fabian collectivism and Welfare Statism require a view of the State diametrically opposed to the Marxist view'.[22]

Thus Fabianism contained within itself tendencies towards elitism which were strengthened by certain other characteristics of social democratic thought as a whole. Yet paradoxically it has been in societies officially committed to Marxism-Leninism that the greatest concentration of power in the hands of the state and its functionaries has taken place. One factor which has inhibited Fabians and social democrats in their use of state power to make radical changes has been the influence of a conception of the scientific different from, and in some ways the direct opposite of, that which influenced the Marxist tradition. Yet, odd as it may seem, this conception too bears witness to the impact of Positivism.

According to this conception the scientific is identified with the empirical. Science deals with facts, not speculations; with the objective, the ascertainable and measurable, not with entities whose existence can only be inferred or conjectured. Such entities are all categorised, pejoratively, as 'metaphysical'. This is an outlook wholly in harmony with the tradition of British empiricism, and it helps to explain, for example, the strongly behaviourist bias of Anglo-Saxon academic psychology and the persistent hostility towards Freud and psycho-analysis as a whole. Within politics it has taken the myopic form of treating people's present and expressed desires, habits and inclinations as an irreducible, unalterable *datum* of policy. 'People don't want culture'; 'they do want motor cars and semi-detached suburban houses'. It is elitist and undemocratic not to recognise such popular tastes and accept them as the basis of policy-making.

We do not take the argument any further by denouncing such a position as 'populist', since it is clear that 'populist' and 'democratic' are words which are used interchangeably according to the position of the speaker or writer. The beginnings of a serious critique of such a position consist in the recognition that, beyond a certain minimal level, people's desires and aspirations are not the freely formed expression of their innate nature or character, but are themselves conditioned and limited by their particular social and economic setting. Such a recognition grows naturally out of a Marxist perspective. But social democrats are generally either unable to else unwilling to achieve it. They have perceived the dangers of manipulation which lie in any distinction between people's expressed wishes and what are presumed to be their 'real' or 'objective' interests. They have perceived them so clearly that they have deprived their own politics of radical impetus by their refusal to look far beyond what is to what could be. If the impact of Positivism helped to push revolutionary Marxism in the direction of a ruthlessly manipulative elitism, the adherence to a narrowly empirical interpretation of the scientific has contributed to the steady erosion of the socialist dynamic within social democracy, which also, as we noted, has not been immune from elitist tendencies.

In a fascinating, if uneven, recent book, *Towards Deep Subjectivity,* Roger Poole has developed a radical critique of current notions of 'science', 'fact' and 'objectivity' initiated by such writers as Marcuse and Chomsky. Such notions are not only limited and inadequate, he suggests, but also inherently conservative in tendency:

'Objectivity is what is commonly received as objectively valid, all the attitudes, presuppositions, unquestioned assumptions typical of any given society. Objectivity implies the acceptance of the dominant social, ethical and religious views in that society.'[23]

Poole suggests that the cult of objectivity involves not merely recognising certain facts *as* facts, but also, and much more ominously, accepting those facts at the moral level. Objectivity, he contends, 'carries with it . . . a mature, rich and integrated acceptance of the evils in the world'.[24] At first sight this may seem implausible. The recognition of something as being the case, as a fact, need not undermine the determination to change it; it might even strengthen that determination. Yet it is also clear that in practice there is an easy and often imperceptible slide from recognising something as a fact and resigning oneself to it as being, in practice, an unalterable fact. It is not far from the apparently neutral observation that *apartheid* exists, to the 'realism' of the politician and businessman who is willing to adapt his policy and his principles to that 'fact' by not challenging it. The term 'realism' is of course tendentious, but its use confirms that Poole is right to be suspicious of conventional conceptions of fact and reality.

Poole is surely right, too, when he says that 'the facts of human suffering are non-facts for objectivity, are merely subjective'.[25] Suffering is undoubtedly a fact, as the Utilitarians understood very well, yet today even to mention, let alone to dwell on the human suffering caused by any particular political policy, whether the context be Vietnam or Northern Ireland or homelessness, is to invite the accusation of introducing 'emotional' or even, so help us, 'subjective' factors into what would otherwise be a rational and objective discussion. The fact that social democratic politicians are as anxious as any others to proclaim and prove their 'pragmatism' is one among many indications of the extent to which gradualist socialism has fallen victim to conventional and restrictive conceptions of the objective and the scientific.

Utopianism invariably gets a bad press. Conservative realists of all shades from the social democrats rightwards attack it for disregarding the alleged facts of 'human nature'; while Marxists, who also want to be realists, denounce it for the vices of 'idealism', 'intellectualism', and 'voluntarism'; as, in a word, 'unscientific'. Yet a sheer pedestrian absence of imagination or vision is one of the things which has harmed the cause of Socialism in this century, and, as a character in one of Christopher Fry's plays remarks:

> There's a dreariness in dedicated spirits
> That makes the promised land seem older than the fish.[26]

I believe that Marcuse is right to argue that it has been a characteristic fault of the Left to be not too utopian, but not utopian enough. By this he means that it has placed too many restrictions upon its hopes and dreams, and also has *under*estimated the depth and scope of the changes that would be necessary to create a truly human and egalitarian society. Too much faith has been placed in the transforming efficacy of the seizure of power and the elimination of private property in the means of production. Not enough attention has been paid to the destruction of capitalism as a total system whose fundamental characteristics, such as the division of labour, fragmentation and alienation, are reflected at every level, including its thought and values. (Mao and the Chinese would seem to have understood this, and to have grasped that a revolutionary transformation of people's thought and values is not something that can be achieved overnight, but can only be the product of a long period of struggle and education. This accounts for much of the interest and sympathy which China currently inspires on the Left.) Socialists have failed to grasp the extent to which a socioeconomic system like capitalism survives and prospers just because it *is* a total system, with a system's internal coherence, with values and a world-view which correspond to its economic and political character. They have relied too heavily on the inherent contradictions within capitalism to do their work for them, and have neglected both to study and to challenge the comprehensive, pervasive ideology of bourgeois society.

Neither the critique of bourgeois society nor the alternative socialist perspective have been sufficiently thorough and radical. Which means that today, after more than a century of socialist thought and practice, socialism also has to be radical in its self-criticism, in making its own *auto-critique.* I have tried to suggest in this essay why it is necessary that this criticism should be extended even to such apparently neutral, common ground as the concepts of science, fact, objectivity and rationality. The willingness of both revolutionary Marxists and social democrats simply to inherit the bourgeois forms of these concepts and incorporate them into their own thinking has done great damage to socialism. Hence the effort to develop new and radical ways of thought in this area is a political as well as a philosophical necessity.

NOTES

1. Peter Sedgwick: 'Varieties of Socialist Thought', in *Protest and Discontent* Penguin, 1971 edited Bernard Crick and W.A. Robson.
2. Quoted by Noam Chomsky in *American Power and the New Mandarins* Penguin, 1969 p.21.
3. Quoted by Chomsky, *op. cit.,* p.38.
4. Quoted by Herbert Marcuse in *Reason and Revolution* Routledge, 1955 p.331.
5. *ibid,* p.326.
6. McNamara himself, quoted by Theodore Roszak in *The Making of a Counter-Culture* Faber, 1971 p.12.
7. In *Encounter,* August 1965.
8. Quoted in Chomsky, *op. cit.,* p.265.
9. Stuart Hampshire: 'Russell, Radicalism, and Reason', a review of the third volume of Bertrand Russell's autobiography, *New York Review of Books,* 8 October 1970.
10. *ibid.*
11. See Roszak, *op.cit.,* especially the Appendix on 'Objectivity Unlimited'.

12. See *Lenin's Last Struggle* by Moshe Lewin Faber, 1969 *passim,* but especially chapters 1 and 9.
13. See Isaac Deutscher, 'The Moral Dilemmas of Lenin' in *Ironies of History* Oxford University Press, 1966 esp. p. 170.
14. Quoted in Isaac Deutscher, *The Prophet Armed* Oxford University Press, 1954 p.90.
15. *ibid,* pp. 92-3.
16. Quoted in Lewin, *op. cit.,* p.6.
17. *ibid.,* pp. 6-7.
18. *ibid.,* p.12.
19. Rosa Luxemburg: *The Russian Revolution* Ann Arbor, 1961 p.69.
20. *ibid.,* p.62.
21. R.H.S. Crossman: 'Towards a New Philosophy of Socialism' in *Planning for Freedom* Hamish Hamilton, 1965 p.56. Originally published, appropriately enough, as the first essay in *New Fabian Essays,* 1952. See also C.A.F. Crosland: *The Future of Socialism* Cape, 1956 Part II 'The Aims of Socialism'.
22. Crosland, *op. cit.,* p.87.
23. Roger Poole: *Towards Deep Subjectivity* Allen Lane, 1972 p.44.
24. *ibid.,* pp. 46-7.
25. *ibid.,* p.47.
26. Christopher Fry: *The Dark is Light Enough* Oxford University Press, 1954 p.18.

8 SOCIALISM AND THE DIVISION OF LABOUR

Tom Bottomore

'I don't like work — no man does — but I like what is in the work — the chance to find yourself. Your own reality — for yourself, not for others — what no other man can ever know.'

Joseph Conrad, Heart of Darkness

'Perhaps after all the division of labour is a necessary evil . . . Let us then accept the division of labour where it is proved necessary, but with the hope that the machine will increasingly take over all simplified jobs; and let us insist with the same urgency as for the workers of other classes, that the workers of this class should receive an education not only saving them from mental torpor, but also stimulating them to find a way of controlling the machine instead of being themselves the machine — controlled.'

Anthime Corbon, Worker, Vice-President
of the Constituent Assembly of 1848[1]

Few socialist thinkers have been ready to accept the division of labour, at any rate in the forms which it has assumed in the industrial capitalist societies, as an inalterable condition. In one way or another they have been concerned to find some means of modifying its operation, mitigating its effects, or even 'abolishing' it. Marx formulated, at different times, ideas about the division of labour which have played a major part in all later criticism and have found, in diverse guises, a practical application.

In *The German Ideology,* Marx outlined a broad criticism, and an equally sweeping alternative:

' . . . as soon as the division of labour begins each man has a particular, exclusive sphere of activity, which is forced upon him and from which he cannot escape. He is a hunter, a fisherman, a shepherd, or a critical critic, and must remain so if he does not want to lose his means of livelihood; whereas in communist society, where nobody has one exclusive sphere of activity but each can become accomplished in any branch he wishes, production as a whole is

154

regulated by society, thus making it possible for me to do one thing today and another tomorrow, to hunt in the morning, fish in the afternoon, rear cattle in the evening, criticise after dinner, in accordance with my inclination, without ever becoming hunter, fisherman, shepherd or critic.'

Later on Marx expressed alternative, or at least modified ideas about how the division of labour might be changed or superseded. In *Capital*, Vol.I, he argued that, in a future condition of society, ' . . . the detail worker of today, the limited individual, the mere bearer of a particular social function, will be replaced by the fully developed individual, for whom the different social functions he performs are but so many alternative modes of activity'; and he went on to suggest that the development of education, especially scientific and technical education, would help to accomplish these ends in a socialist society. But in a later discussion, in *Capital*, Vol. III, Marx emphasised more strongly that man's struggle with nature in order to maintain and reproduce his life, which he must undertake 'under any possible mode of production', remains always a realm of necessity: 'Beyond it begins that development of human potentiality for its own sake, the true realm of freedom, which however can only flourish upon that realm of necessity as its basis. The shortening of the working day is its fundamental prerequisite.'

These different judgements are not, however, contradictory. They embody diverse approaches to a problem which Marx treats in a consistent and systematic way. In the first place, Marx's concern is always the same: it is a concern with human liberation, with the possibility of constructing, and the means of achieving, a form of society in which each individual would be able to develop to the fullest extent his own talents and interests, instead of being confined within a narrow and imposed sphere of labour. The ideal is a society in which free, creative activity, as against *forced* labour, predominates. Throughout all his work, and not only in his early writings, Marx was guided by this vision of a liberated society, in which the division of labour too would be subjected to rational human control instead of developing as an apparently objective necessity determined by economic and technological imperatives. In the first drafts of *Capital*[2] Marx returns frequently to this theme: he writes, for example, 'In fact, however, when the limited bourgeois form is stripped away, what is wealth other than the universality of individual needs, capacities, pleasures, productive forces, etc., created through universal exchange? The full development of human mastery over the forces of nature, those of so-called nature as well as of humanity's own nature? The absolute working out of his creative potentialities, with no presupposition other than the previous historic development . . . Where he does not reproduce himself in one

155

specificity, but produces his totality? Strives not to remain something he has become, but is in the absolute movement of becoming?'[3]

Secondly, Marx always analysed the division of labour in a more general economic and social context, and with reference to particular forms of society. In *The German Ideology,* he observed that 'The division of labour implies from the outset the division of the *pre-requisites of labour,* tools and materials, and thus the partitioning of accumulated capital among different owners. This also involves the separation of capital and labour and the different forms of property itself. The more the division of labour develops and accumulation increases, the more sharply this differentiation emerges.' Hence, Marx analysed not only the division of labour, in the narrower sense of the specialisation of tasks within a productive enterprise, but also the differentiation of social functions which made one individual a land-owner or capitalist, another an agricultural labourer or factory worker. The division of labour, in its more restricted sense, is only one aspect of this larger differentiation of functions, and the specific form that it takes is influenced not merely by the development of technology (which results in the creation of new occupations and new ways of organising the productive process), but also by the particular interests, objectives and tendencies within a given social mode of production.

It also follows from Marx's historical treatment of the division of labour that it is only with the rise of modern capitalism, the rapid growth of productive forces and the systematic application of science to production, that it becomes possible to think realistically of a new type of society in which men would not simply accept their ascribed social roles within a system that appears to exist and function on a basis of natural necessity, but would organise their production for definite social objectives and seek to achieve a balance between the need for specialised labour in production and the claims of individuals to develop freely and fully their personal talents and capacities. To use Marx's own phrase, the post-capitalist society would be one in which men could ' . . . regulate their interchange with Nature rationally, bring it under their common control, instead of being ruled by it as by some blind power . . .'.

It is worthwhile to note here that Durkheim, who attributed a greater significance, and paid more attention, to the division of labour than did any other modern social thinker, although he approached the subject in a very different spirit from Marx arrived at conclusions which are not entirely divergent. Durkheim regarded the division of labour as a beneficent element in social life, as being essentially a source of solidarity;[4] but what he presented as its 'natural course' was a highly idealised picture, and only when he turned to discuss, in the third part of his book, the 'abnormal forms' of the division of labour did he seem to be describing its real features and effects in modern capitalist society. The two principal abnormal forms that he distinguished were the 'anomic' division of labour characterised by an insufficient regulation of the diverse functions, which resulted in economic crises and the conflict between capital and labour; and the 'forced' division of labour, in which the crucial element was the existence of class inequalities, which brought about a discordance between the distribution of social functions and the distribution of natural abilities, and unjust contractual relationships.

Thus Durkheim, like Marx, recognised the profound importance of class structure and class conflict in the actually existing division of labour, but he assumed that this is a temporary deviation from the inherent, natural tendency of the division of labour which will somehow bring about, through the progress of the collective consciousness and the activities of an impartial State embodying this consciousness, a condition of social harmony and solidarity. But this is no more than a vaguely formulated hope, and as Bougle observed in a comprehensive review of the theories about the division of labour ' . . . there emerges from Durkheim's apologia an impression which is very nearly as pessimistic as that which the socialist critics attempted to give . . . '.[5] Later critics of Durkheim have pointed out that the increased coordination of functions in an enterprise, in accordance with doctrines of 'scientific management', does not necessarily enhance solidarity; and Georges Friedmann, in particular, has noted that two different kinds of solidarity may be engendered by the capitalist system of production — either the solidarity of all those engated in production in an enterprise or branch of industry, or the solidarity of workers as a class.[6] In fact, it is the second type of solidarity which has grown most notably up to the present time.

Let us now examine more closely Marx's ideas about how the division of labour might be transformed in a socialist society, and consider how relevant these ideas are to present day conditions. The passage in *The German Ideology,* where Marx talks about hunting, fishing, etc. has sometimes been ridiculed by anti-socialist writers, but the notion it expresses is by no means so foolish and impractical as they suggest, although it needs to be put in a less romantic and archaic form. Of course, in an advanced industrial society a man cannot be an airline pilot in the morning, a nuclear physicist in the afternoon, and so on, but it is not altogether out of the question that many people, whatever their principal occupation might be, could become 'critical critics' in the evening; and the progress of a society in liberty and civilisation might well be gauged by the numbers of citizens who participate significantly in its intellectual life and become, for at least a part of their lives 'intellectuals'.

There is another social function which could also, with great benefit, be much more widely distributed; namely, political leadership. The traditional category of 'professional politician' is one that would need to be greatly modified in a thoroughly democratic society; for if men are really to govern themselves (in a collective fashion, not as isolated individuals) then the experience of governing should be widely diffused, and this is incompatible with the concentration of political experience and leadership in a small minority of people who, in Weber's phrase, live 'off' politics. There are several ways of extending more widely the experience of policy making, especially by the devolution of political responsibilities upon a larger range of regional and other associations and by the development of 'workers' self-management' in an increasing number of organisations, especially business enterprises. The progress of such a movement would be marked by a decline in the numbers of those who made politics their lifetime career, and a considerable increase in the numbers of those who devoted a part of their lives — perhaps a few years — to the exercise of political functions. At the present time, the evident mediocrity of professional politicians in so many countries should allow us to contemplate the prospect of a decline in their function without undue anxiety.

Even in the narrower sphere of occupational specialisation Marx's idea of an alternation of activities is not altogether impractical, and indeed it has found some practical applications. 'Work rotation' and 'job enlargement' have been widely discussed in studies of the organ- isation of industrial work and many experiments have been carried out with a view to making routine jobs more varied and interesting.[7] It is true that such experiments have been mainly concerned to raise productivity, by reducing absenteeism, accidents, high labour turnover, etc., but there has also been some element of concern about the effect of monotonous, assembly line work upon the worker himself, and the experiments do suggest that much more could be done along these lines to improve the situation of the industrial worker without any very adverse effects upon production. Of course, the scope of this kind of job rotation is still quite limited, but I think there would be opportunities for more extensive changes of occupation in a society which actually aimed to organise its production in the rational and humane way that Marx envisaged.

In any case, as we have seen, Marx also proposed two other means of limiting the harmful effects of the division of labour. One was the development of technical education which Marx thought would allow the worker to grasp the nature of the whole process of production in which he was engaged and thus make his own particular task more interesting as well as enabling him to move more easily from one specialised job to another. The second was, quite simply, to reduce the hours of work and increase the amount of leisure time, 'the true realm of freedom'.

Both these lines of thought have been followed by many students of industrial work since Marx's time. In the USSR especially, considerable efforts were made in the 1930s to develop polytechnical education, inspired in part at least by the idea of overcoming the narrowness of subdivided industrial tasks, though this kind of education was also well adapted to the needs of Soviet industrialisation during that period. More recently, similar questions have been discussed in the context of a more advanced stage of industrialisation, and there is an excellent analysis in the Czechoslovak study by Radovan Richta and his colleagues.[8] The authors describe two main tendencies in the development of industrial work: one is the extension of mechanised industrial production which gives rise to subdivided, monotonous tasks on the assembly line, the other, which they think will become predominant, the growth of automated, computer-controlled production lines, in which the unskilled repetitive operations are performed entirely by machines, while the activity of the worker is directed to the general regulation, maintenance and repair of the machinery. At a still later stage even these functions require fewer workers, and the most important human participation in production becomes the preparation and planning of the whole productive process. Thus it may be argued, there is a continuing transfer of labour to more creative activities, and this trend can be reinforced by the planned transformation of labour into a scientific activity, in which the producer can experience his work as both a means and an end.

Richta and his colleagues, although they attribute great importance to this scientific and technological progress, which makes possible an entirely new organisation of the labour process, also regard its consequences as depending upon the social conditions in which it takes place. From one aspect, it may establish some of the prerequisites of socialism; from another aspect, the realisation of its potential benefits presupposes socialist institutions and a socialist culture in which the system of production would be directed not simply by the striving for maximum output and consumption, but also by the desire to provide, in the work process itself, the greatest possible scope for each individual to exercise his judgment, take responsibility, and find satisfaction in the employment of his creative abilities.

In any case, the benefits that are likely to flow from purely technological developments should not be exaggerated. The sphere in which automation can eliminate disagreeable and tedious kinds of work, though it is quite large, is still limited. Moreover, this process is accompanied by an opposite one in which computer-controlled operations encroach upon more skilled occupations — for example, tool-making or industrial design, and a variety of white-collar jobs – and diminish the element of creativity and independent judgment in such work. But on balance the shift from manual to white-collar occupations which is going on in all the advanced industrial societies does probably represent a movement from more routine and irksome jobs to those which are more interesting, require greater initiative, and allow the individual more freedom of choice in the execution of the work.

This trend toward the expansion of more interesting, more intellectually demanding kinds of work, which results directly from technological change, could be reinforced in various ways through political choices. For example, the investment in education could be substantially increased in order to raise the general educational level, and to provide new types of education, which might be more directly associated with productive work, or be made available during periods of leave from work for people of all ages. One important innovation worth considering here would be the extension of an arrangement such as 'sabbatical leave' from the universities to all kinds of occupation, so that individuals could pursue their education, visit similar enterprises in other countries, and generally broaden their experience as well as adding to the variety and interest of their jobs.[9] Another more fundamental change would be to involve employees much more fully in the management of their enterprise, along the lines of the Yugoslav system of workers' self-management; this again would provide the individual with opportunities for a greater variety of activities during working hours and would perhaps enhance the interest of even the most fragmented jobs. Finally, the possibilities of job mobility, discussed earlier, might be greatly enlarged by a policy which set out deliberately to organise production in terms of providing the conditions for maximum satisfaction at work. William Morris once wrote an essay on 'A Factory as it might be',[10] in which he outlined the character that factory production might assume in a socialist society; but socialists, for a long time, and for various reasons (which I shall examine later), have sadly neglected these issues, while still arguing in an abstract way that the division of labour would need to be modified under socialism.

Even if the changes I have outlined above were successfully brought about, the sphere of production would still remain, in Marx's words, 'a realm of necessity', in which large numbers of people, at least, would not be developing freely their own activities, but would be more or less strongly *constrained* to produce. Hence the importance of Marx's third argument, that the growth of individual freedom in a socialist society would have as its fundamental prerequisite 'the shortening of the working day'.[11] This theme has been taken up by many later writers, both socialist and nonsocialist, who have seen in the expansion of 'leisure time' a possible compensation for the unavoidable constraints and dissatisfactions of work in an industrial society.

But the relation between work and leisure is a complex one, and we have to consider several different aspects. For some occupations, especially those of a professional or intellectual kind, the division between work and leisure may not be very clear cut; the interests of the occupation are often continued in leisure time, and even the distinction between home and workplace may not be very significant. Equally, in such occupations elements of leisure time activity may be introduced into the sphere of work; business lunches, conferences, travel on business affairs, all have some features of leisure. On the other hand, for those engaged in routine manual or clerical occupations which are strictly regulated, there is likely to be a sharp distinction between work and leisure; but the extent to which leisure activities in this case provide a 'compensation' for work depends upon a variety of factors. Routine work may predispose the individual to equally routine leisure pursuits, or it may lead him to more active recreations in which he can satisfy a need for self expression. Much depends upon what facilities are available, and how they are organised. It should not be overlooked that in the capitalist societies leisure activities themselves have become a large scale industry, and the transition from work to leisure assumes to some extent the character of a move from one sphere of mass production to another.

The impact of leisure upon work, however, may be just as important. Insofar as individuals do enjoy increasing leisure in which they can engage in freely chosen, self-directed activities, they may become more critical of the authoritarian organisation of work, and seek to modify it in various ways. Marx foresaw this possibility when he wrote that: 'Free time — which is both idle time and time for higher activity — has naturally transformed its possessor into a different subject, and he then enters into the direct production process as this different subject. This process is then both discipline . . . and, at the same time, practice, experimental science, materially creative and objectifying science . . .'[12] During the past decade much stronger demands for participation in the planning of work have been formulated by trade unions (and also in other spheres of activity, such as education), and one of the sources of this movement is probably the experience of greater independence and freedom of choice in leisure time which has accompanied increasing prosperity. In a more general way, material prosperity may have had some effects just the opposite of those which Marcuse outlined so pessimistically in *One Dimensional Man;* namely, the stimulation of a more widespread critical concern about the quality of life, which necessarily includes a more profound questioning of the quality of working life.

The industrial societies, in the course of the twentieth century, have undergone considerable changes in all those aspects of the division of labour that were of concern to Marx and other socialist thinkers. Job rotation is taken more seriously though the chances of extending it were limited for a long time by the development of assembly line production; social mobility has probably increased somewhat as the structure of occupations has changed, so that there is now more congruence between ability and occupation; some of the more unpleasant and monotonous kinds of work have disappeared or are disappearing; above all leisure time has increased, by the shortening of the working week, and especially by the extension of paid holidays.

But the advance in all these directions has been slow, and there are two factors above all that are responsible for this. In the first place, all the industrial societies, whether capitalist or socialist, have concentrated their main effort upon increasing the total output of goods and services, much more than upon reducing hours of work or transforming the whole organisation of labour. This phenomenon itself has various causes: in the capitalist societies it resulted from the struggle, led mainly by working-class organisations, to escape from the mass poverty of the 1930s, and at a later stage, from the interest of capitalist industry itself in creating ever larger mass markets; in the socialist countries of Eastern Europe it was engendered mainly by the initial poverty of agrarian societies, the requirements of industrialisation, and the need — for ideological and political reasons — to approach more closely the consumption levels of the capitalist countries. This element of competition has also a more general significance; high levels of production form one of the essential bases of national power, and international rivalries thus strengthen further the commitment to unrestricted technological advance and ever rising output.

The second factor that has impeded radical changes in the division of labour is the persistence of the class structure based upon property ownership in the capitalist societies, and the emergence of a new type of hierarchical structure in the socialist countries of Eastern Europe. In both cases, a strict and inegalitarian differentiation of social functions is maintained; in society as a whole, between those who direct the process of social development and those who are 'dependent participants',[13] and in the individual enterprise, between 'managers' and 'workers'.

Only in Yugoslavia has there been a sustained attempt to reduce substantially such distinctions, through the system of workers' self-management; and this attempt has revealed some of the difficulties involved in reconciling the aims of technological development, efficient economic administration, and general participation in the planning of production, especially in conditions where the need to raise the overall level of output is very pressing. It seems indeed that a high level of production, such as has been attained only since the war in the more advanced industrial countries, is a crucial precondition for tackling in a radical way the problems of the division of labour, and for making the reorganisation of the work process a *major* aspect of socialist policy. Previously, in conditions where a large part of the population was badly housed, undernourished, and often unemployed, the main weight of socialist activity had clearly to be directed toward eliminating mass poverty.

Thus, it may be said that only now are the circumstances favourable, in some parts of the world, for attempting large-scale changes in the organisation of work. They are favourable not only in the sense I have just outlined, that the material basis for a comfortable life for all citizens exists at present in many of the industrial countries, but also in another sense; namely, that there is now a widespread recognition of possible limits to economic growth, so that the task of creating a good society can no longer simply be thrust upon a more or less automatic process of endlessly increasing prosperity, which might be expected to provide compensation for the disagreeable consequences of the division of labour – for both the boredom of routine work and the more general inequality of social functions.[14]

The change in attitudes arising from this relative prosperity, and at the same time from the growing doubts about the possibility or desirability of ever increasing consumption, are now becoming very clear in a number of different ways. There has been a marked increase in the scope and activities of egalitarian movements, which have taken shape in a great variety of organisations – in sections of the established Labour Movement, in ethnic groups, in Women's Lib, and so on. The idea of 'participatory democracy', although it is no longer expressed in the dramatic manner of the 1960s, is still very much alive; and one of its most important manifestations is the growing interest, in the trade unions, in the possibilities of workers' control or self-management. There is also apparent, especially among the young, a new attitude towards occupations. Many young people, after completing their formal education, are extremely disillusioned by the kinds of occupation that are available to them; some opt out, in communes, or in temporary and intermittent work, but many more, while taking their place in the apparatus of production, nevertheless remain critical of a form of society in which, for all its prosperity, there seem to be so few opportunities for enjoyable productive activity. Thus, in one way or another, they express the notion that the division of labour should be made for man, should correspond more closely with his own needs for creative activity, and that man should not be shaped to fit the division of labour. The concern with the environment, and with the 'quality of life', again particularly in the younger generation, embodies a similar outlook; it raises questions about the reorganisation of social life as a whole — work, leisure, institutional arrangements and personal relations — in such a way as to satisfy as fully as possible in all spheres the great diversity of human needs. The trends which I have described — the rapid progress of science and technology, and the emergence of a new social consciousness — have already reached a stage where it is reasonable to think about practical policies designed to bring about a radical reorganisation of the division of labour. It is not too fanciful to suppose that a socialist Ministry of Employment, sometime before the end of this century, might be devoting a major part of its activities to developing schemes of self-management and to fostering the variety, interest and human value of work. Indeed, some reorientation of activities toward this end might be undertaken very quickly in many of the industrial countries.

Of course, there will remain very considerable problems. One of the most formidable of these is presented by the enormous gap, in the world as a whole, between the rich and poor countries, and by the tendency of the international division of labour to reproduce and reinforce this distinction. In the long term — the very long term — the problems of industrial work can only be solved on a world scale. But still, the poor countries, just as they can, in favourable circumstances, leap over some of the intermediate stages of industrialisation by introducing the most advanced technology, might also be able to avoid some of the most disagreeable features of the division of labour if an alternative model of the organisation of production were available for them to follow.

There are other problems arising directly out of technological progress — its enormous destructive potential in military uses, its threat to the environment — which can lead one to a very gloomy assessment of the likely future for mankind, such as Robert Heilbroner has recently outlined.[15] Nevertheless, without lapsing into a Panglossian optimism, it may be remarked that this 'oppressive anticipation of the future',[16] induced by the immensity of our problems and the failure to cope with them in any effective way during the past decade, is counterbalanced, to some extent, by the much more widespread awareness of the need to establish a conscious, enlightened human control over the whole process of social life. The question that Marx posed — how men can 'regulate their interchange with nature rationally, bring it under their common control, instead of being ruled by it as by some blind power' — has become the central question of our age for very large groups of people. To work out in detail the meaning of this 'rational interchange', its implications for the organisation of production and consumption, for the relations between nations, and for the elaboration of entirely new forms of society, is now the foremost intellectual obligation of social

164

thinkers.

NOTES

1. Quoted from Georges Friedmann, *The Anatomy of Work* London 1961.
2. Karl Marx, *Grundrisse* Penguin Books 1973.
3. *op. cit.,* p.488.
4. Emile Durkheim, *The Division of Labour in Society.* Like much else in Durkheim's sociology this is an elaboration of an idea derived from Comte.
5. C. Bougle, 'Theories sur la division du travail', *Année Sociologique,* VI, 1903.
6. Georges Friedmann, *op. cit.,* p.78.
7. See the review of work in this field in George Friedmann, *op. cit.,* Chapter III. In recent years a number of automobile firms, notably Volvo in Sweden, have changed over from a system of production involving highly subdivided routine tasks performed repetitively by each individual worker to a system based upon the organisation of complete sections of the production line by teams of workers.
8. Radovan Richta *et al., Civilization at the Crossroads,* 3rd ed. White Plains: Internationational Arts and Sciences Press, 1969. See especially Part II on the radical changes in the nature of work, skill, and education.
9. Some modest experiments along these lines have been introduced, but I do not think they are very widespread as yet. One case is mentioned in A. Rubner, *Fringe Benefits* London 1962 p.26. In some professional occupations, however, there are already opportunities for periods of leave in order to attend courses, which may last for a month or longer, and this practice could be much more widely adopted.
10. Reprinted as a pamphlet London 1907. I visited in the 1950s a factory which had some of the qualities that Morris envisaged, the *communauté de travail* 'Boimondau', at Valence in France; but so far there have only been isolated examples of this kind of factory organisation, though it may be that the numbers have increased since Morris's time.
11. Marx discussed this question at several points in the *Grundrisse,* and in one passage he quoted approvingly the comment of the anonymous author of *The Source and Remedy of the National Difficulties, Deduced from Principles of Political Economy* London 1821: 'Truly wealthy a nation, when the working day is 6 rather than 12 hours. *Wealth* is not command over surplus labour time [real wealth], but rather, *disposable* time outside that needed in direct production, for *every individual* and the whole society.' *Grundrisse,* p.706.
12. *Grundrisse,* p.712.
13. As Alain Touraine describes them in his analysis of the new class structure, in *The Post-Industrial Society* Random House 1971.
14. J.K. Galbraith, in one short chapter of *The Affluent Society* devoted to the subject of equality, argued that there had been a 'decline of interest in equality as an economic issue', and that the progressive increase of aggregate output was seen as an alternative to redistribution. This is clearly no longer the case, if it ever was; egalitarian movements have become much stronger and, as they have always done, set the issue of economic equality in the context of a broader discussion of the whole inegalitarian structure of

industrial societies. For an analysis of some trends in the USA see the recent study by Herbert J. Gans, *More Equality,* New York 1973.

15. Robert L. Heilbroner, 'The Human Prospect', *New York Review of Books,* XX, 21-22, 24 January 1974.
16. Heilbroner, *op. cit.,* p.21.

9 MARXIST CRITIQUES OF THE STATE

Leslie Macfarlane

The purpose of this essay is briefly to analyse the way in which the concept of the state outlined by Marx and Engels was developed and used by other Marxists, in particular by Kautsky and Lenin. This is not a simple task since the 'founding fathers' themselves never provided a comprehensive and systematic theory of the state. References to the state are scattered over many works, with the emphasis shifting not only with the passage of time and the maturing of judgement, but with the nature and purpose of the work concerned. Ralph Miliband has suggested that Marx developed two views of the state.[1] The primary view is that expressed in the *Communist Manifesto* — 'The executive of the modern state is but a committee for managing the common affairs of the whole bourgeoisie.'[2] The secondary view, exhibited most strikingly in *The Eighteenth Brumaire of Louis Bonaparte,* is, in Miliband's words, 'that of the state as independent from and superior to all social classes, as being the dominant force in society rather than the instrument of a dominant class.'[3] In Miliband's opinion the impact of the secondary position is to introduce, not simply an element of flexibility, but a strong anti-authoritarian and anti-beaurocratic bias into Marx's critique of the state. In contrast Miliband notes fewer signs of these characteristics in Engels' writings. A few years earlier John Plamenatz had suggested that Marx had produced two quite separate theories of the state, as an instrument of class rule and as a parasite on society;[4] while a few years later Shlomo Avineri put forward the thesis that Marx and Engels had held different views of the state.[5] But as I argued in *Modern Political Theory* it is difficult to believe wither that Marx and Engels could have collaborated so closely together for so many years without realising that they differed from each other on such a fundamental question as the nature of the state, or that they produced two quite different theories without noticing it.

The most detailed treatment of the state is to be found in Engels' *The Origin of the Family, Private Property and the State,* written a year after Marx's death. Engels wrote 'As the state arose from the need to keep class antagonisms in check, but also arose in the thick of the fight between classes, it is *normally* [italics added] the state of the most powerful, economically ruling class which by its means becomes also the politically ruling class, and so acquires new means of holding down and exploiting the oppressed class . . . . Exceptional periods, however, occur when the warring classes are so nearly equal in forces that the state power, as apparent mediator, acquires for the moment a certain independence in relation to both.' This, argued Engels, was the position during the Second French Empire 'which played off the proletariat against the bourgeoisie and the bourgeoisie against the proletariat'.[6] Marx's own account of the Second French Empire at the time of its downfall was couched in very similar terms.

'The Empire, with the *coup d'etat* for its certificate of birth, universal suffrage for its sanction and the sword for its sceptre, professed to rest upon the peasantry, the large mass of producers not directly involved in the struggle of capital and labour. It professed to save the working class by breaking down parliamentarianism, and, with it, the undisguised subserviency of government to the propertied classes. It professed to save the propertied classes by upholding their economic supremacy over the working class; and, finally it professed to unite all classes by reviving for all the chimera of national glory. In reality, it was the only form of government possible at a time when the bourgeoisie had already lost, and the working class had not yet acquired, the faculty of ruling the nation. It was acclaimed throughout the world as the saviour of society. Under its sway bourgeois society, freed from political cares, attained a development unexpected even by itself.'[7]

It is apparent that both Marx and Engels had arrived at the conclusion that the econonic interests of the bourgeoisie did not necessary require that it should as a class directly wield political power. In a letter to Marx in 1866 Engels wrote 'It is always becoming clearer to me that the bourgeoisie had not the stuff in it for ruling directly itself';[8] while Marx in his *Critique of the Gotha Programme* of the German Social Democratic Party in 1875 pointed out that 'The different states of the different civilised countries, in spite of their manifold diversity of form' were all 'based on modern bourgeois society, only one more or less capitalistically developed'.[9] Though the bourgeois democratic republic was for Marx and Engels the natural or logical form for the state to assume under the conditions of bourgeois society, they recognised that in many countries this form had not, and might never be, realised.

Marx in *The Eighteenth Brumaire* makes abundantly clear his bitter opposition to and distaste of the Napoleonic state 'with its enormous bureaucratic and military organisation, with its artificial state machinery, with a host of officials numbering half a million, besides an army of another half million, this appalling parasitic growth', which had grown up since the first French Revolution.[10] Under successive

168

governments 'every *common* interest was straightaway severed from society, counterpoised to it as a higher, *general* interest, snatched from the self-activity of society's members and made an object of governmental activity, from the bridge, the schoolhouse and the communal property of a village community to the railways, the national wealth and the national university of France.'[11] The great 'artificial caste' of bureaucrats created for these purposes was dependent for its existence on the maintenance of the regime and imposed a heavy burden of taxation on the populace at large. 'Strong government and heavy taxes are identical', remarked Marx.[12] Bureaucracy was for Marx only 'the low and brutal form' of the 'state centralization that modern society requires'.[13]

For Marx the 'direct antithesis' to the Second Napoleonic Empire was the 1871 Paris Commune, whose constitution would have restored to the social body all the forces hitherto absorbed by the state parasites feeding upon and clogging the free movement of society'.[14] The Commune made 'cheap government' a reality by destroying the two greatest sources of expenditure — the standing army, which it replaced by the armed people, and the state bureaucracy (including the judiciary) for which it substituted elected officials paid workmen's wages.

> 'While the merely repressive organs of the old governmental power were to be amputated, its legitimate functions were to be wrestled from an authority usurping pre-eminence over society itself, and restored to the responsible agents of society. Instead of deciding once in three or six years which member of the ruling class was to mis-represent the people in Parliament, universal suffrage was to serve the people.'[15]

The importance of the Commune for Marx was that it was essentially a working class government, the product of the struggle of the producing against the appropriating class, the political form at last discovered under which to work out the economical emancipation of labour'.[16] It is true that Marx unlike Engles did not categorise the Paris Commune as the dictatorship of the proletariat; but this is almost certainly, as Miliband suggests, because for Marx that form of government would be the out-come of a socialist revolution on a national scale; rather than through any disagreement with the principles the Commune put into operation. Years earlier Marx had written in *Class Struggles in France, 1848-50* of the dictatorship of the proletariat as 'the inevitable transit point to the *abolition of class differences generally,* to the abolition of all the productive relations on which they rest, to the abolition of all the social relations that correspond to these relations of production, to the revolutionizing of all the ideas that result from these social connections'.[17] In his notes for *The Civil War in France* Marx is even more explicit. The Commune, he insisted, 'was a Revolution not against this or that, legitimate, constituional, republican or Imperialist form of State power. It was a revolution against the State itself, at this supernaturalist abortion of society, a resumption by the people for the people of its social life.[18] The Commune had not made the mistake of all previous revolutions in France of perfecting the state machine 'instead of smashing it.'[19]

While it is generally true, as Miliband argues, that Marx chose to emphasise the liberating rather than the repressive aspects of the dictatorship of the proletariat, there is one passage from a short polemic against Bakunin compiled in 1875, (not referred to by Miliband) in which Marx strongly asserts the need for proletarian coercion. In answer to Bakunin's question ' "if the proletariat will be the ruling class . . . whom will it rule?" ', Marx responded — 'it means that as long as other classes, and the capitalist class in particular, still exist, and as long as the proletariat fights against them (for its enemies and the old organization of society did not vanish as a result of its coming to power) it must employ *coercive* [Marx's italics] meansures, that is, government measures; so long it is a class itself, and the economic conditions which give rise to the class struggle and the existence of classes have not yet disappeared and must be forcibly removed or transformed, and the process of their transformation accelerated by the use of force.'[20] This is completely in line with the oft-quoted remarks of Engels to Babel that 'so long as the proletariat still *uses* the state, it does not use it in the interests of freedom but in order to hold down its adversaries, . . .[21] Engels had earlier written a short piece *On Authority* in which he took an even sharper line. In reply to the anti-authoritarians who 'demand that the authoritarian political state be abolished at one stroke, even before the social conditions that gave birth to it have been destroyed', Engels retorted:

'Have these gentlemen ever seen a revolution? A revolution is . . . the act whereby one part of the population imposes its will upon the other part by means of rifles, bayonets and cannon . . . and if the victorious party does not want to have fought in vain, it must maintain this rule by means of the terror which its arms inspire in the reactionaries reactionaries.'[22]

In 1891 Karl Kautsky, the leading theorist of the German Social Democratic Party, drafted a new Party Programme which he submitted to Engels for comment. In his reply Engels criticised the absence of any specific reference to the Party's attitude to the German state. While accepting that this was a difficult and dangerous topic for the Party to take a public stand on, for fear of a revival of the laws banning socialist parties, Engels could not accept th 'the present legal position of the Party in Germany is now all of a sudden to be treated as sufficient for carrying out all of the demands of the Party by peaceful means' — especially Germany 'where the government is almost almighty and the *Reichstag* and all other representative bodies have no real power, to proclaim such a thing in Germany — and moreover when there is no need to do so — is to remove the fig-leaf from absolutism, and to become oneself a screen for its nakedness'.[23] The Programme as adopted showed no evidence that Engels' views had any impact. The only reference to the political struggle in the Programme was the simple statement that the working class 'cannot bring about the transference of the means of production into the possession of the community, without having obtained political power'.[24] In the same year, however, Kautsky published an exposition of the Programme (titled *The Erfurt Programme*) which Engels found much better than the Programme itself, although he thought it over-long.[25]

Kautsky's *The Erfurt Programme* became widely accepted as the official exposition of the basic principles, not simply of German Social Democracy, but of orthodox Marxism. While Kautsky makes a number of interesting and perceptive points his treatment of the state is sketchy and unsystematic. 'The modern state', writes Kautsky, 'grew with and through the capitalist class, just as, in turn it has become the most powerful support of that class. Each has promoted the interests of the other. The capitalist class cannot forgo the assistance of the state. It needs the powerful hand of government to protect it against foes within and without.'[26] As the friction between the classes grows the capitalist system of exploitation finds it necessary to rely more and more on an ever growing army of officials and police to enforce its laws, as well as an army of soldiers to protect it from its foreign competitors. The result is that the burden of state expenditure ever increases, and in spite of efforts to shift that burden on to other classes, 'the exploiters are obliged to increase the share of profits which they turn over to the state'.[27] In England, the birthplace of industrial capitalism, the capitalist class was initially hostile to the interference of the state in the economic life of the community; and this doctrine of the 'Manchester School' led many to erroneously conclude that socialism and the interference of the state in economic affairs were identical. That doctrine, wrote Kautsky, was now dead — the economical and political needs of the capitalist class have themselves necessitated the extension of the functions of the state. 'While the economic functions and the economic power of the state are thus steadily increased, the whole economic mechanism becomes more and more complicated, more sensitive, and the separate capitalist undertakings become, as we have seen, proportionately more interdependent upon one another. Along with this grows the dependence of the capitalist class upon the greatest

171

of all their establishments — the state or government.' This increased dependence, however, only serves to increase the disorders to which the economic system is subject and gives rise to calls for further state assistance and intervention. 'Accordingly, in modern society the state is called upon more and more to step in and take a hand in the regulation and management of the economic mechanism, and ever-stronger are the means placed at its disposal and employed by it in the fulfilment of this function.'[28] Kautsky is concerned to stress that such state intervention is in no way hostile to the interests or position of the capitalist class. Even where the modern state nationalises certain industries it does so for the purpose of protecting the capitalist system. 'The state will not cease to be a capitalist institution until the proletariat, the working class, has become the ruling class; not until then will it become possible to turn it into a cooperative commonwealth.'[29]

The basic weakness of Kautsky's analysis, from a Marxist point of view, is seen most clearly in the section of *The Erfurt Programme* on 'The Political Struggle' which deals almost exclusively with parliamentary activity. 'Whenever the proletariat engages in parliamentary activity as a self-conscious class, parliamentarianism begins to change its character. It ceases to be a mere tool in the hands of the bourgeoisie [and becomes] the most powerful lever that can be utilized to raise the proletariat out of its economic, social and moral degradation.'[30] While Kautsky is not explicit he appears to envisage a German Social Democratic Party victorious at the polls using the *existing* machinery of state to establish a new socialist system.[31] This interpretation is confirmed in Kautsky's *The Social Revolution*, based on lectures given in 1902, where he writes 'the governmental power was never so strong as now, nor the military, bureaucratic and economic forces so powerfully developed. It follows from this that the proletariat, when it shall have conquered the governmental powers, will have thereby obtained the power to at once bring about the most extensive social changes'.[32] The issue of parliamentarianism, on the other hand, receives both more detailed and more sceptical treatment in *The Social Revolution* than in *The Erfurt Programme*. In the former Kautsky observes that 'at the same time that the influence of social democracy grows in Parliament the influence of Parliament decreases' — a consequence of Parliament's increasing lack of united majority parties pursuing firm social goals. 'The Parliament which was formerly the means of pressing the government forward upon the road to progress becomes ever more and more the means to nullify the little progress that conditions compel the government to make.'[33] The conclusion which Kautsky draws from this development is that 'Parliamentarianism, far from making a revolution useless and superfluous, is itself in need of a revolution in order to vivify it'.[34]

The decisive battle between the proletariat and the ruling class will not, it appears, be fought out on the floors of the parliamentary chamber or in the voting booths. On the contrary, Kautsky talks of 'the approaching revolution', which will be quite unlike its predecessors, 'much less of a sudden uprising against the authorities than a long-drawn out *civil war,* if one does not necessarily join to these last words the idea of actual slaughter and battle'.[35] He suggests that neither armed uprising nor financial collapse are likely to be the prelude to revolution under modern conditions. Instead he stresses the importance of the strike as a political weapon, though he ridicules the idea of *the* great strike which will bring capitalism to its knees. The strike must supplement and strengthen, not displace, other means of political struggle, including the parliamentary struggle.[36] Moreover it is likely that in the course of the struggle new methods and organs of battle will develop 'of which we do not even dream today'.[37] Finally Kautsky speaks of the possibility that war may play a part in bringing about the overthrow of the ruling class in those countries where 'revolution is necessary to the further progress of society but where the revolutionary classes are still too weak to overthrow the ruling powers'.[38] But, he prophetically declares,

'It (i.e. war) brings such terrible destruction and creates such gigantic demands upon the state that any revolution springing from it is heavily loaded with tasks that are not essential to it but which momentarily absorb all its means and energy. Consequently a revolution which rises from war is a sign of the weakness of the revolutionary class, and often the cause of further weakness, just because of the sacrifice that it brings with it, as well as by the moral and intellectual degradation to which war gives rise. It also increases enormously the tasks of the revolutionary regime and simultaneously weakens its powers. Accordingly a revolution springing from a war is easier wrecked or sooner loses its motive force.'[39]

In Part II of *The Social Revolution* Kautsky examines the problems that will arise out of the conquest of power by the proletariat. The first objective would be to 'realise that democratic programme for which the bourgeoisie once stood'[40]; but beyond looms the problem of 'bringing the capitalist means of production into social possession', mainly the possession of the State and the municipalities. Kautsky, unlike Marx and Engels,[41] does not expect any strong resistance in Germany to this fundamental change; indeed he suggests that 'Capitalists would themselves demand that their means of production be purchased'.[42] The only important question which would arise is whether capitalist property should be confiscated or compensated for. Kautsky's own preference is for confiscation through heavy taxation over a decade. He optimistically sees the expropriation of the means of production as 'relatively the simplest incident among the great transformation of the social revolution'.[43] The major problems are to ensure the continuance and increase of production, in the absence of the discipline and sanctions imposed by capitalism. The answer must be found, not in regimentation by a 'prison-like State', but through 'the introduction of union discipline into the processes of production' — 'a democratic discipline, a free will submission to a self-chosen leadership, and to the decisions of the majority of comrades. If this democratic discipline operates in the factory, it presupposes a democratic organisation of labour, and that a democratic factory would take the place of the present aristocratic one.'[44]

Kautsky was to add nothing of significance to his writings on the State,[45] until he was faced with the advent of the Bolsheviks to power. From the obscurity of backward Russia, the leader of the minority faction of the Russian Social Democratic Party had risen to claim Marx's mantle and to label Kautsky as a revisionist and renegade. Until the collapse of the Second International in 1914 Lenin had no disputes with Kautsky, whose work he admired. In this period Lenin's concern was with the special problems facing the Russian people who, in his view, had still to win for themselves the political liberty which other European people had achieved long ago. In the midst of the 1905 revolution Lenin produced a leaflet which admirably sums up his assessment of the issues of state power in terms of the class interests of the major groups concerned.[46] (reproduced in Appendix).

As Lenin made clear in *Two Tactics of Social Democracy in the Democratic Revolution* (1905) the democratic republic he wanted to secure differed fundamentally, not only from Russian liberal conceptions of constitutional monarchy, but from existing Western forms of bourgeois democratic republic of the French or United States type. Lenin's democratic republic was 'the revolutionary-democratic dictatorship of the proletariat and the peasantry'[47] which involved 'paralysing the bourgeoisie's instability' and 'smashing and crushing the autocracy'.[48] Yet Lenin also envisaged such a democratic republic somehow laying 'the foundations for a really extensive development of capitalism'[49], under expected conditions of ever intensifying class struggle leading to the socialist revolution. In March 1906 Lenin made a detailed study of revolutionary-democratic dictatorship in *The Victory of the Cadets and the Task of the Workers Party*.[50] He points to the creation of 'new organs of revolutionary authority' (Soviets of Workers', Soldiers', Railwaymen's and Peasants' Deputies etc.) as 'the rudiments of the dictatorship of the revolutionary elements of the people', 'a dictatorship in embryo' which 'recognised *no* other authority, *no* law and *no* standards, no matter by whom established'. Their power was 'based on the mass of the people' and was used by them as 'an instrument of the rule of the people, of the workers and peasants, over the minority, over a handful of police bullies, over a handful of privileged nobles and government officials'. 'As the dictatorship of the overwhelming majority, the new authority maintained itself and could maintain itself solely because it enjoyed the confidence of the vast masses, solely because it, in the freest widest and most resolute manner, enlisted all the masses in the task of government. It concealed nothing, it had no secrets, no regulations, no formalities.'[51] Lenin goes on to make clear that the dictatorship is to be exercised not by the whole people, but only by 'the *revolutionary* people' who, however, 'do not shun the whole people', but, 'explain to all the people the motives of their actions in all their details, and who willingly enlist the *whole* people not only in "administering" the state, but in governing it too'.[52]

Lenin was able to apply this formulation without much difficulty to the rapidly shifting and disorganised conditions he found on his return to Russia after the February 1917 Revolution. In *The Tasks of the Proletariat in Our Revolution* he summed up the political situation as one in which 'the dictatorship of the bourgeoisie', in the form of the Provisional Government, was confronted by 'the dictatorship of the proletariat and the peasantry', in the form of the Soviets of Workers' and Soldiers' Deputies – one was bound to perish.[53] Throughout his writings Lenin talks of the state only in the primary sense in which Marx used the term, as an instrument of class rule.[54] The state in the proper sense of the term', he writes in *The Task of the Proletariat in Our Revolution* 'is domination over the people by contingents of armed men divorced from the people. Our *emergent* new state is also a state, for we too need contingents of armed men, we too need the strictest order, and must *ruthlessly* crush by force all attempts at . . . counter-revolution. But our *emergent,* new state is *no longer* a state in the proper sense of the term, for in some parts of Russia these contingents of armed men are the *masses themselves,* the entire people, and not certain privileged persons placed over the people, and divorced from the people.'[55] In August-September 1917, while Lenin was in hiding, he wrote his major work on the state – *State and Revolution: The Marxist Theory of the State and the Task of the Proletariat in the Revolution.* Lenin's main concern was to show that the position he had consistently taken up with regard to the state and the dictatorship of the proletariat was strictly in line with the views put forward by Marx and Engels. The main part of the book is therefore devoted to extensive quotation from, and detailed analysis of, the limited number of Marx and Engels' writings bearing on this question. In my view Lenin cannot be accused of distorting the position taken up by Marx and Engels; rather he draws their scattered writings together, tightens them up and produces an integrated, sharper and less flexible doctrine. Lenin's appraisal is well summed up in the following passage. 'The essence of Marx's doctrine of the state is assimilated only by those who understand that the dictatorship of a *single* class is necessary not only for class society in general, not only for the *proletariat* which has overthrown the bourgeoisie, but for the entire *historical period* which separates capitalism from "classless society" from Communism.'[56] Lenin argues that until the 'higher' state of communism is reached,[57] it is necessary to have 'the *strictest* control by society *and by the state* over the measure of labour and the measure of consumption' but insists that 'this control must *start* with the expropriation of the capitalists, with the establishment of workers' control over the capitalists, and must be exercised not by a state of bureaucrats, but by a state of *armed workers'.*[58]

All this does not mean that Lenin had rejected Engels' celebrated dictum of 'the withering away of the state'. Lenin, correctly in my opinion, argues that 'the withering away' refers to 'the remnants of the *proletarian* state *after* the socialist revolution', and after the bourgeois state has been abolished by the proletariat.[59] During the transition period to the higher stage of communism the need for the state as 'a *special machine* of suppression will begin to disappear'; for the suppression of the minority of exploiters by the majority of the wage slaves of yesterday is a comparatively easy task — *'the people* can suppress the exploiters even with a very simple "machine", almost without a "machine", without a special apparatus, by the simple *organisation* of the *armed people* (such as the Soviets of Workers' and Soldiers' Deputies . . .)'[60] What, indeed, is striking about Lenin's views is not their authoritarian nature, but his optimistic belief in the capacity of the common man to run the state. Given universal literacy and numeracy, and the training and discipline provided by industrial society (conditions which did not exist in Russia), Lenin believed 'all members of society, or at least the vast majority' will quickly learn to administer the state themselves.[61] State officials will still be required under socialism but they will cease to be bureaucrats 'i.e. privileged persons divorced from the people and standing *above* the people'; since they will be elected, subject to recall, paid workmen's wages and made responsible to working bodies combining both executive and legislative functions (as in the Paris Commune).[62]

A few weeks later Lenin returned to and expanded on this theme in *Can the Bolsheviks Retain State Power?* (completed on 1 October 1917). As Marx had done in writing of the Commune, Lenin distinguished between 'the chiefly "oppressive" apparatus — the standing army, the police and the bureaucracy' and the 'apparatus which performs an enormous amount of accounting and registration work', and which has close connections with the banks and industrial syndicates. This latter apparatus he insisted must not be smashed. 'It must be wrested from the control of the capitalists; the capitalists and the wires they pull must be *cut off, lopped off, chopped away* from this apparatus; it must be *subordinated* to the proletarian Soviets; it must be expanded, made more comprehensive and nation-wide.'[63] The achievements of large scale capitalism, especially the big banks, and the innovations of the state in wartime, such as the grain monopoly, bread rationing and conscription of labour, must be taken over and utilised for the building of socialism.[64] Capitalists and the higher officials could be expected to offer resistance to the new regime and it would be necessary, not only to break their resistance, but to compel them to work within the framework of the new state on the principle that 'he who does not work, neither shall he eat'.[65] Specialists would also be employed, initially at higher than average salaries, but would, like the capitalists and officials, be subject to *'workers' control'*. The core of the new state apparatus would be the Bolshevik Party with its 240,000 members, backed up by the million adults who voted for the Party. This core could, however, be enlarged 'tenfold at once', if class conscious workers and soldiers drew the poor, the working people into the daily work of state administration; training them to allocate housing, food, clothing and land in the interests of the many, not the few. 'For the administration of the state in *this* spirit we can *at once set in motion a state* apparatus consisting of ten if not twenty million people.' 'The chief thing now is to abandon the prejudiced bourgeois-intellectualist view that only special officials . . . can administer the state . . . The chief thing is to imbue the oppressed and the working people with confidence in their own strength, to prove to them in practice that they can and must themselves ensure the *proper,* most strictly regulated and organised distribution of bread, all kinds of food, milk, clothing, etc. in *the interests of the poor.* Unless this is done, Russia *cannot* be saved from ruin.'[66]

Experience, however, soon revealed the enormous difficulties in giving effect to these conceptions. In *The Immediate Tasks of the Soviet Government* published in April 1918 Lenin was forced to admit that 'we have not yet introduced accounting and control in those enterprises and in those branches and fields of economy which we have taken away from the bourgeoisie; and without this there can be no thought of achieving the second and equally essential condition for introducing socialism, namely raising the productivity of labour on a national scale.'[67] He now argued, contrary to the position he had taken up in October 1917, that the rapid realisation of this objective had been 'impossible owing to the war and the backwardness of Russia', and that it would take some time yet to achieve.[68] In place of the earlier prospect of 'a million new fighters' for socialism for every ten thousand overt and concealed enemies of working-class rule, Lenin now spoke of the need for 'time', for 'an *iron-hand*' to put down 'the increasing crime, hooliganism, corruption, profiteering and outrages of every kind', and for 'unquestioning submission to a single will' (that of the executive director) in the management of the railways and large-scale machine industry, in place of workers' control.[69] Lenin concluded, 'The more resolutely we now have to stand for a ruthlessly firm government, for the dictatorship of individual persons, *for definite processes of work*, for definite aspects of *purely executive* functions, the more varied must be the forms and methods of control from below in order to counter every shadow of possibility of distorting the Soviet power, in order repeatedly and tirelessly to weed out bureaucracy.'[70] A year later at the Eighth Congress of the Russian Communist Party (March 1919), Lenin was forced to admit that, because of the low cultural level of the mass of the population, the Soviets, instead of being 'organs of government *by the working people*, are in fact organs of government *for the working people* by the advanced section of the proletariat, but not by the working people as a whole' − 'the section of workers who are governing is inordinately, incredibly small'.[71] By 'the advanced section of the proletariat' Lenin meant the Bolshevik Party, as was made clear in *'Left-Wing' Communism: An Infantile Disorder* (June 1920),[72] and his *Thesis on the Fundamental Task of the Second Congress of the Communist International* adopted in July 1920.[73]

In spite of the heady optimism of the Second Communist International Congress (in session as the Red Army advanced to the outskirts of Warsaw) the revolution in the West failed to materialise and Soviet Russia was left, after seven years of World War and civil war, in a calamitous condition. At the Second All-Russia Congress of Miners in January 1921 Lenin acknowledged that production was 'at a standstill' and that only 'a few thousand' workers throughout Russia were engaged in government. It would take 'a number of years' before the trade unions could turn out millions of working-class administrators. 'To govern', he insisted 'you need an army of steeled revolutionary communists. We have it and it is called the Party.'[74] At the Tenth Congress of the Russian Communist Party, held at the time of the Kronstadt Revolt in March 1921, Lenin reiterated that 'the dictatorship of the proletariat would not work without the Communist Party' and spoke of that dictatorship lasting for as long as classes hostile to the proletariat still existed in Russia, which would be 'many many years' in view of the predominantly peasant population of Russia.[75] In the meantime the Party continued to face 'the malaise' of bureaucracy within the state system, which it would take 'decades to overcome'.[76]

The success of the Bolsheviks in seizing power inevitably brought Kautsky, as the leading theoretician of Social Democracy, into conflict with Lenin. Towards the end of 1918 Kautsky published *The Dictatorship of the Proletariat* to which Lenin immediately responded with *The Proletarian Revolution and the Renegade Kautsky*. Kautsky's basic argument was that conditions had not been ripe in Russia for a proletarian revolution, and that this was the cause of the difficulties which the new regime faced and the mistakes it had made. 'State organization of production by a bureaucracy, or the dictatorship of a single section of the people, does not mean Socialism. Socialism presupposes that broad masses of the people have been accustomed to organization, that numerous economic and political organisations exist, and can develop in perfect freedom. The socialist organisation of labour is not an affair of barracks.'[77] The Bolsheviks had ignored Marx's teaching and attempted to build a socialist state before the necessary material and intellectual resources had been established by capitalism. They had also twisted Marx's teaching on the dictatorship of the proletariat which 'was for him a condition which necessarily arose only in a real democracy, because of the overwhelming numbers of the proletariat.' Kautsky further argued that it was necessary to distinguish between dictatorship as a *condition* of proletarian government (as with Marx), and dictatorship as a *form* of government, involving disarming the opposition by removing from them rights of franchise, press and combination. Dictatorship as a *form* of government necessarily means the dictatorship 'of a single person, or of an organisation, not of the proletariat, but of a proletarian party', since 'a class can only rule, not govern'.[78] 'Parties', wrote Kautsky, 'are not synonymous with classes, though they may represent a class interest, but a class can split between various parties and a party may consist of members of different classes.'[79] Dictatorship as a form of government 'compels the party which is in possession of power to maintain it by all means, whether fair or foul, because its fall means its complete ruin'.[80] This is what the Bolsheviks did when they dissolved the Constituent Assembly, turned the Soviets into organs of government and got rid of the opposition parties.[81] 'Starting with the idea of establishing the dictatorship of the proletariat the Bolshevist regime was bound to become the dictatorship of a party within the proletariat.'[82]

Lenin in his reply insisted, that Kautsky 'fails to see the *class* nature of the state apparatus, of the machinery of state'. 'The working people are *barred* from participation in bourgeois parliaments (they *never decide* important questions under bourgeois democracy, which are decided by the stock exchange and banks) by thousands of obstacles, and the workers know and feel, see and realise perfectly well that the bourgeois parliaments are institutions *alien* to them, *instruments for the oppression* of the workers by the bourgeoisie, institutions of a hostile class, of the exploiting minority.'[83] In Russia, on the other hand, '*far more accessible* representation has been given to the workers and peasants; *their* Soviets have replaced the bureaucrats, or *their* Soviets have been put in control of the bureaucrats, and *their* Soviets have been authorised to elect the judges. This fact alone is enough for all the oppressed classes to recognise that Soviet power, i.e. the present form of the dictatorship of the proletariat, is a million times more democratic than the most democratic bourgeois republic.'[84]

Kautsky returned to the attack in *Terrorism and Communism* written in the middle of 1919. Russia, he declared, had been ripe for the abolition of absolutism but not for the abolition of capitalism. In consequence what was developing in Russia under the Bolsheviks was state capitalism, through the merger of both state and capitalist bureaucracy into one arbitrary system of rule — 'the most oppressive of all forms of despotism that Russia has ever had'.[85] Although the Bolsheviks had started off with the intention of destroying the military and bureaucratic apparatus of the state they were compelled by the conditions of civil war and chaos which inevitably ensued from their seizure of power 'to erect anew the self-same apparatus', in order to maintain themselves in power. The Soldiers' and Workers' Councils, which were to be the repositories of power, were quickly turned into 'mere shadows', their powers reduced, new elections postponed and every possible form of opposition excluded.[86] To maintain 'their dictatorship in the name of "the dictatorship of the proletariat" ', the Bolsheviks had resorted to terror; in the form of a network of revolutionary tribunals and extraordinary commissions with complete arbitrary power to condemn anyone denounced as a counter-revolutionary or a speculator.[87] The Bolsheviks by seeking to force socialism on the majority were being forced themselves to abandon the very principles for which they took power. They had found it necessary 'to make all sorts of possible concessions to bureaucracy, to militarism, and to capitalism'. Any concession to democracy, on the other hand, appeared to the Bolsheviks as 'sheer suicide'; and indeed under the conditions they had themselves created it would inevitably mean the defeat not only of the Bolsheviks but of the proletariat.[88]

It was Trotsky who took it upon himself to reply to Kautsky's espousal of the democratic road to socialism. Trotsky forcefully argued that 'the bourgeois democratic state not only creates more favourable conditions for the political education of the workers, as compared with absolutism, but also sets a limit to that development in the shape of bourgeois legality, which skilfully accumulates and builds on the upper strata of the proletariat, opportunist habits and law-abiding prejudices.'[89] The 'hypnotic suggestion of peaceful legality' resulted in the working classes of the so-called democratic states 'under the united pressure of imperialist governments and Socialist patriotic parties' being dragged into the Imperialist War of 1914-18.[90] The lesson of that bloody catastrophe was that 'violent revolution has become a necessity

180

precisely because the imminent requirements of history are helpless to find a road through the apparatus of parliamentary democracy'.[91]

Trotsky is less successful in dealing with Kautsky's criticisms of the form and nature of Bolshevik rule, but his explanations are in some ways more revealing than those put forward by Lenin. Trotsky's justification for 'the exclusive role of the Communist Party' in controlling the country, is that the dictatorship of the proletariat could not be secured in any other way.

> 'The question is of the dictatorship of a class. In the composition of that class there enter various elements, heterogeneous moods, different levels of development. Yet the dictatorship presupposes unity of will, unity of direction, unity of action. By what other path can it be obtained? The revolutionary supremacy of the proletariat presupposes within the proletariat itself the political supremacy of a party with a clear programme of action and a faultless internal discipline.'[92]

This ' "substitution" of the power of the party for the power of the working class' is 'in reality no substitution at all' since 'the Communists express the fundamental interests of the working class'.[93] In reply to the charge 'how do you know what your party expresses these historical interests, especially since you deny other parties the right to compete with you and test your line of action?' Trotsky baldly retorts that survival is the test.

> 'Noske [in Germany] crushes the Communists, but they grow. We have suppressed the Mensheviks and the SRs [Social Revolutionaries] — and they have disappeared. This criterion is sufficient for us ... our problem is not at every given moment statistically to measure the grouping of tendencies; but to render victory for our tendency secure. For that tendency is the tendency of the revolutionary dictatorship; and in the course of the latter, in its internal friction, we must find a sufficient criterion for self-examination.'[94]

Trotsky is also very revealing when he discusses his own project for the militarisation of labour. 'Why do we speak of militarisation?' he asks, 'Of course this is only an analogy but an analogy very rich in content. No social organisation except the army has ever considered itself justified in subordinating citizens to itself in such a measure, and to control them by its will on all sides to such a degree, as the State of the proletarian dictatorship considers itself justified in doing and does.'[95] The transition to socialism requires 'the centralised distribution of labour-power in harmony with the general State plan. The Labour State considers itself empowered to send every worker to the place where his work is necessary.'[96] Although 'under socialism there will not exist the apparatus of compulsion itself, namely the State: for it will have melted away entirely into a producing and consuming commune' . . . 'the road to Socialism lies through a period of the highest possible intensification of the principle of the State'.[97] And if one should ask, as the Menshevik Abramovitch does, ' "Wherein, then, does your Socialism differ from Egyptian slavery?" '; the answer is that unlike the Pharaohs 'Our compulsion is applied by a workers' and peasants' government, in the name of the interests of the labouring masses.'[98]

In 1924 Kautsky wrote *The Labour Revolution* in which he developed a detailed criticism of Lenin's conception of the state, on the basis that Lenin had misinterpreted Marx's writings. Marx, in the passages which Lenin had quoted from *The Eighteenth Brumaire* and *The Civil War in France* in *State and Revolution*, 'did not', wrote Kautsky, 'in any way mean that the workers could under no circumstances establish their rule without destroying the transmitted State machinery. Marx rejected only a special form of this machine, the bureaucratic-militarist form, which had reached an exceptionally high stage of development in the second French Empire.' Marx had expressly declared that the destruction of the bureaucratic-militarist machinery was ' "the preliminary condition of every real people's revolution on the Continent" ', thus excluding England.[99] In the light of the discussion at the beginning of this paper this seems a doubtful assertion. Marx certainly spoke of the possibility of the working class achieving power by peaceful means through the established constitutional machinery of state (in 1872 he mentioned America, England and Holland); but not of being able to use that machinery to build socialism. While his remarks in *The Eighteenth Brumaire* certainly refer specifically only to France; it was to the France of the parliamentary republic as much to that of Louis Bonaparte – 'all the revolutions perfected this machine instead of smashing it'.[100] Further, notes on the Paris Commune make abundantly clear Marx's enthusiastic approval of the Commune's rejection of 'the State itself' and not just 'this or that, legitimate, constitutional, republican or Imperialist form of State power' (see p.170 above). Kautsky is also on shaky ground in arguing that, because Engels in 1871 had spoken of the Paris Commune as the dictatorship of the proletariat, and in 1891 had written that the working class could only achieve power under 'a form of the democratic republic . . . the specific form for the dictatorship of the proletariat'; it followed that there was now no need to destroy the state machine, since almost everywhere in Europe the workers 'find the democratic Republic already in existence'.[101] Kautsky appears to believe that the post-war states of

Western Europe were democratic Republics, in the sense in which the Paris Commune was a democratic Republic. He is on stronger ground in arguing that if, as Lenin insisted on the basis of the experience of the Commune, the essential distinction between bourgeois democracy and proletarian democracy was the extirpation of bureaucracy in the latter, 'then no State is further removed from "proletarian democracy" than the State that was governed by Lenin.'[102] Kautsky deals at some length with the other conditions of proletarian democracy in the Paris Commune to which Marx drew attention and to which Lenin attached such importance — payment of workers' wages to officials, recall of deputies, union of executive and legislative power. The first, Kautsky argues, is very difficult to achieve in the transition period, as Lenin himself found when he came to realise that state administration was not something which any literate person could carry out. The recall of deputies was, in Kautsky's view, no longer of major importance now that Socialist deputies were subject to the discipline of the Party group; while the merging of executive and legislative power was undesirable, since it would strengthen an existing tendency in large states for the executive to assimilate both legislative and judicial power at the expense of the popular will and lead to the suppression of all opposition to the governing party. Finally, Kautsky argues, the merging of executive and legislative power, which Marx briefly described but did not elucidate, is 'the only one to which the Bolsheviks now cling' — 'because it facilitates their dictatorship'.[103]

Kautsky summed up his case in the following words which may perhaps serve as a conclusion to this essay, in the sense that they bring out the fundamental points at issue in the Marxist critique of the State and provide a basis for further discussion and analysis.

'The dictatorship of the proletariat soon became untenable. It had led to the most rapid economic collapse of Russia. But the anarchy of this kind of dictatorship formed the soil out of which grew another kind of dictatorship, that of the Communist Party, which is in reality nothing less than the dictatorship of its leaders. The Communist Party was able to survive as the only firm organization in the general chaos, thanks to its unparalleled opportunism, which allowed it to maintain its power by throwing overboard the most important principles for the realization of which it had captured power.
'From the loose state of anarchy in town and country Russia passed immediately into the tightest grip of a privileged bureaucracy, police, and standing army, invested with absolute power, whose operations culminated in the bloodiest terrorism.
'According to Marx's conception, which we fully accept, and which

Lenin also championed in 1917, the proletariat cannot liberate itself without abolishing the machinery of domination of the bureaucracy, the political police, and of the standing army. If dictatorship cannot be maintained without this machinery, it proves what an unsuitable instrument it is for the political rule and the economic emancipation of the proletariat.'[104]

NOTES

1. Ralph Miliband 'Marx and the State' in *The Socialist Register 1965* The Merlin Press 1965 pp. 278-96.
2. *Karl Marx Selected Works* (2 vols.) prepared by the Marx-Engels-Lenin Institute Moscow under the editorship of V. Adoratsky Lawrence & Wishart 1942 vol. I, p.207, Hereafter noted as *SW*.
3. Ralph Miliband, *op. cit.,* p. 283.
4. John Plamenatz, *German Marxism and Russian Communism* Longmans 1954 Ch. 7, s. III 'The Marxian Theory of the State'.
5. Shlomo Avineri, *The Social and Political Thought of Karl Marx* Cambridge University Press 1968 pp. 202-4.
6. Frederich Engels, *The Origin of the Family, Private Property and the State,* translated by Alick West and Dona Torr Lawrence & Wishart 1942, p.196.
7. Karl Marx, *The Civil War in France* May 1871 in *SW* p. 497. The assessment here is at variance in important respects with that given in *The Eighteenth Brumaire of Louis Bonaparte,* written in 1852. There Marx writes of Louis Bonaparte as representing the interests of 'the most numerous class of French society . . . the *small peasants',* who since they lack unity and political organisation must have a representative who appears 'as their master, as an authority over them, as an unlimited governmental power that protects them against other classes . . . ' 'The political influence of the small peasants, therefore, finds its final expression in the executive power subordinating society to itself.' *SW* vol. 2, pp. 414-5.
8. *Karl Marx and Friedrich Engels Correspondence 1846-1895: A Selection with Commentary and Notes,* edited by V. Adoratsky, Martin Lawrence 1934, pp. 205-6, hereafter noted as *Selected Correspondence.*
9. *Critique of the Gotha Programme,* 1875, *SW* vol. II, p. 577.
10. Marx and Engels, writings on this point are not always consistent. See my *Modern Political Theory* Nelson 1970, pp. 254-5.
11. *The Eighteenth Brumaire, SW* vol. II, pp. 412-3.
12. *ibid., SW* vol. II, pp. 419-20.
13. *ibid., SW* vol. II, p. 422.
14. *The Civil War in France,* 1871, *SW* vol. II, pp. 501-2.
15. *ibid., SW* vol. II, pp. 500-1.
16. *ibid., SW* vol. II, pp. 502-3.
17. *The Class Struggles in France 1848-1850, SW* vol. II, p. 289.
18. Quoted by Miliband *op. cit.,* p.290 from *Marx-Engels Archives* Moscow, 1934, vol. III (VIII), p. 324.
19. *The Eighteenth Brumaire of Louis Bonaparte, SW* vol. II, p. 413.
20. 'From the Conspectus of Bakunin's Book *State and Anarchy'* 1874-5 in *Marx, Engels, Lenin: Anarchism and Anarcho-Syndicalism* Progress Publishers,

Moscow 1972, p. 147. As this article was not published until 1926 it was not available to Lenin when he wrote *State and Revolution* in 1917. It would certainly have provided reinforcement for his thesis (see below).

21. *Selected Correspondence,* Engels to Bebel 18-28 March 1875, p. 337.

22. *On Authority* published December 1873 in *Marx, Engels, Lenin: Anarchism and Anarcho-Syndicalism,* pp. 103-4. See also Engels' letter to Van Patten, 18 April 1875; 'it was always our (i.e. Marx and Engels) view . . . that . . the working class must first take possession of the organised political power of the state and by its aid crush the resistance of the capitalist class and organise society anew' – 'after its victory the sole organisation which the proletariat finds already in existence is precisely the state. This state may require very considerable alterations before it can fulfil its new functions. But to destroy it at such a moment would be to destroy the only organism by means of which the victorious proletariat can asset its newly-conquered power, hold down its capitalist adversaries and carry out that economic revolution of society without which the whole victory must end in a new defeat . . . ' *Selected Correspondence,* pp. 416-7.

23. Published in *Neue Zeit* in 1901 and quoted by Lenin in *State and Revolution,* Ch. IV, s. 4 Criticism of the Draft of the Erfurt Program', *The Essentials of Lenin in Two Volumes,* vol. II, pp. 187-8 Lawrence & Wishart 1947. Lenin Collected Works .

24. The Erfurt Programme in Bertrand Russell *German Social Democracy* Longmans Green 1896, p. 139.

25. Letter from Engels to Kautsky 28 Sept. 1891 in *Friedrich Engels' Briefwechsel Mit Karl Kautsky* edited by Benedikt Kautsky Danubia-Verlag, Universitatsbuchandlung Wilhelm Braumüller & Sohn, Wien, 1955.

26. Karl Kautsky *The Class Struggle (Erfurt Program),* translated and abridged by William E. Bohn from the 8th German edition 1907. Charles H. Kerr, Chicago 1910, pp. 55-6.

27. *ibid.,* p. 58.

28. *ibid.,* pp. 108-9.

29. *ibid.,* p. 110.

30. *ibid.,* p. 188.

31. *ibid.,* p. 191.

32. Karl Kautsky *The Social Revolution,* translated by A.M. and May Wood Simons, Charles H. Kerr, Chicago 1916, p. 36. In *The Road to Power* translated by A.M. Simons, Samuel A. Bloch, Chicago 1909, Kautsky writes of the need for the proletariat not simply to protect itself from attack, but to conquer new positions in the national life 'which will enable it to utilize the governmental institutions in the service of its class interests'. (p. 97).

33. *ibid.,* pp. 78-9. Kautsky also writes 'Even if the governments are but agents of the ruling classes, still they have more insight into the sum of political and social relations, and, however willing a servant the official bureaucracy is to the government, it nevertheless develops its own life and its own tendencies that react upon the government. Moreover the bureaucracy is recruited from the intellectuals, in which, as we have already seen, an understanding of the significance of the proletariat is advancing even though timidly.' (p. 78).

34. *ibid.,* p. 80.

35. *ibid.,* p. 88. Rosa Luxemburg in *The Mass Strike, the Political Party and the Trade Unions,* 1906, translated by Patrick Lavin, Detroit 1925 writes that the Russian Revolution of 1905 had shown that the mass strike, as '*the method of motion of the proletarian mass*', was not one isolated action, but 'the

indication, the rallying idea, of a whole period of the class struggle lasting for years, perhaps for decades'. *Rosa Luxemburg: Selected Political Writings,* edited by Robert Looker, Jonathan Cape 1972, p. 122.

36. *The Social Revolution,* p. 95. 'We are now entering upon a time where opposed to the overwhelming power of organised capital an isolated non-political strike will be just as hopeless as is the isolated parliamentary action of the labour parties opposed to the pressure of the capitalistically dominated governmental powers.' (p. 91). A similar point is made more forcibly by Rosa Luxemburg in *Social Democracy and Parliamentarianism,* 1904: The danger to universal suffrage will be lessened to the degree that we can make the ruling classes clearly aware that the real power of Social Democracy by no means rests on the influence of the deputies in the *Reichstag,* but that it lies outside, in the people themselves, "in the streets", and that if the need arise Social Democracy is able and willing to mobilise the people directly for the protection of their political rights.' *Rosa Luxemburg: Selected Political Writings,* p. 114.

37. *The Social Revolution,* p. 92.

38. *ibid.,* p. 93.

39. *ibid.,* pp. 97-8.

40. *ibid.,* p. 107.

41. In his preface to the *English Edition of Capital* vol. I, 1887, Moscow 1965, Engels wrote 'At least in Europe, England is the only country where the inevitable social revolution might be effected entirely by peaceful and legal means. He (Marx) certainly never forgot to add that he hardly expected the English ruling classes to submit, without "pro-slavery rebellion" to this peaceful and legal revolution.' In *K. Marx, F. Engels, V.I. Lenin: On Scientific Communism* Progress Publishers, Moscow, 1967, p. 200.

42. *The Social Revolution,* p. 113.

43. *ibid.,* p. 123.

44. *ibid.,* p. 126. These conceptions owed much to the ideas and writings of the syndicalists, especially the French syndicalists. Georges Sorel in *The Socialist Future of the Syndicats* (1898) argued that the proletariat must struggle 'to strip the State and the municipality, one by one, of all their attributes, thereby to enrich the proletarian organisms in process of formation, namely the syndicats': while Emile Pouget in *La Confederation génerale du Travail* 1908 declared 'syndicalism does not look to a simple modification of the governmental personnel, but rather to a reduction of the State to zero, by transplanting into the syndicalist organs the few useful functions which keep up the illusion of the value of government and by suppressing the others purely and simply'. Quoted in Emile Vandervelde *Socialism Versus the State* Charles H. Kerr, Chicago 1919 p. 29 and p. 40 respectively. Vandervelde, a leading Belgian Social Democrat, was himself influenced by these doctrines and declared 'Now, with a proletariat powerfully organized, we may admit that it would be far less a question of utilising the bourgeois State for other ends than of substituting for it a new State which is, from now on, in process of formation in the great trade-union co-operative and political federations of the working-class' *(ibid.,* p. 130). Vandervelde argues that it is necessary both to transform the present State from an organ of domination of one class over another into the People's Labour State, through the proletarian conquest of political power; and to separate the State, as an organ of authority, from the State, as organ of management – minimising the former and maximising and decentralising the latter. 'Socialists', he concludes, 'act on the State to constrain it to enact reforms. They are demanding, even

now, extensions of its domain. They are striving to conquer it, to turn its coercive force against capitalism. The all-important thing is that *this action for the conquest or for the utilization of the State does not prevent the struggle against the State, in so far as it is an agent of State rule.'* pp. 227-8.

45. Kautsky's *The Road to Power,* 1909, is most disappointing not only in this respect but in its general failure to provide a Marxist appraisal of the road ahead. What the proletariat mainly lacks in advanced capitalist states like Germany and England, he writes, is 'a consciousness of its own strength', which it is the task of the Socialist movement to develop through struggle. (p. 45) The immediate task of the German proletariat was to fight for a democratic state, and of the international proletariat to fight against imperialism, colonialism and militarism (p. 100); but these goals could not be secured without the proletariat 'itself attaining to a dominant position in the State' (p. 102). It is interesting to compare Kautsky's formulation of the conditions for a successful revolutionary struggle with those set out by Lenin in *Left-Wing Communism, An Infantile Disorder.* They are virtually identical except in one crucial aspect, that while Lenin argues in terms of *class,* Kautsky argues in terms of *the mass of the people* (p. 64).

46. Lenin *Collected Works, vol. 8, Jan.-July 1905* Foreign Languages Publishing House, Moscow, 1962 pp. 557-9.

47. Lenin *Collected Works, vol. 9, June-Nov. 1905,* p. 113.

48. *ibid.,* 'Socialism and the Peasantry', p. 308.

49. *ibid.,* p. 309.

50. Lenin quoted fourteen pages of this pamphlet in an article 'Contribution to History of Dictatorship Question', published in *The Communist International* Petrograd in 1920. *Collected Works, vol. 31,* pp. 340-61.

51. Lenin *Collected Works, vol. 10, Nov. 1905-June 1906,* pp. 243-5.

52. *ibid.,* p. 247.

53. Lenin *Collected Works, vol. 24, April-June 1917,* p. 61.

54. It is interesting to note, however, that in his important early work, *To the Rural Poor* 1903 Lenin writes of the Tsarist Autocracy, both as government 'by a handful of the richest and most high-born officials', and of 'an army of officials', 'towering above the voiceless people like a dark forest', officials who have woven a thick web of red tape in which 'men and women struggle like flies'. *Collected Works, vol. 6,* pp. 368-70.

55. Lenin *Collected Works, vol. 24,* p. 85.

56. Lenin *Collected Works, vol. 25, June-Sept. 1917,* p. 413. This is in line with Marx's own formulation in *Critique of the Gotha Programme:* 'Between capitalist and Communist society lies the period of the revolutionary transformation of the one into the other. There corresponds to this also a political transition period in which the state can be nothing but the *revolutionary dictatorship of the proletariat.'* (quoted by Lenin, p. 459).

57. The higher and lower stages of communism are discussed by Marx in his *Critique of the Gotha Programme.* Briefly under the former bourgeois conceptions still remain and workers are paid for what they do; under the latter, with the all-round development of the individual, the principle will be 'from each according to his ability, to each according to his need'. Karl Marx *SW,* pp. 563-6.

58. Lenin *Collected Works, vol. 25,* p. 470.

59. *ibid.,* p. 397. At the Seventh Congress of the Russian Communist Party in March 1918 Lenin opposed Bukharin's proposal that the new Party Programme should contain a description of socialism in its developed form (i.e. communism), 'where the state has ceased to exist'. 'The bricks of which

socialism will be composed have not yet been made', Lenin declared. To speak of 'the withering away of the state' was premature and the distortion of historical perspective. Lenin *Collected Works, vol. 27, February-July 1918,* pp. 147-8. Engels had written 'As soon as there is no longer any class of society to be held in subjection; as soon as, along with class domination and the struggle for individual existence based on the former anarchy of production, the collisions and excesses arising from these have been also abolished, there is nothing more to be repressed which would make a special repressive force, a state, necessary. The first act in which the state really comes forward as the representative of society as a whole – the taking possession of the means of production in the name of society – is at the same time its last independent act as a state. The interference of the state power in social relations becomes superfluous in one sphere after another, and then ceases of itself. The government of persons is replaced by the administration of things, and the direction of the processes of production. The state is not "abolished", *it withers away.'* Herr Eugen Dühring's *Revolution in Science (anti-Duhring),* translated by Emile Burns, Lawrence & Wishart, 1934 p. 107.

60. Lenin *Collected Works, vol. 25,* p. 463.
61. *ibid.,* pp. 473-4.
62. *ibid.,* pp. 486-7.
63. Lenin *Collected Works, vol. 26, Sept. 1917-Feb. 1918,* p. 106.
64. *ibid.,* pp. 106-9. Lenin goes so far as to assert that 'A single State Bank, the biggest of the big, with branches in every rural district, in every factory, will constitute as much as nine-tenths of the socialist apparatus. This will be country-wide *book-keeping,* country-wide *accounting* of the production and distribution of goods, this will be, so to speak, something in the nature of the *skeleton* of socialist society.' (p. 106).
65. *ibid.,* p. 104.
66. *ibid.,* pp. 114-5.
67. Lenin *Collected Works, vol. 27, February-July 1918,* p. 245.
68. *ibid.,* p. 248.
69. *ibid.,* pp. 264-9.
70. *ibid.,* p. 275.
71. Lenin *Collected Works, vol. 29, March-August 1919,* p. 183. Lenin's aim was to make the trade unions the main bodies for involving the masses in government 'by directly working in all government bodies, by organising mass control over their activities etc., and by setting up new bodies for the registration, control and regulation of all production and distribution . . . ' 'The trade unions', he said, 'have to be governmentalised; they have to be fused with state bodies.' 'Report at the Second All-Russia Trade Union Congress, January 1919', Lenin *Collected Works, vol. 28, July 1918-March 1919,* pp. 421 and 424.
72. In *Left-Wing Communism* Lenin writes of 'the class-conscious vanguard of the international working-class movement, i.e. the Communist Parties, groups and trends', having the mission 'to overthrow the bourgeoisie and transform the whole of society'. Lenin *Collected Works, vol. 31, April-December 1920,* p. 93 and pp. 24-5.
73. In the *Theses* Lenin writes that 'only the Communist Party . . . is capable of leading the proletariat in a final, most ruthless and decisive struggle against all the forces of capitalism'. *(ibid.,* pp. 187-8), and called on Communist Parties to make 'preparations for the dictatorship of the proletariat' by forming 'groups or cells of Communists' in all organisations of the working class and the toiling and exploited masses. *(ibid.,* pp. 191-2). Neither Marx

nor Engels had referred to the dictatorship of the proletariat in party terms.

74. Lenin *Collected Works, vol. 32, Dec. 1920-August 1921,* p. 61 and 62.

75. *ibid.,* p. 199 and p. 251. Lenin also stated that 'it will take us at least ten years to organise large-scale industry to produce a reserve and secure control of agriculture'. (p. 250).

76. *ibid.,* p. 56 and pp. 190-1.

77. Karl Kautsky *The Dictatorship of the Proletariat,* translated by H.J. Stenning, I.L.P. Library, The National Labour Press, Manchester N.D. p. 51.

78. *ibid.,* p. 45.

79. *ibid.,* pp. 31-2.

80. *ibid.,* p. 133 and pp. 37-8.

81. *ibid.,* p. 74.

82. *ibid.,* p. 85. Rosa Luxemburg just before her murder in January 1919 made similar criticisms of the Bolsheviks in *The Russian Revolution* 1918, 'In place of the representative bodies created by general, popular elections, Lenin and Trotsky have laid down the Soviets as the only true representation of the labouring masses. But with the repression of political life in the land as a whole, life in the Soviet must become more and more crippled. Without general elections, without unrestricted freedom of press and assembly, without a free struggle of opinion, life dies out in every public institution, becomes a mere semblance of life, in which only the bureaucracy remains as the active element. Public life gradually falls asleep, a few dozen party leaders of inexhaustible energy and boundless experience direct and rule. Among them, in reality only a dozen outstanding heads do the leading and an elite of the working class is invited from time to time to meetings where they are to applaud the speeches of the leaders and to approve proposed resolutions unanimously – at bottom, then, a clique affair – a dictatorship, to be sure, not the dictatorship of the proletariat, however, but only the dictatorship of handful of politicians, that is a dictatorship in the bourgeois sense, in the rule of the Jacobins . . . Yes we can go even further: such conditions must inevitably cause a brutalisation of public life: attempted assassinations, shooting of hostages etc.' (pp. 71-2). She repudiates, however, both Kautsky's rejection of dictatorship in favour of democracy and Lenin and Trotsky's rejection of democracy in favour of dictatorship. 'But socialist democracy is not something which begins only in the promised land after the foundations of socialist economy are created: It does not come as some sort of Christmas present for the worthy people who, in the interim, have merely supported a handful of socialist dictators. Socialist democracy begins simultaneously with the beginnings of the destruction of class rule and of the construction of socialism. It begins at the very moment of the seizure of power by the socialist party. It is the same thing as the dictatorship of the proletariat. Yes dictatorship! But this dictatorship consists in the *manner of applying democracy* not in its *elimination,* in energetic, resolute attacks upon the well-entrenched rights, and economic relationships of bourgeois society, without which a socialist transformation cannot be accomplished. But this dictatorship must be the work of the *class* and not of a little leading minority in the name of the class.' (p. 77). Rosa Luxemburg *The Russian Revolution and Leninism or Marxism,* with an introduction by Bertram D. Wolfe, Ann Arbor, 1961. ›l.

83. Lenin *Collected Works, vol. 28, July 1918-March 1919,* p. 247.

84. *ibid.,* p. 249. In dealing with Kautsky's criticism of the Bolsheviks having turned the Soviets into organs of state power, Lenin makes the extraordinary charge that Martov, the leading Menshevik Marxist theoretician, in opposing

this and urging that the Soviets remain 'the "militant organisations" of one "class" ', was 'embellishing by this innocent wish the fact that under Menshevik leadership the Soviets were *an instrument for the subjection of the workers to the bourgeoisie' (ibid.,* p. 259).

85. Karl Kautsky *Terrorism and Communism: A Contribution to the Natural History of Revolution,* translated by W.H. Kerridge, The National Labour Press, 1920, p. 202. As the result of his visit to the Menshevik-controlled Georgian Republic in 1920 Kautsky came to the conclusion that 'a socialist regime is thus possible under economically backward conditions, if the State is democratic, and the industrial proletariat is superior in intelligence and organisation to the other classes which express their strength by and through democracy. Provided also that the Socialist Government remains always conscious of the limits of its power and does not attempt more than it can achieve with the strength and resources at its disposal, and if, finally it is anxious to develop the productive forces and strength of the proletariat. From being the champion of the special interests of the proletariat it will become the representative of the general social interests. In this capacity it will be enabled to marshal behind it the majority of the nation and maintain their allegiance.' *Georgia: A Social-Democratic Republic: Impressions and Observations,* translated by H.J. Stenning and revised by the author International Bookshop, London 1921, pp. 68-9. Trotsky dealt with the issue of the Georgian-Menshevik Republic, which the Bolsheviks overthrew in 1921, in *Between Red and White: A Study of some Fundamental Questions of Revolution with Particular Reference to Georgia,* Communist Party of Great Britain, 1922. Trotsky dealt at some length with Kautsky's book and justified the Bolshevik intervention – 'when the principle of self-determination became . . . a juridical guarantee for counterrevolution which was preparing a new attack upon us – we did not and could not see any moral obstacle in introducing, at the call of the revolutionary vanguard of Georgia, our Red Army, in order to help the workers and protect the peasants with the least possible delay and sacrifice to overthrow the pitiful democracy which had destroyed itself by its own policy' – 'for while recognising the right of national self-determination, we take care to explain to the masses its limited historical experience, and we never put it above the interests of the proletarian revolution.' (p. 86).
86. *Terrorism and Communism,* p. 205.
87. *ibid.,* p. 197 and p. 209.
88. *ibid.,* p. 221.
89. Leon Trotsky *The Defence of Terrorism (Terrorism and Communism: A Reply to Karl Kautsky,* with a Preface by H.N. Brailsford, The Labour Publishing Company and George Allen & Unwin, 1921 pp. 29-30.
90. *ibid.,* p. 18.
91. *ibid.,* p. 35.
92. *ibid.,* p. 100.
93. *ibid.,* p. 101.
94. *ibid.,* pp. 101-2.
95. *ibid.,* p. 130.
96. *ibid.,* p. 131.
97. *ibid.,* p. 157.
98. *ibid.,* pp. 158-9.
99. Karl Kautsky *The Labour Revolution,* translated by H.J. Stenning George Allen & Unwin 1925 p. 66.
100. Karl Marx *SW* vol. II, p. 413.

101. *The Labour Revolution*, p. 67.
102. *ibid.*, p. 68.
103. *ibid.*, p. 83. Kautsky argues that, since in writing of the Paris Commune, Marx spoke of the need for a ' "national delegation in Paris confronting a central government with few but very important functions" ' this 'implied the same separation of legislative and executive powers [at national level] which Marx desired to see abolished so far as the Commune was concerned.' (*ibid.*, p. 83). This seems a doubtful reading of what is certainly a brief and incomplete discussion in the text.
104. *ibid.*, pp. 85-6.

APPENDIX

THREE CONSTITUTIONS OR THREE SYSTEMS
OF GOVERNMENT[46]

What do the police and officials want?	What do the most liberal of the bourgeois (the people of the *Osvobozhdeniye,* or the Constitutional-Democratic Party) want?	What do the class-conscious workers (the Social Democrats) want?
The absolute monarchy	The constitutional monarchy	The democratic republic

OF WHAT DO THESE SYSTEMS OF GOVERNMENT CONSIST?

Absolute Monarchy	Constitutional Monarchy	Democratic Republic
1. The tsar — an absolute monarch.	1. The tsar — a constitutional monarch.	1. No tsar.
2. A Council of State (officials appointed by the tsar).	2. An Upper House of popular representatives (indirect, not quite equal and not quite universal elections).	2. No Upper House.

3. A State *Duma,* or consultative body of popular representatives (indirect, unequal and nonuniversal elections).	3. A Lower House (universal, direct, and equal elections by secret ballot).	3. A single republican house (universal, direct, and equal elections by secret ballot).

WHAT IS THE SIGNIFICANCE OF THESE SYSTEMS OF GOVERNMENT?

Absolute Monarchy	Constitutional Monarchy	Democratic Republic
1. and 2. Complete power of the police and the officials over the people.	1. One-third of the power in the hands of the police and the officials, headed by the tsar.	1. No independent power for either the police or the officials; their complete subordination to the people.
3. Consultative voice of the big bourgeois and the rich landlords.	2. One-third of the power in the hands of the big bourgeoisie and the rich landlords.	2. No privileges for either the capitalists or the landlords.
No power for the people.	3. One-third of the power in the hands of the whole people.	3. All power – wholly, completely and indivisibly – in the hands of the whole people.

WHAT PURPOSE SHALL THESE SYSTEMS OF GOVERNMENT SERVE?

Absolute Monarchy	Constitutional Monarchy	Democratic Republic
That the courtiers, the police, and the officials may live on the fat of the land; that the rich may rob the workers and peasants at their own free will; that the people may remain for ever without rights and live in darkness and ignorance.	That the police and the officials may be dependent on the capitalists and landlords; that the capitalists, landlords, and rich peasants may freely and easily rob the workers of town and country, by right and not by arbitrary rule.	That the free and enlightened people may learn to run things themselves, and, principally, that the working class may be free to struggle for socialism, for a system under which there will be neither rich nor poor and all the land, all the factories and works will belong to all the working people.

June-July 1905

10   SOCIALISM AND VIOLENCE

Neil Harding

Most commentators have it that modern socialism as a continuous and selfconscious tradition began with Babeuf's Conspiracy for Equality. If we grant this then modern socialism began with the express declaration that the realm of justice and equality could not be realised without a strong dose of therapeutic violence. Ever since, the history of socialist thought has been punctuated by recurrent controversy over the role and function of violence in creating socialism. To some extent the importance and immediacy of the controversy depends upon the historical period involved and the necessity of defining one's attitude towards the *grandes journees* of the revolutionary calendar. 1789, 1830, 1848, 1871, 1917 and 1949, the years of climacteric in this respect, leave behind them an ambiguous and repeatedly disputed legacy. To some socialists the events of these years confirm them in their view that reason and patient propaganda are, of themselves, insufficient to accomplish radical change within society. The main cause of the failures suffered by the movement they attribute to its excessive and misplaced humaneness, its lack of resolution, its failure to appreciate the crucial need for a preponderance of force at the right time and place. For others the initial heady enthusiasms which greeted these periodic outbursts, were followed by the anguish of hopes unfulfilled. The lesson they learned, painfully and repeatedly, was that political violence tended to excite expectations which the economic and cultural level of society could not translate into realities. The revolutionary rebirth so frequently and loudly proclaimed seemed to lead to new tyrannies and new sufferings for the people so long as they remained unprepared for the tasks ahead.

The debate within socialist thought over the role of violence can, in some ways, be reduced to this historiographical controversy about the consequences of past experience of political violence and its appropriateness in a current situation. More basically the debate highlights the eclecticism, the profusion of patterns of argument embraced by the generic term 'socialism'. At root the debate is intelligible only when we make explicit the two alternative accounts offered of how the people are to be prepared for the tasks ahead. The debate over violence becomes essentially a debate between rival epistemologies, between two competing accounts of how the mass is to be made conscious of its mission. This historical data selectively employed by each side is used to substantiate its own account of this progress towards consciousness. We shall return to this theme later.

Babeuf, as we have noticed, stands at the fountainhead of one side of the dispute and his apology for the utilisation of violent means has been taken up and reapplied by many socialists who fancied themselves to be in an analagous situation. Babeuf defends resort to arms and the installation of a transitional dictatorship, not because these means are desirable, but because they are the only viable means of realising social justice. His justificatory argument was contingent not principled and flowed from the situation in which, he alleged, the proponents of equality were placed. They were, he contended, precluded from any possibility of open organisation and peaceful propagation of their views by governmental persecution. His partisans, he maintained, were driven underground, persecuted and executed for fear that they might bring the people to an awareness of their true interests. Centuries of priestly and royal propaganda kept the people enslaved and debased, unable therefore to engineer their own salvation. For the people to attain their true stature the incubus of the past had to be destroyed by those dedicated and virtuous men who had already escaped its spell. Babeuf is quite clear that where the 'sovereign nation' decides its destiny openly and freely, no man may arrogate to himself the role of deciding things for his fellow citizens:

'where the people is free, and may be consulted, it is not to be presumed that others can judge better of its interests than the people itself can.

'The case is different when a people is in chains — when tyranny has placed it in a state of impotence to emit its will on all that concerns it . . . when it has been rendered incapable of wresting from them the usurped power, of which they take advantage to make it suffer and languish in despair . . .

'It becomes, then, just — it becomes necessary that the most intrepid — men most capable of devoting themselves — men endowed with the greatest amount of energy, fire and force . . . it is just and necessary that such men should invest themselves with the dictatorship of insurrection — that they should assume the initiative — that they should arrogate the glorious title of "Conspirators for liberty" — in a word, that they should erect themselves into magistrates to save their fellow-citizens.'[1]

If Babeuf's justification for resort to violence is simply stated, his thoughts on the organisation of political violence were a deal more complicated, entailing among other things, plans for a Plebeian Vendeé, which, through the excellence of its institutions and pattern of life would act as an example to all of how social life could be organised. The revolution would then gradually consolidate itself by spreading the influence of the 'provisional administration' outwards from this base area.[2] At times Babeuf advocates this almost Maoist tactic of utilising expanding base areas spreading from the periphery to the centre, but he is most renowned for his ideas on the organisation of the *coup d'état*. In either case he is unambiguous — nothing will be achieved without civil war, without 'reducing the past to dust'. 'Let us repeat once again: our afflictions are at their apogee; they cannot get worse; they can only be ameliorated by a total overthrow! Let everything be confounded! . . . let all the elements be thrown into confusion, mingled and dashed against each other! . . . let everything relapse into chaos, that from chaos there emerge a new and regenerated world!'[3]

The first condition for the educative reconstitution of the people's nature was possession of the governmental machine, possession of the requisite force to meet the inevitable resistance. The only effective means of acquiring this was to build the secret organisation of a revolutionary society bound together by a common social and political credo which would, through the subsidiary (or 'front') organisations it controlled, seize power by an armed coup in order to reconstitute property and social attitudes. The Babeuvist apology for violence was powerful in its simplicity and in variant forms reappears throughout the history of socialist thought. It argues that in conditions of illegality and suppression of free speech and association, the only possible form of organisation is a conspiracy which cannot, if it is to be a credible alternative to the existing régime, reject violence on principle. To do so would deliver the movement into the hands of the existing régime, amounting to a declaration of its own impotence. Babeuf's justificatory argument also broaches many of the elements of what is later to be taken up by Marxian historiography. Classes and groups throughout history, Babeuf maintained, have confirmed their social superiority through the violent seizure of political power. They guaranteed their pre-eminence through their control over the agencies of governmental coercion; the police and army. History afforded no examples of a ruling group peacefully yielding place to a rival. On the contrary, Babeuf maintained that the recent history of France demonstrated that only popular violence dislodged the monarchy and only violence could oust the new privileged dictatorship of lawyers, journalists and clerks, place-seekers of the Third Estate who had reneged on all the progressive social measures beneficial to the Fourth Estate. The *sans culottes* who had made the revolution had been cheated of the fruits of victory and effectively denied the franchise and all opportunity of peaceably influencing public policy. Usurpers had insinuated themselves into positions of privilege and power and one last shove was needed to oust them. The cry went up, which was to reverberate among the extreme left of every succeeding revolution — 'la révolution est à refaire'. The foundation of government becomes in this view of history violence exercised by a class or group, opposition is met by violence and can only reply in like measure if it is to succeed.

It is difficult to deny the cogency of the line of argument. If socialists find themselves in a situation where the propagation of their views is met with violence, if they have no hope of peacefully affecting and altering existing society what other option is open to them apart from a resort to violence? This kind of argument from contingency has had a continuous existence within socialist and radical thought. The Babeuvist doctrine on violence was of obvious appeal to socialists in all countries where the mass of the people had no prospect of peacefully influencing affairs of state. It was disseminated throughout Europe by Buonarrotti's tireless zeal in conspiratorial activity and by his publication of the *History of the Conspiracy for Equality* which rapidly became the bible of extreme revolutionaries in Europe. Translated by Bronterre O'Brien it found adherents amongst those Chartists impatient for reform and tired of the stalling tactics of a parliamentary régime which seemed dedicated to denying the working man the vote. In Russia in the seventies the Populists, faced with a total ban on political opposition, rapidly became converts to the Babeuvist operational *schema* which, in the opinion of many commentators left its enduring imprint upon Bolshevik and Communist organisational structures. Most socialists in the West were prepared to concede that in countries like Russia there was no alternative to the violent overthrow of the autocratic régime. The same arguments were later applied to the plight of socialists in China and might still be applied to the situation prevailing in many countries of Africa, South-East Asia and South and Central America. To be consistent it should be added that by the same rationale a recourse to violence by non-Communist socialists in contemporary Eastern Europe, Russia and China might be justified.

At its minimum specification the justification for resort to violence unites socialists with democrats in general. There is indeed a considerable and little-explored case for arguing that, in Europe at least, socialists have been the most consistent and determined supporters of democracy and civil liberties. This identification of socialism with democracy stemmed from the fact that both currents were steeped in a rationalist tradition according to which all men being creatures of reason are amenable to persuasion. All men have an intrinsic dignity and are worthy of respect by virtue of their faculty of reason. The majority of socialist theorists would therefore agree with a much broader spectrum of rationalist and radical thinkers that to oblige a man to act under

threat of violence would be to affront his dignity as a man.[4] In terms of
this rationalism the only political violence which could conceivably be
justified was that bare minimum requisite to establish the primary
conditions for the progress of reason itself. Evidently there is considerable room for dissent here on what would constitute the minimum
violence requisite in any concrete situation. Furthermore, the primary
conditions referred to, have themselves been the subject of the most
diverse interpretations. To generalise and simplify, the majority of
socialists would interpret those conditions as equivalent to the ground
rules for the operation of an effective democracy; freedom of press and
association, equality before the law, representative assemblies elected
by universal, direct and secret ballot, etc. In the voicing of these
objectives European socialists stood in the forefront of the democratic
movement. In their preparedness to organise, suffer if need be and fight
when necessary to secure them, the movement has matched its
professions with its deeds. The role of socialists in the Chartist
movement, in the European revolutions of 1848, the struggle for
democracy in Belgium, Germany and Spain and in the Russian
Revolution of 1905, demonstrates a resoluteness in pursuit of democratic values which is unmatched. For the majority of socialists in the
nineteenth and twentieth centuries the issue of violence disappeared
however when the democratic preconditions of a rational and orderly
advance toward social justice had been secured.

'It is the madness of Bedlam to talk about the overthrow of the
capitalist system in democratic countries by arming the proletariat and
waging a war of extermination upon the bourgeoisie.'[5] Philip Snowden's
argument against proletarian violence where democratic conditions
prevailed may be taken as typical. Violence, he contended, was not only
unnecessary, it was unrealistic. To imagine a proletariat so lacking in
intelligence and organisational ability that it would forsake the open
and easy road of constitutionally depriving the ruling classes of power,
yet somehow able to undertake the far more rigorous and dangerous
path of armed insurrection; was, he maintained, a hopeless delusion.
The social democrats state their ground clearly, no great changes are
accomplished without the conscious support of the majority, 'All
change that is permanent must be a change of consent',[6] but the
conscious support of the majority in democratic society renders talk of
violence quite superfluous, it is indeed retrogressive for it plays into the
hands of the reaction. For the majority of socialists in the nineteenth
and twentieth centuries, violence has been seen not as an instrument of
politics, not as a means whereby rational ends can be promoted; on the
contrary it has been seen as an unfortunate vehicle for the establishment
of politics. Once this is accomplished it becomes irrelevant because it
cannot contribute to the goals in hand; it is in fact corrosive of them.

If the objective is a more rational, freer society where utility is maximised, then the intellect and education of the people and of the government too, must be the main focus. If the objective is the establishment of a more efficient means of producing and a more equitable manner of distributing the products of society, then here too the complex problems involved will come not a whit closer to solution in mass political violence. What is needed in this case is a variant of the Saint Simonian-Fabian tutorship of the best qualified, an approach which was considerably bolstered in the late nineteenth century by Spencer's notions of specialisation of function as the key to human progress.

In either case the present imperative is for enlightenment. Until the people's cultural and educational level has been raised they will not comprehend the responsibilities the new society involves them in; they cannot therefore immediately assume the rights it confers nor even assume the leadership of the party working out their own emancipation. Hyndman, with typical patrician bluntness, wrote what some other socialist leaders doubtless believed but dared not utter: 'a slave class cannot be freed by the slaves themselves. The leadership, the initiative, the teaching, the organisation, must come from these comrades in a different position and who are trained to use their faculties in early life.'[7] The objective in hand, according to Hyndman, Snowden,[8] Vandervelde[9] and all social democrats, is to educate the people, to make them understand and be able to utilise the opportunities the franchise opened up. A comprehensive system of national education through schools, parliament, trade union and cooperative associations and party propaganda is necessary in order that the people shall come to a rational awareness of the necessity of the transformed society which is envisaged. Each variant of this pacific radicalism is confident that when this state is reached its precepts will be adopted. In the meantime it is the duty of socialists to forestall lapses into political violence, lapses which must injure the prospects for the rationally ordered harmony of the future.

There was, particularly in the nineteenth century an awesome awareness on the part of most socialists and radicals alike that they were sitting on a volcano. The people had been miserably abused and the clear danger existed that they would be forced into revolutionary violence through the cupidity, savagery or stupidity of the governing classes. Each successive European crisis reawakened these fears which lingered on well into the twentieth century. Writing of the consequences of the First World War Ramsay MacDonald eloquently expresses them:

'The state in which Europe is today is ominous. Society has been rent and civilization has been riven. A settled order of politics, of governments, of production and international exchange has been absolutely destroyed, and the peoples have returned to the social and mental chaos of pre-mediaeval times. In the midst of these earthquake upheavals both in States and in the minds of men, the peoples of the more favoured countries take too little warning by the cracks and the crashes. They are surrounded by a great collapse and hardly know it. The distress, famine and bankruptcy may so weightily overwhelm people that they will be crushed and emerge broken, spiritless, enslaved; these calamities on the other hand, may rouse a mad wrath which will burst into revolution and hurl order into a deeper night. Whichever happens it will be evil, and against the spread of that evil every intelligent being and every disciple of progress must strive. Obedient to a blind fear, there are signs that the classes in authority may resort to repression and to police government. There lies calamity and disgrace . . . The reform movement, barred from its natural road of advance and deprived of its liberty of thought, expression and action, would become a destructive force within Society, blasting the outlets it requires, and in due time it would win. The incidents of the struggle, however, would make but a sorry chapter in the history of the nation.'[10]

This lengthy extract expresses a central dilemma of the peaceable social democrat, he had to walk the tightrope between the potentially destructive violence of the mass and the selfish coercion of the ruling élite. Each form of violence excites relatiation from the other, both are corrosive of progress. The social democrats for long conceived their role as mediators between the understandable irrationality of the mass and the more culpable irrationality of the elite. Macdonald brings out well another point too frequently disregarded by critics of social democracy who ignore their acute and sensitive awareness that the veneer of civilisation lay perilously thin sustained as it was by the mass of the people who were largely outside its pale. Too sharp a critique, raising too extravagant expectations might provoke a justifiable onslaught resulting in violent anarchy and barbarism. The central dilemma faced by moderate socialists was that they realised that the present institutions and morals were corrupt and had to be transformed for reason or science to prevail. But beware the abyss, lest civilisation itself and all the centuries of man's cultural achievement go down in a deluge of violence.

Those, of course, were counsels of conservativism as well as a feature of socialist thought, the apocalyptic vision was present as much in the conservative and moderate socialist outlook as in that of the extreme revolutionaries. With the moderate socialists, as for MacDonald, the very voicing of the fear of imminent catastrophe became a main lever of their efforts to reform the existing structure. Socialism becomes in this sense the last defence available to civilisation against a threatening barbarism. It becomes a holding operation in which the mass of the people, illiterate and prejudiced through no fault of their own, are progressively raised to the level of rational appreciation of their situation and are treated as worthy of dignity and respect. Reforms along these lines are pressed upon the existing status quo as the only way to forestall the threat of popular violence; they are pre-emptive palliatives. 'Reform' as Snowden reminds us 'is the surest preventive of revolution. If statesmen wish to avoid revolution they will deal with the conditions which provoke it.'[11]

A variant of this general position was embraced by the German social democrats who maintained the historic inevitability of the violent transformation of society very largely as a propaganda weapon. The message of eventual retribution dealt out by the oppressed to their masters had too potent an appeal to be lightly abandoned. Even when the day to day attributes of the Party quite belied any intention to hasten or prepare for this judgement day, it was retained as a beautiful vision to sustain enthusiasm — a factor quite neglected by Bernstein's sober analysis. For the SPD the assurance that the ruling class would go down before the violence of the working class was a vital propagandist tool the function of which is broadly similar to the repeated warnings about imminent revolution and the British working man being at the end of his tether, which MacDonald and Snowden utilised to exert pressure for reform. If it helped to inspire awe in the middle classes and the Imperial Government to such an extent that it was prepared to offer reforms in the vain expectation of forestalling this eventuality, so much the better. The orthodox social democrats of the late nineteenth and twentieth centuries belong nonetheless with the rationalists in their attitude towards violence. They asserted that socialism cannot be established without the attainment of a requisite cultural and educational level among the masses. This development is itself linked with the development of the productive forces which alone can guarantee the material basis of socialism. As the productive forces mature and become more complex they demand an increased level of education and ability amongst the operatives, a more refined division of labour and therewith of labour organisation. The working class is educated and organised by the processes generated by capitalist industry itself — augmented of course by Party propaganda. This propaganda must never, however, in its immediate claims, run far ahead of those demands which are immediately realisable on the basis of present organisational strength. It must never indulge in utopian fancies of imminent total success, for to do so would be to ignore one of the ancillary effects of technological development — the way in which it enormously strengthened the power of the state to resist insurgent violence. This was in short Engels' celebrated message of 1895 which was represented as his testament to the SPD and to the socialists of Europe. The era of street fighting and barricades, when working men, arms in hand, could storm the centres of power, was at an end. The rapid-firing rifle, developments in artillery, improved discipline in the army, improved communications, changes in town planning – all these factors enormously augmented the power of governments. The new road to power lay through the ballot box 'transformed from a means of deception, which it was before, into an instrument of emancipation'.[12] Ultimately of course violence might still have to be used – the propaganda centrepiece was still potent – but in the meanwhile 'win the battle for democracy'. That 'meanwhile' indicated, of course, a prolonged period of peaceful electoral and pastoral work in which a magnificent party machine was built up, the like of which Europe had never before (nor since) witnessed. That machine itself, as Michel's sociological study, and Schorske's more recent historical work[13] demonstrates, became through internal pressures progressively more modest (some would say timid) in its demands as its scope and power increased. It had too much to lose in its coffers, its vote, and above all in its respectability, to hazard all by responding to the calls to action, however heroic, uttered by its own left activists. Engels' optimistic words that 'We the "revolutionists", the "overthrowers" – we are thriving far better on legal methods than on illegal methods and overthrow',[14] came to have a double irony. In the proportion that they succeeded and built the requisite electoral machine the SPD ceased to be revolutionary. The Party came to constitute an end in itself; the product of generations of travail could not be threatened by leaps in the dark. This was the burden of Bebel's famous reply to those who advocated a general strike or open revolutionary measures in the event of war. Such a course he declared could not be contemplated. 'We cannot proceed with methods of struggle which could destroy the normal life, and in some conditons, the very existence of the party.'[15]

The orthodox social democrats of Europe, heavily influenced by the Germans adopted a similar stance. If violence there had to be, to wrest power from the recalcitrant bourgeoisie, if the prospect of a future Armageddon appealed to the working-class electorate, then let it be an abstract probability of a more or less remote future, a revolution of infinite regression (what Lenin contemptuously termed the revolution on credit). In the meantime the task ahead was to organise and educate – *organisieren, studieren, propagandieren* was the gradualist watchword that Liebknecht bequeathed the Party. To prepare the people for the responsibilities ahead in a peaceful and responsible manner became the duty of responsible 'revolutionaries'. Violent activity in the present would only harm the prospects for socialism, lose votes, play into the hands of the reactionaries and would be likely to incur governmental retribution in the form of a re-enactment of the Anti-Socialist Laws — perhaps worse. More essentially violence had no creative role to play in forging the organisation and broad culture of future socialist man. Socialism in this guise, according to critics on the left, became a new methodism, a corporative anodyme for the violent passions produced by industrial society.

What unites social democrats in their disparagement of violence, their general refusal to play to the savage instincts of the people, is their commitment to the precepts of rationalism. Violence by its nature is irrational, spontaneous and anarchic; it threatens not merely bourgeois society but civilisation itself. The values it prompts are the inverse of those desired, those appropriate to a rationally ordered policy. Until the mass of the people have attained a degree of rationality and can responsibly manage the privileges which the new society is to give to them,there can be no fundamental change. The means for attaining this level of development must of course exist and where freedom of association, of the press, freedom before the law, where in other words the basic fundaments of rational progress do not exist — there political violence may be justified. Where they do exist liberals and social democrats alike share a sublime confidence that the peaceful education of the populace will suffice to demonstrate the correctness of their respective views. They have the optimism of a Godwin or a Mill, that the diffusion of knowledge, the ever-questing role of enquiry and reason would put things to right.

This confidence was periodically fractured by particular political or economic crises. In 1848 for example socialists, radicals and liberals had been united in enthusiastic support of democracy and the peaceful road. This enthusiasm could not long survive the European-wide failures that swiftly followed, the apostasy of liberals to their erstwhile principles of one man, one vote and their meek acquiescence in the restoration of the *ancien régime*. There is a measure of truth in Marx's contention that the bourgeoisie was the first to renege on the implementation of democracy, that it tended to join with the reaction as soon as the radical implications of democracy threatened its social power. The position of Europe in 1848 became analogous to that which England had earlier experienced. The middle-class radicals encouraged and assisted the development of mass popular movements in demanding manhood suffrage. But when the sops were thrown out to them, when their political goals were realised in the 1832 Reform Bill, they preached responsibility and order. As in England the continental exponents of physical force derived their strength from the impossibility of a reasoned explanation of franchise restriction. The climate of disillusion which followed 1832, exacerbated by the punitive terms of the new Poor Law, created the milieu in which the advocates of violence in the Chartist movement found eager audiences.

1848 marks a similar watershed in Europe. A socialist could no longer be automatically identified with the peaceful transformation of society along the road to integral democracy. The good will of men, their obligation to act according to rational principles had been found sorely wanting. Corrosive self-interest was found to be every bit as much a radical or liberal-bourgeois trait as an aristocratic or monarchical one. It appeared to be a more potent motive force in politics than all the fine words of radical rhetoric. How then to effect radical change when the men with power in the state had turned a deaf ear to popular demands and the implementation of true civic and democratic right?

Almost exclusively on the basis of the events of 1848-51, particularly in France, Marx was to articulate a new political tactic of proletarian revolution. His preparedness to counsel violence differs dramatically from his restraint in the earlier period of radical hope expressed in his optimistic and 'democratic' articles in the *Neue Rheinische Zeitung*. His disgust at the treachery of the liberals leads directly to his advocacy of violent revolution in the famous 'Address of the Central Committee to the Communist League' with its call to arms and vindication of political terrorism. The recourse to violence, both in its theoretical exposition, and in the extent to which the call is taken up, is clearly a function of the disillusion with the fragile nature of democracy.

Once articulated however, the theory that proletarian violence was necessary in order to realise socialism assumed a life of its own. It was stamped with the authority of the founder of social democracy and within the movement itself it served the function of an article of faith distinguishing believer from nonbeliever. The theory might well have held good of Continental Europe in the 1850s and the 1860s, but by the 1890s it was clear to all but the most obtuse that there were other channels for the voicing of grievances and real opportunities for achieving reform quite peaceably. By this time economic and political changes made retention of the orthodox Marxist belief in the necessity of violence increasingly difficult. In the first place the economic rationale upon which that belief was established encountered not merely the theoretical attack of revisionist economists, but seemed to be contradicted by the facts of life as experienced by party members. Europe had enjoyed an unprecedented period of sustained prosperity, the proletariat had undoubtedly shared in that prosperity, their economic situation was improving year by year. The concentration of capital might be proceeding but there was little evidence to support the Marxian prediction that the bourgeoisie would be reduced to a handful of wealthy magnates. In other words the twin predictions upon which the economic rationale for violent revolution had been established were not being realised. The proletariat was not becoming increasingly desperate and impoverished, forced into armed revolution by a system 'unfit to rule because it is incompetent to assure an existence to its slave within his slavery'.[16] Society was not becoming polarised into two homogeneous and antagonistic classes. There was evidence aplenty to suggest that mature capitalism spawned a whole host of small-scale enterprises, distributive, managerial and technical personnel standing between the magnates of capital and the proletariat. These economic questionings coincided with the rise of socialist party machines dedicated to winning votes. As the parties grew, so did the role of the functionaries. They conceived of their objective, quite naturally, as extending as far as possible the influence of the party, in practical terms this meant the winning of votes. They had an equally natural interest in the career structure the party afforded — the move up the ladder from district to regional secretary. Both objectives would be threatened by any excess of spontaneous disorder. Violent activity associated in any way with the party would be utilised to the utmost by rivals, votes would be lost, membership numbers jeopardised and subscriptions would fall, the prospects for the party and for promotion and advance would undoubtedly suffer. In this way the interests of the party and those of the functionaries became identified and both militated against any violent or disorderly activity. The more the party grew, the more it became insistent upon the need for discipline, responsibility and order.

The war and the Bolshevik revolution were clearly another climacteric. Just as Marx universalised from the particular, so too did the Bolsheviks. Many European socialists, appalled at the senseless carnage of the war and the punitive nature of the peace, were ready to lend an attentive ear to the Bolshevik slogan of a civil war to end all wars and establish a United States of Europe. Many were prepared to accede to the rigour of the Twenty One Points of Admission to the Communist International, for Bolshevik organisation and Bolshevik tactics appeared the only sure road to success. The fact that the Bolsheviks had emerged from obscurity to success only because of a unique concatenation of circumstances was, in this atmosphere, quite ignored. For decades Western Communists laboured on, and retained the faith in the dictatorship of the proletariat and revolutionary violence, for, once again, it was precisely these tenets of faith that provided the internal cement of the movement — however outmoded or irrelevant they appeared in changing times. When at last this set of Leninist attitudes was discarded in 1956, as no longer appropriate to the situation of the Soviet Union and its client parties, the insistence upon the necessity of violence was restated in strident terms by the Chinese. It was their road to power, it seemed the only road open to radicals in neighbouring countries and throughout much of the Third World. As was the case earlier, the peculiarities of the Chinese experience were given generalised universal expression. The rural areas of the world would through guerilla action gradually encircle the North American and European urban strongholds of imperialism.

Each new revolution tends to universalise its experience and, at least in the initial enthusiasm that a new beginning is to be made, lends fresh credence to the possibility of root and branch change by violent means. Each establishes a new orthodoxy in which the acceptance of violence is a cardinal feature. Gradually, however, countervailing pressures build up to negate the *practical* import of this doctrinal pose. The political sect, in its avarice for votes, does as little as possible to disturb the present enjoyment of ameliorations and expectations for the future. Similarly the isolated and weak regime grows in power and prestige and seeks to augment both by conventional diplomatic means. A belligerent foreign policy generally involves high allocations to heavy industry and armaments, but pressure from below for consumer goods and services has a way of making itself felt on even the most insensitive régime. The very success of revolutionary régimes in maintaining power and achieving their material goals itself creates the milieu for the advocacy of the doctrine of the inevitability of gradualness. Each successful revolutionary movement it seems becomes vulnerable to its Bernstein, Khrushchev or Liu Shao Chi. This is not to go the whole way with the theorists of convergence, but simply to admit that all successful revolutionary movements have, in the interests of prudence, come to temper their militant espousal of the cataclysmic solution.

Up to this point we have been largely concerned with the variety of responses available to socialists within the framework of rationalism. The differing degrees of tolerance of political violence they exhibit is, by and large, a function of time and place. The general disposition which unites them is that violence is to be resorted to only where all other avenues of change are closed. Violent activity for them has no creative role to play in producing the positive attributes of socialism, when embraced it is regarded as an unfortunate preliminary to be treated with extreme caution for fear that its effects will poison the subsequent attempt to transform man and society. To this extent Babeuf and Blanqui share a common disposition with MacDonald and Jaurés, their argument in defence of violence is always an argument from contingency and sad necessity, it is always an apology for violence from within the precepts of rationalism and never a vindication of it.

Let us turn to the numerically far smaller but nonetheless persistent tendency which argues that violent conflict *can* constitute a moralising and educative force. This equally disparate group of thinkers was earlier characterised as sharing a common 'romantic' pattern of ideas as distinct from the 'rationalists' discussed above. To some extent the romantic vindicators of the creative role of violence are the more cohesive of our two groups for in spite of all the differences of emphases and levels of articulation, their stock-in-trade of ideas can be directly traced to notions which had a long pedigree in German Romantic thought. They seized in particular upon the element of practice and gave it a radical twist by attributing to it not the activity through which the individual becomes self-conscious, and therefore, free, but the process through which the mass struggles to realise its freedom and humanity. The activity, from being internal, individual, and concerned with thought, becomes a mass struggle directed against people and institutions fettering the people's freedom. The idea of the group realising its freedom and consciousness through the process of struggle with other groups was a clear transposition of romantic ideas. It provided for many socialists a satisfying theoretical justification for the violent conflict inherent in French ideas of society and history as the arena of class war. German preoccupations were wedded to French ones and a potent rationale for regarding violence as a creative and necessary element in establishing socialism soon emerged.

Moses Hess was one of the first to attempt to fuse the ideas of French socialism and German Romanticism in his article *The Philosophy of the Act*.[17] He insists that the goals of freedom and equality loudly proclaimed by the French Revolution and refined through the prism of German thought cannot be realised by further refinements in the realm of thought and consciousness but only by resolute action.

'It is now the task of the philosophy of the spirit to become the philosophy of the act. Not only thought but all human activity, must be brought to the point at which all oppositions fade away. The heavenly egoism, that is, the theological consciousness, against which German philosophy is now so zealously crusading, has thus far hindered us from stepping forth into the act.'[18]

Socialism, Hess goes on to argue, will be the issue not of speculative thought but of action. Revolution and anarchy in politics — the bequest of Babeuf and the French Revolution is the means to unmask the 'lies of religion and politics . . . the entrenchments, the enemy's secret hiding places, the bridge of asses and of devils must be burned down and annihilated'.[19] German philosophy must realise that the problems of thought and consciousness are in fact practical problems; that the path to self-consciousness and freedom is not through cerebration to perfect self-knowledge but through revolutionary activity to a society in which freedom and equality are realised. Hess in this way anticipated by some years Marx's imperative to action enshrined in the famous eleventh thesis on Feuerbach. He provided the basis from which many subsequent theorists of socialism have justified violent action as a creative force. Man, he argued, finds and makes himself in his own activity. That activity is, however, fettered on all sides by oppressive institutions and outmoded thought-patterns. French socialism in its emphasis on class struggle provided the means whereby the fetters were to be broken down and a radical transformation effected. The class struggle must be viewed not simply as a means to realise the economic objectives of a partial group but as the activity in and through which man affirms his own freedom and comes to self-consciousness.

'Without revolution, no new history can begin. As strong as was the approval of the French Revolution in Germany, its essence, which consisted in nothing less than tearing down the pillars upon which the old social life had stood, was just as strongly misunderstood everywhere. The value of negation was perceived in Germany in the realm of thought, but not in the realm of action. The value of anarchy consists in the fact that the individual must once again rely upon himself and proceed from himself.'[20]

The year before Hess wrote this, Bakunin was already coming to similar conclusions. In his celebrated article 'The Reaction in Germany' he too points to the necessity of practical activity to overcome the transparent contradictions of social life. In particular the 'contradiction of freedom and unfreedom has advanced and soared to its last and highest summit in our time, otherwise a time so similar to the period of dissolution of the heathen world. Have you not read the mysterious and awesome words, *Liberté, Egalité and Fraternité*, on the foreground of the Temple of Freedom erected by the Revolution? And do you not know and feel that these words intimate the complete annihilation of the present political and social world?' [21] Invoking variously the authority of the Apocalypse and the primacy of the negative over the positive in all contradiction, warning of the rise of wrathful indignation among the poor, Bakunin ends with his much-quoted invocation to elemental destruction:

'even in Russia dark clouds are gathering, heralding storm,
Oh, the air is sultry and filled with lightning.
And therefore we call to our deluded brothers,
Repent, repent, the Kingdom of the Lord is at hand! . . .
Let us therefore trust the eternal Spirit which
destroys and annihilates only because it is the unfathomable
and eternally creative source of all life. The passion for
destruction is at the same time a creative urge.'[22]

According to Bakunin man's urge to freedom and self-activity and instinct of revolt constitute his distinguishing marks. 'L'homme est *forcé* de conquérir sa liberté ... L'homme ne devient realement homme, il ne conquiert la possibilité de son émancipation interieure, qu'autant qu'il est parvenu à rompre les chaines d'esclave que la nature extérieure fait peser sur tous les vivants.'[23] To realise freedom involved however, as French socialism pointed out, a life and death struggle against those whose interest lay in restricting it. Freedom was possible only on the basis of persistent struggle in the course of which whole groups of men and institutions would necessarily perish: 'a war of extermination is bound to erupt, with no quarter and no respite'.[24]

Violence in this view is fundamentally creative in that it rouses the masses to self-activity, to assert themselves as men. For Bakunin, as for Sorel, this Satanic instinct of revolt was the sole agency of historical progress. In it, man, throughout all ages, had found himself as properly human: not as the servile instrument of an outmoded authority secular or religious, but as a free creative being. For them progress was not a peaceful movement of gradualist inevitability. It came into the world with heroic defiance, its success was dependent upon the will and endeavour of those few innovators who had the resolve not to be crushed. It was their duty to stimulate the less developed, but never entirely crushed instinct of revolt in the masses. Here in short is the romantic notion of the *minorité agissante*. Its pre-eminent role derives from its will and preparedness to act to realise freedom. Its idea of freedom is not, like Mill's, amenable to logical examination of the separate phases of its justificatory argument; it is a totality of impressions that must be taken as a whole. Whether bolstered by Sorel's Bergensonian notions or Bakunin's more expressly romantic conceits, it is clear that the faculty of reason alone cannot embrace these truths. They are indeed better apprehended by those who are unimpeded by cautious reason, by those who retain their natural spontaneity and instincts. These new barbarians will generate spontaneously a new and revivifying idea, not through the toils of philosophy but simply through asserting their natural humanity not yet extinguished by industrial civilisation. It is in this way that Marx early conceives of the proletariat as as a force 'outside of civil society', proclaiming the end of philosophy through its commitment to act to assert its threatened humanity. Marx's romantic quest for a class 'outside of civil society' regenerating a corrupt civilisation has remained a persistent one among the extreme left radicals. Marx found this class in the proletariat. Bakunin discerns it variously in the peasantry, the *lumpenproletariat* and the bandits. Sorel envisages his closed corporation of the proletariat evolving a cultural pattern and an idea, in hermetic isolation from the bourgeoisie. His whole notion of prosecuting an unceasing war to the knife with the bourgeoisie is designed to ensure that the proletariat remains uncontaminated by contact with the bourgeoisie. Marcuse insists that the only truly revolutionary class in contemporary society consists of 'the outcasts and outsiders, the exploited and persecuted of other races and colours, the unemployed and the unemployable . . . [who] exist outside the democratic process'.[25] Fanon, Debray and Mao likewise argue that the true radical revolutionaries are those least corrupted by contact with urban capitalist values, precisely the group which produced Hobsbawm's 'Primitive Rebels'.[26] It is hardly surprising that all of these theorists adopt an epistemology consonant with their romantic view of the liberating group. This group is by prior definition that least touched by bourgeois mores and ideology. It must consequently be the least educated and literate group, for that, after all, is part of the guarantee of its pristine nature. It is similarly dispersed and ill-organised, otherwise it would already play its part in the political process. Clearly this group cannot be reached through printed propaganda and is difficult to recruit into an orthodox political party. It is aware of the ills it suffers not as particular abuses but as the encapsulation of all the woes of society and the consummate inversion of its proper humanity.[27] It is that 'class which is really rid of all the old world and at the same time stands pitted against it'.[28]

The goals and objectives of this class in permanent exile from society are portrayed as quite distinct from those of bourgeois civilisation. Social democrats and Fabians, *possibilistes* and integral socialists might find the consumer or utilitarian ethic a natural complement to their view of society as an organic integral whole, i.e. they accepted that society was a unitary whole, they accepted that there was a moral community of shared values, and all they were concerned to do was to press these to what seemed their logical conclusion. Had not good liberals themselves admitted that a greater equalisation of wealth was necessary to the maintenance of freedom and the implementation of equality of opportunity. The attainment of abundance, the raising of the working class to the level of opportunity enjoyed by the middle class was, and perhaps remains, the Social Democratic dream. As such it was a plan of social integration (as MacDonald never tired of repeating) which was being proffered. None of this will do for the revolutionary apologists of violence. Society is no organic whole. That, Sorel maintains with the superb contempt he reserves for sociologists, is the predominant myth of 'the little science'. Society is riven into mutually hostile camps. The aims and objectives of the one are fundamentally antagonistic to those of the other. For such varied revolutionaries as Bakunin, Marx, William Morris, Sorel, Lenin[29] and Marcuse, man's species being cannot be reduced to the striving for plenty. The goal of the exile class is far more sublime; it is the pursuit of freedom.

Its *leitmotif* is the self-acting creative being, freed from external authority, from religious and prescriptive law. It seeks for that which bourgeois society cannot possibly grant.

The romantic objective is complemented by an appropriate epistemological structure quite different from that embraced by the rationalists. If the SPD, emphasising one side of Marx, placed its faith in the evolution of productive forces, themselves occasioning consciousness with the careful assistance of the Party, the radical disciples of Marx placed their faith in *praxis.* It is not the rational apprehension that forces of production are being fettered that will be the transforming agency. Activity, in its paradigm form of violent conflict will be the solvent. They argue that the oppressed people do not learn from theoretical disquisitions about the nature of capitalism and class antagonism, they do not learn from electoral broadsides delivered by ever-so-able parliamentary candidates; nor do they learn from words spoken 'through the windows' of parliaments. They learn through their own practice the most heightened and compressed form of which is violent conflict.

This lesson, it can be argued, is the burden of Marx's *Theses on Feuerbach,* more emphatically of his analyses of French history in the nineteenth century.[30] The proletariat, Marx contends, does not *commence* the revolution with anything like adequate consciousness. At the outset it is inclined to follow the utopian dreams of all kinds of crackpots. It is lulled by the illusion that its interests and those of the bourgeoisie are not irreconcilable, that they can both be accommodated within the framework of the bourgeois republic. Only the painful experience of revolutionary action itself can purge the proletariat of these illusions. The revolution of 1848 progressed, Marx said, by building up the reaction. The bourgeoisie reneges on its promises, it progressively eliminates the social gains made by the other classes and provokes them into a protest which can be met with governmental retribution on a savage scale. Its erstwhile allies it pronounces its enemy and deals with them accordingly. The bloodbath of the July days marked a most important step in the education of the working class for at that moment the state revealed itself for what it was – an instrument of violence created and sustained to protect the interests of a specific economic group. No prior theoretical arguments, however cogent, could have taught the proletariat this lesson, only their experience and suffering as actors in the historical drama could reveal it. The violence of revolution clarifies the issues, obliges millions to declare their position, it enormously accelerates the growth of consciousness. The rapid march of the European counter-revolution; the glorious Hungarian fight; the armed uprisings in Germany; the Roman expedition; the ignominious defeat of the French army before Rome – in this vortex of the movement, in this torment of historical unrest, in this dramatic ebb and flow of revolutionary passions, hopes and disappointments the different classes of French society had to count their epochs of development in weeks where they had previously counted them in half centuries.'[31]

The proletariat, Marx argued, learns from its own mistakes. In action it draws in the mass of the unorganised, for, in the breach of blood that revolution occasions, the dialectical choice is posed. It is either their camp or ours, there can be no middle ground. Spontaneously and instinctively the proletariat feels its solidarity and its power. It apprehends in its practice and in the violence meted out to it the truths of the theoretical analysis evolved by revolutionary socialism. These truths, arrived at from economic theory, that society is split into two irreconcilable camps with diametrically opposed objectives, are now firmly established in the feelings and the minds of the masses.

One of the problems in Marx, and for subsequent Marxists is that violent conflict lauded as an instrument of acceleration, as the means whereby the essential dichotomy within society is clarified, made apparent and felt, can be taken to be *the* determining factor in the growth of that consciousness appropriate to socialist society. The problem evidently arises of how this is related to Marx's more Saint-Simonian determinist structure where the progress of the productive forces is held to be of decisive importance. In terms of Marx's basically romantic ideas on revolutionary *praxis*, action would appear to be its own justification. The possibility of what might be termed 'premature' revolution could hardly arise if all revolutionary experience is useful in extending, developing and clarifying the struggle. Marx's epigram that *'Revolutions are the locomotives of history'*[32] has indeed been transposed into Debray's ultraromantic formulation that the guerilla *foco* can itself, through armed propaganda create its own preconditions or objective basis.

Engels makes one of the few attempts in the literature of Marxism to pinpoint the problem of reconciling the romantic philosophy of activity with the determining role of productive forces. He poses the question, significantly in his *Introduction to the Class Struggles in France* (1895), of how the one is to be kept in step with the other. His conclusion is that the task is methodologically impossible. In a revolutionary situation the revolutionary theorist and leader must respond to every shift of the wind, he must be able to formulate a decisive plan of action in a rapidly changing balance of forces, he must above all be clear and forthright in his appraisal of when the time has arrived for violent conflict. In all of this, as Engels concedes, knowledge of the recent and contemporary economic trends cannot help — for the good reason that it is unobtainable. (Exactly how it would help, even *if* available, would pose further problems).

> 'A clear survey of the economic history of a given period can never be obtained contemporaneously, but only subsequently, after a collecting and sifting of the material has taken place. Statistics are a necessary auxiliary means here, and they always lag behind. For this reason, it is only too often necessary, in current history to treat this, the most decisive, factor as constant . . . It is self-evident that this unavoidable neglect of contemporaneous changes in the economic situation, the very basis of all the processes to be examined, must be a source of error.'[33]

Engels is clearly understating the difficulty for it follows from his admission that the point at which violent action, or revolution, becomes appropriate is not capable of prediction within the framework of economic determination. Economic analysis can only point up *a postereori* the conditions which prompted the outbreak, it is inherently incapable of predicting or advocating the immediate necessity for such action. The connection between revolutionary theory and revolutionary practice would seem to be thinnest precisely during revolutionary periods. It is indeed difficult to see what the revolutionary leader can do other than adhere to the Napoleonic precept *on s'engage, puis on voit.*

William Morris, during his career as a revolutionary, escaped the problems of dualism by frankly declaring himself a romantic who saw in socialism the potential for an aesthetic revolution. Morris is preoccupied with the plight of man as a free, creative and artistic being, crushed and extinguished by a capitalism intent on persuing crass ornamentation and extravagant uselessness. The irremediable flaw of capitalism is its division of labour, the 'division between gentleman designer and mechanic executant had brought about the final degradation of art'.[34] Morris' grudge against capitalism is not the Fabian grudge that capitalism is inefficient, nor is it the revisionist one that the workers are underpaid, it is rather that the whole system is endemically inhuman; it cannot sustain true art or creativity, it governs men and has an abhorrence of the prospect of men governing themselves. He sets himself the task of creating a new myth which will demonstrate what life might become. In his *News from Nowhere* he sets out the sublime ideal of what will and imagination might achieve.

The scheme Morris outlines for the realisation of his utopia bears an almost uncanny resemblance to that set out by Sorel and Bakunin and, on many points that of Marx. He leans, as Marx does, upon a conception of men's species-essence in which the instinct for free creativity plays a preponderant role. This instinct is almost submerged by the enslaving process of capitalist production but its residue will suffice to save the people.[35] It is stirred and reanimated by the counterrevolutionary violence meted out to them by the selfish governing minority. The people begin to think and act for themselves, they establish their own organisations to conduct a general strike, their own leaders emerge and therewith the end of the old order is signalled. The mass of the people are stirred from their customary sloth and cowardice, they confront the old order with restless heroism born of the conviction that the new world of their imagination can be realised if only men *will* its realisation. Governmental violence is the factor which brings the people to consciousness of the fact that the possessors will not voluntarily relinquish their positions. Only in violent resistance do they acquire a sense of their own power, that the dream can be realised. Violent action resolves prevarication, it poses the essential choice between polarities. 'All ideas of peace on a basis of compromise had disappeared on either side. The end, it was seen clearly, must be either absolute slavery for all but the privileged, or a system of life founded on equality and Communism. The sloth, the hopelessness, and, if I may say so, the cowardice of the last century, had given place to the larger, restless heroism of a declared revolutionary period.'[36]

The Romantics are generally agreed that the mode of knowing of the masses is preeminently through action. It follows that this is a process which cannot be mediated or represented. Its essence must be participatory. If the rational approval of considered schemes of reform is the objective of rational socialism or of liberalism, all that is demanded of the masses is approval in the form of a vote, and a vote is the conferring of a right upon someone else to represent a shared viewpoint. The issue can then be rationally considered in the gladiatorial verbal combat of representative institutions. In the romantic mode there can be no conferring of a proxy. The issue cannot be settled by eloquent gladiators confronting liberals and conservatives on their own chosen ground; it is settled in the will of the masses to re-assert their humanity and freedom. Action, culminating in violent conflict, is, according to this view *the* medium of proletarian self-expression. A recent syndicalist appraisal of the significance of the Paris Commune expresses the position very neatly.

'The workers, artisans and ordinary people of the period did not conceive of social life, least of all their own, in terms of universal concepts but in terms of action. Nine workers out of ten still do so today. Action is their language. It is in fact the only language of which they have acquired complete mastery. For intellectuals words are often a substitute for action. For workers, actions are a form of speech.'[37]

The ethic of Social Democracy is essentially passive and utilitarian, its object is the satisfaction of needs. These needs may well be best satisfied in the future through the quiescent discipline of the masses assenting to a rational scientific management of state and industry effected through an elaborate institutional mechanism. Its ethic is a consumer ethic, the expectation of plenty. The mode of prerevolutionary activity appropriate to this would take the form of a highly disciplined and mass thoroughly organised by an elaborate party structure.

The other ethic, that of the romantics, is an activist one; it is producer-orientated and its inspirational force is not a situation of plenty but a condition of freedom. It places little faith in formal institutions, relying rather upon the self-governing agencies thrown up in the revolution. Its mode of prerevolutionary activity would stress the spontaneous creativity of the masses which would only be encumbered and restricted by a flabby all-embracing party machine. From this point of view there is nothing incongruous about Lenin, Bakunin and Sorel vaunting the role of the activist minority — their authority derives not, as commentators tirelessly repeat, from their presumption to represent the working class in history and to make the revolution on its behalf. On the contrary, their authority derives from their committed activism, from their ability to stimulate and coordinate the activity of the masses. Only in the course of that activity do the people come to consciousness; if this is the case, then the minority plays the crucial role of a catalyst in organising and preparing the masses for action.

Lenin came round to this viewpoint early in his career, in 1895-6. The Russian Social Democrats had attempted to build bridges to the workers by means of workers' circles. The best-educated, most intelligent workmen were recruited and inducted into the theorems of Marxist determinism. Armed with theory, it was hoped, they would then return to proselytise their workmates and raise them to revolutionary consciousness. The project foundered. The trained workmen were loath to return to their unkempt and uncomprehending comrades. Lenin came to the conclusion — which he consistently maintained throughout his career as a Marxist, that it is not from books, not from theoretical induction in previous socialist seminar groups that mass consciousness is attained. It will come from the struggle against capital and eventually with the state. The state being by definition an instrument of violence this latter struggle must eventually assume a violent form. In initiating their struggle against capital the working class begins with all sorts of illusions that their grievances are due to particular abuses which are easily curable within the present structure of property ownership. Only in the course of the struggle do they realise that the abuses are general and endemic and can be resolved only through the total overthrow of private property. At this stage they come into conflict with the state which undertakes the protection of property. Still they begin their political activity with the belief that the state is amenable to peaceable reform, that their interests can be reconciled with those of the bourgeoisie, that they are in fact fighting the same fight as the liberals. Only when the liberal bourgeoisie in the course of the revolution moves over to the side of the reaction and comes out in defence of the autocracy are these illusions shattered. Only then does the mass come to adequate revolutionary consciousness.

For the revolutionary Marxists what was needed was an organisation of activists, a cadre party whose function was to so guide and stimulate the revolutionary impulses so that the polarities long discerned by theory and immanent in society would be actualised in political groupings. They would be actualised above all in the utilisation of state violence by the ruling class, desperate to retain its power. Then and only then would the veil be lifted from the people's eyes, the state revealed for what it was, an instrument of coercive violence to protect the interests of a class. The extensive utilisation of violence by the state would strip it of its facade as impartial arbiter amongst competing interests, it would convince the masses as no theoretical argument could, that they cannot realise their objectives without the destruction of the existing state and the establishment of a new transitional force wielded by the proletariat. Modern theories of 'confrontation' are no more than a simplified gloss to the Leninist original. They see in violence a fundamentally creative role in the transformation of society for only in violent confrontation is the true nature of things made plain and apparent for all to see. Only then does the state manifest itself as naked violence shorn of its trappings, only then do the revolutionary forces themselves close their ranks. The time for prevarication and qualified support is over; in class war as in any other, identification must be total. Violent confrontation is the necessary climax and pure expression of this war. In its face all intermediary and subsidiary groupings and ideologies, which in times of peace are taken seriously, are abruptly swept aside. The sharp polarities emerge, the two armies close their ranks and clarify their essential objectives.

It is in very similar vein that the Syndicalists vaunt the creative role of violence in the political process. It eliminates the middle. It condemns to deserved obscurity all that host of meddlesome social democrats swollen with sociology. The brahmins of the labour movement imagine that their science of society will save civilisation, and that all that is needed is that the masses be organised to vote them into power. They are matched in their desire for conciliation and gradual but sure progress only by the insipid and spineless philanthropic employers. These renegade bourgeois, full of concern for the 'social problem', declaiming in tones of the highest sincerity their desire to improve the lot of labour, are the most mischievous and deluded of men. Both social democrat and philanthropic bourgeois demean and pervert the grandeur of the true historical drama which is unfolding. The social democrats in their pursuit of petty 'proximate goals' their *possiblisme* and 'integral socialism' peacefully attained through gradual progress, reason and experimentation — they offer nothing to galvanise the proletariat to assert the dignity of labour. Worse, they become the trouble-shooters of capitalism, pacifying every outbreak of proletarian assertiveness which can only lead to an upset of the complicated organic inter-relationship of the society to which the socialists are heirs presumptive. They have no wish to see their patrimony destroyed by the violence of men who fail to appreciate the delicate mechanisms of progress. Every bit as much as the well-meaning bourgeois, radical in his own way, the socialists and radical socialists obfuscate the true nature of things and this arises from the very structure of representative democracy. They must strive to attract *all* the discontented to their cause, and in so doing their propaganda must emphasise the lowest common denominator or dissent. The particularity of the proletarian position must be discarded in favour of an all-embracing appeal which is neutral in its class bias. They disguise the polarities inherent in the class war. They envisage it as a series of parleys in which the actual troops are never brought in to play. Their numbers are assessed at the polls, their strategic disposition is calmly considered by both general staffs in parliament, and territory is graciously yielded by the loser until he admits his situation to be untenable. Like players who respect each other's skill they build up their pieces and concede defeat without having to go through the unseemly savagery of the endgame.

Like all theatre, parliament vicariously plays out the real drama. The real drama, the syndicalists maintain, cannot be played out by proxies. It can be played out only by the proletariat where it encounters the bourgeoisie — in industry itself. The field of battle is clearly defined and so too are the weapons which are available to the proletariat — sabotage, boycott, strike and general strike. Each partial protest is given meaning by its contribution to the final cataclysm of the General Strike, each militant driven by the sublime vision of a society of free creative producers. This goal capitalism cannot possibly concede, and precisely for that reason it is the goal appropriate for the proletariat. It destroys at a blow the credibility of the social democrats proximate and immediately realisable demands. It repays with black ingratitude all the ingratiating concessions of employers. It demonstrates above all the hollow unreality of the polite parliamentary game, for the class war is fought outside of parliament and renders superfluous all the cumber-some vote-catching political machines. The function of violence in bringing an end to this sham and hypocritical game is, for Sorel at least, central.

Only the self-activity of the proletariat as an embattled and insulated corporation can, according to Sorel, cleanse society of its self-evident putrefaction.[38] It can accomplish this only if it is pure, and it attains the purity only through struggle. Only violence and the surety that catastrophic conflict is ahead can continually reanimate the sublime and epic character of the struggle. It rouses the bourgeoisie from its torpor, teaching it to mind its own business and aggressively pursue its proper self-interest. It teaches the proletariat to value heroism and self-denial – not the flesh pots of utilitarian satisfaction desired on their behalf by social democrats and earnest students of the social question. Only struggle and violent confrontation *par excellence* can beget that distinct community and total commitment necessary for the proletariat to accomplish its mission. Sorel constantly bolsters his argument by reference to the experience of early Christianity. So long as it was a distinct and embattled group, so long as it was heroic, it preserved the purity of its original aim. When the church militant became the established church it necessarily degenerated.

The central thesis that Sorel presents is that the vocation of the proletariat is not political, its mode of expression is not political. The political is the way of compromise, alignments, duplicity, personal aggrandisement and all manner of things abhorrent to the sublime, the heroic and self-denying. It is vainglorious and essentially individual, the war of debators' words and nice constructions which must always favour the socially confident and best educated who sniff the wind and attach themselves to that party which promises them the greatest power. It is the means *par excellence* whereby the bourgeois intelligentsia waylays and misleads the proletariat in history. Bakunin in his 'Appendix A' to *Statism and Anarchy* predicts this new tutelage to which the proletariat will fall prey, a technocratic intelligentsia arrogating to itself all decision-making and establishing a new despotism over the proletariat all the more odious for its scientific pretensions. This new autocracy is in essence fundamentally conservative, for in its superior wisdom it must frown on all spontaneity and self-activity. It becomes a reactionary force in that it must tend to undermine the goals of socialism itself. These insights Machajski raised to an integrated anti-intellectual theory whose truth appeared to be borne out by Michels' findings on the inherent conservativism of party machines. For Bakunin and Machajski, for the Russian populists, the Syndicalists and for Lenin, for Guevara and Debray there is a clear agreement that the organisation must be kept to a minimum. Its uncontrolled growth will lead to a threat to its ideals and the best means of guaranteeing its purity and its activism, of guarding against place-seekers is by engaging in revolutionary violence. There are thus reasons of prudence and reasons of principle for preferring the violent road. Violence cleanses the élite of its hangers-on and solidifies the group. Only through violence, by prosecuting it and experiencing the retributive violence meted out by opponents are the masses steeled and made aware of the polarities within society, compelled to choose sides.

The radical justification of violence it has been argued is closely connected with the romantic critique of rationalism. The degree to which it has been accepted is largely a function of the credibility of the rationalist ideas of progress. Where rational debate and exhortation is perceived of as effective in achieving desired reform the ground is cut from under the feet of the antirationalist radical. Where civil rights leaders and nonviolent demonstrations are met with state violence or assassins' bullets, the situation is inverted. As Eldridge Cleaver said of the death of Martin Luther King 'The assassin's bullet not only killed Dr King, it killed a period of history. It killed a hope, and it killed a dream.'[39] Rapidly the Black movement, or at least a section of it, shifted its ground from humanitarian precepts of rationalism to an almost archetypal romantic structure of thought. The eulogy of violence as the means whereby the group found and reasserted its identity overcame its castration complex and vindicated its manhood, though bolstered with Fanon's excursions into psychology, is basically the same mixture as before – the romantic philosophy of action. Let us cite Cleaver again – this time on the message of Fanon's *Wretched of the Earth:* 'What this book does is legitimize the revolutionary impulse to violence. It teaches colonial subjects that it is perfectly normal for them to want to rise up and cut off the heads of the slave-masters, that it is a way to achieve their manhood, and that they must oppose the oppressor in order to experience themselves as men.'[40] The awful simplicity of the Manichean vision reasserts itself, and, whatever its socialist trappings or professions, amounts to no more than an assertion that the war of blacks against whites will be an ennobling experience. It is a line of argument that can as easily and as facilely be utilised to justify a war of Jews against gentiles or gentiles against Jews or Germans against Russians or whatever, in an endless progression to Armageddon.

The problem and danger of the Romantic view is that it must presume the fiction of a single proletarian purpose. It writes the scenario beforehand, and its concern is to get the actors to know their lines, to play out their foreordained role. The romantics know with a terrible certitude what the proletarian interest is and must be. Marx's arrogance in this connection may be taken as typical. 'The question is not what this or that proletarian, or even the whole of the proletariat at the moment *considers* as its aim. The question is *what the proletariat is,* and what, consequent on that *being,* it will be compelled to do. Its aim and historical action is irrevocably and obviously demonstrated in its own life situation as well as in the whole organisation of bourgeois society today.'[41] The 'essential' being of the proletariat has, it seems no connection with the variety and contention of views and objectives, the odd improvisations and clashes of interests which have formed the fabric of socialism and working-class politics. The obviously 'demonstrable' has to be revealed unto it by those who presume to know its true interests. The proletariat becomes an idealised and arbitrary essence, existing as proletariat only insofar as it conforms to the pattern of actions laid down for it from without. Revolutionary *praxis,* preparedness to prosecute violence, are used as arbitrary external yardsticks to gauge the degree of proletarianisation of the working class. Lengthy historical disquisitions are penned to demonstrate how and why the working class of particular countries were waylaid from fulfilling their proper or essential role.

So long as the romantics remain a sect with little influence or power there is evidently little for the social democrat to fear. It may even be argued that their very presence and activity is a stimulant to the more moderate in that they keep up a constant, and often justified critique of the sloth, dilatoriness and lack of radical innovation of social democracy. In power the story is different. Power born of violence perpetuates itself by the same means. There is a consistency in this, if the myth is to be sustained after the revolution it must know no alternatives. Sublime objectives can only be realised if the masses are enthusiastic for their implementation. Their will to realise these objectives is the crucial factor in their implementation. The two elements are inseparable: they represent the integrity of the romantic design and any attempt to assault this integrity, whether wilful or not, is treasonable. The grand design and its subsidiary policies define the proletarian interest. To sow doubt, to canvass alternatives, is to council inactivity and induce scepticism. Decisive action, the wholehearted will of the masses to implement policies can however only issue from certainty. Criticism becomes apostasy, the positing of alternatives must proceed from bourgeois premises for the proletarian line is unique and declared. For all who take issue with the regime punishment must be of the most severe since it is central to the preservation of myth that the objective it expresses is beset on all sides with enemies, it must ever be embattled against a hostile exterior and enemies within − both must be met with resolute violence. Sorel perceived, in his commentaries on Christianity and Syndicalism, that it is as applicable to the 'heroic' phase of Communist states. All criticism now becomes not only anti-proletarian it becomes treachery to the socialist fatherland. With a remorseless logic which has frequently been recounted, revolutionary violence turns in upon itself and devours its own children. Bids for power are bids to define the proletarian interest but the integrity of the design demands that only one definition be admitted. The unsuccessful must be cut down lest their alternatives induce doubts, dissaffection and the sapping of revolutionary will. Those who, like Trotsky, once vaunted the creative role of violence are left without means of defence when it turns upon them. Reasoned defence and appeal to the facts, claims from natural law or due process are all alike appeals to a different language and tradition of socialism, they express values long condemned by the romantics and cannot therefore be expected to count.

NOTES

1. *The Conspiracy for Equality,* trans. by B.B. [Bronterre O'Brien] London, 1836, pp. 304-5.
2. Babeuf, *Textes Choises,* Paris, 1965, p.200.
3. *ibid.,* p. 219.
4. Godwin and subsequent anarchist theorists do no more it would seem than pursue this precept to its logical conclusion in denying the authority of prescriptive law threatening sanctions for the performance or non-performance of specified actions.
5. Philip Snowden, *Labour and the New World,* London, n.d., p. 48.
6. J. Ramsay MacDonald, *Socialism Critical and Constructive,* London, n.d., p. 265.
7. H.M. Hyndman, *Record of an Adventurous Life,* London 1911, p.432.
8. See e.g. Philip Snowden, *Labour and the New World,* London, n.d. p. 50.
9. Emile Vandervelde, *Collectivism and Industrial Evolution,* London 1907 pp. 208-9.
10. J. Ramsay MacDonald, *Socialism: Critical and Constructive,* London n.d. p. 10.
11. Philip Snowden, *Labour and the New World,* London, n.d., pp. 66,68.
12. F. Engels, *Introduction to The Class Struggles in France,* Karl Marx and Frederick Engels Selected Works, Moscow 1962, vol. 1, p. 129.
13. K. Schorske, *German Social Democracy* 1905-1917, Cambridge, Mass., 1955.
14. Engels, *op. cit.,* p. 136.
15. Quoted in J. Braunthal, *History of the International 1864-1914,* London 1966, vol. I, p. 322.
16. Marx-Engels, *Selected Works,* Moscow, 1962, vol. 1, p. 45.
17. Hess was here reformulating in a somewhat more radical way many of the ideas of A.V. Cieszkowski's *Prolegomena,* See D. McLellan, *The Young Hegelians and Karl Marx,* London 1969, pp. 9-11.
18. Moses Hess, 'The Philosophy of the Act' (1843), in A. Fried and R. Sanders, *A Documentary History of Socialist Thought,* Edinburgh 1964, p.264.
19. *ibid.,* p.256.
20. *ibid.,* p. 267.
21. Michael Bakunin, *Selected Writings,* ed. A. Lehring, London 1973, p. 55.
22. *ibid.,* p. 58.
23. Michel Bakounine, *Oeuvres,* t.III, Paris 1908, pp. 278-9.
24. Michael Bakunin, *Selected Writings, op. cit.,* p.91.
25. H. Marcuse, *One-Dimensional Man,* Boston, 1964, p. 256.

26. E. Hobsbawm, *Primitive Rebels*, Manchester, 1959. 'They do not as yet grow with or into modern society: they are broken into it, or more rarely . . . they break into it.' Hobsbawm's general discussion of the mythology associated with banditry bears a compelling resemblance to the more articulate theories stemming from romanticism. Banditry he maintains is always represented in popular myth as elemental and heroic, a vindication of the common people against wealth, authority, the law and the state. It is for exactly that reason that Bakunin regarded the bandit as a man who in his whole style of life has symbolically removed himself from the State and the trappings of its laws, he is in permanent insurrection against the wealthy — the quintessential barbarian quite outside the pale of civilisation.

27. cf. Marx, *Toward the Critique of Hegel's Philosophy of Law: Introduction* in L.D. Easton and K.H. Guddart *Writings of the Young Marx in Philosophy and Society,* N.Y., 1967.
'If *one* class is to stand for the whole society, all the defects of society must conversely be concentrated in another class. A particular class must be the class of general offense and the incorporation of general limitation. A particular social sphere must stand for the *notorious crime* of society as a whole so that emancipation from this sphere appears as general self-emancipation *par excellence,* conversely another must be the obvious class of oppression.'

28. Marx, Engels, *The German Ideology,* London, 1965, p. 76.

29. This appears peculiar in Lenin's case but how else are we to explain the anarchist tendencies of State and Revolution? To say that it is an aberrant text does not explain the importance Lenin attached to it as a programmatic statement. Nor does it explain why nothing at all like it was ever produced or contemplated by the leaders of German (or any other) Social Democracy.

30. See his *The Class Struggle in France* and *The Eighteenth Brumaire of Louis Bonaparte, passim.* Karl Marx and Frederick Engels, *Selected Works,* vol. 1, Moscow, 1962.

31. Karl Marx and Frederick Engels, *Selected Works,* vol. 1, *op. cit.,* p. 192.

32. Marx/Engels, *Selected Works,* vol. I, *op. cit.,* p. 217.

33. Marx/Engels, *Selected Works, op. cit.,* p. 119.

34. The terrible beauty born of the violence of the Easter Rising, was, according to Yeats, *felt* not thought, and this feeling of exaltation that new worlds are at hand, is best expressed by poets not political theorists. cf. Hobsbawm, *op. cit.,* p. 61.

35. William Morris, *News from Nowhere,* London 1924, p. 123.

36. *ibid.,* p. 150.

37. P. Guillaume and M. Grainger, *The Commune,* Solidarity Pamphlet no. 35, Bromley, 1971, p. 17.

38. Sorel refers of course to the condition of *fin de siècle* France with its constant political intrigues and economic and social scandals.

39. Eldridge Cleaver, *Post-Prison Writings and Speeches,* London, 1971, p. 95.

40. *ibid.,* p. 45.

41. K. Marx and F. Engels, *The Holy Family,* Moscow, 1956, p. 53, emphasis as in the original.

11 WOMEN'S LIBERATION, MARXISM AND THE SOCIALIST FAMILY

Juliet Mitchell

Although my title is wide enough, there are within this several quite distinct issues that I want to isolate. For instance, what has historical materialism, the science of Marxism, to tell us about the position of women? Towards what type of material should we direct the philosophical approach of Marxism – the principles of dialectical materialism? And, finally, at a general level, what can be said of socialist visions of a future family?

I shall leave out any discussion of what either Marx or Engels explicitly said about women. Leaving aside Engels' *Origin of the Family, the State and Private Property,* if we cannot quite limit their explicit utterances about women to the fingers of one hand, we can indeed restrict the general theses to nearly this meagre figure. Raking around in the indexes of their works under the heading 'women' is enough to convince anyone that Marx at least was a male chauvinist *per excellence.* Such a conclusion comes from a ridiculous task. Marx's maleness may have been a precondition of his lack of interest in certain areas, but historical materialism is about the antagonisms and contradictions within the development of *mankind's* history. That a possible antagonism between men and women has escaped analysis is a serious sin of omission but not a sin of omission that of itself would make Marxism a sexist science.

I think we can divide what we learn from historical materialism about the position of women into two areas: work and the family. The two areas are interlinked and the separation is only in the interests of analysis and lucidity.

Very briefly, the main body of Marxist theory relating to this area suggests that an original communal method of production and consumption gave way first to the division of labour, then to the exchange of commodities, produced by different groups according to this division, then to the accumulation of commodities, then to the appropriation by a few and to the appropriation of the labour power that was needed to produce them. In this process the family (originally a very different structure) shifted from being a unit that revealed a non-exploitative division of labour to one which incarnated and incorporated directly or reflectively all forms of social exploitation known to man (as Engels says, within its history there is slave, serf and proletariat).

The original accumulators of commodities were men, and within the family or kinship equivalents women became merely the vehicles for ensuring that the man's property was handed on to his known heirs — hence the wife's enforced sexual fidelity. However, whilst the capitalist stage of development confirms this earlier relegation of the woman to the role of breeding machine — it also contradicts it. For its system of production it needs cheap mass labour (women and, at times, children). It thus takes them out of the family which has been designed to enclose them. It also dispossesses the vast majority of the population: the exploited or oppressed masses, the wretched of the earth. The working-class man has no heritage to hand on (bar his name), and his wife, in early capitalism and in later periods of economic depression, will quite probably be the chief breadwinner. As within the dominant bourgeois ideology a man is supposed only to be a true man in relation to a woman, who should not be a wage slave but instead should only (again within the dominant bourgeois ideology) be the mother to his children who should be the heirs of his fortune, manhood itself — amongst the oppressed — is undermined, womanhood and childhood denied. Capitalist society sets up a miserable struggle between the private and the public and then offers an ideology which tries to obscure the torture-marks of the struggle. Bourgeois ideology suggests that the private is the true and the public the necessary. The family us supposed to be the area of the private, the repository of the true 'individual', so the denial of even this illusion, as it is denied for the majority, can be one of the most painful experiences of the contradictions of capitalism. Under communism the distinction between the private and public would exist no more and real privacy and real individualism would come about alongside the real, unexpropriated social work which would have produced social individuals; the exploitative aspects of all divisions of labour would gradually vanish and with them all that today characterises the family and the economic and sexual subordination of women and children.

From its analysis of the present and the past, historical materialism posits the suggestion that women will be liberated from the status of unpaid servant in the home only with their full and equal entry into social production. Capitalism sets such a process in motion, though typically, in such an exploitative way that, though it utilises women for its own mode of production, it also retains them for merely socially useful work in the home. Their socially useful work in the home is without direct economic value in capitalist terms, for they produce there nothing that they can exchange for anything else of equivalent value. The housewife has thus neither her labour power nor the products of it to sell. It is given in so-called 'free' exchange for capricious maintenance by a husband. That such maintenance is capricious can be tested not only by the fact that there is no 'standard' of maintenance that her work commands – the wife of a poor man goes poorly fed and poorly clad – but also by the fact that on the occasion of death or desertion the State is obliged to continue adequate maintenance only if the male provider has been a State employee or a certain kind – i.e. the Army Widow's pension. The State will try and force the father of a child to give the mother money for its provision, but it will not stand in for the father. Thus in all instances, despite social welfare and welfare statism, the housewife is still, on the whole, dependent on a single man for maintenance. Yet her social usefulness as housewife and mother is clearly of much larger social benefit; she provides the environmental conditions necessary for a man to work within the capitalist mode of production, and, as childbearer, she provides the reproduction of the labour force.

It is clear from this that the institution of the family, at this stage of capitalism, still acts on behalf of the State to provide certain economic conditions. It is quite conceivable that the State should, at some time, take over more of these functions (as it has with school education) providing communal welfare facilities (housing, cleanliness, child-care and nourishment) and even, if we wish to fantasise about the ecological revolution, the extrauterine production of children – test tube babies or what have you. Such a development hypothetically could take place under capitalism and would doubtless contribute in an uneven fashion to an erosion of the family and consequently provide a possible pre-condition for women's liberation just as, Marx and Engels separately observed, the massive and painful entry of women and children into large-scale industry in early capitalism at first also dissolved to a great degree the traditional relationships within the working-class family. Engels drew an honest conclusion from his observation of this phenomenon in *The Condition of the Working Class in England,* written in 1844 before his meeting with Marx:

' . . . we must admit that so total a reversal of the position of the sexes can have come to pass only because the sexes have been placed in a false position from the beginning. If the reign of the wife over the husband, as inevitably brought about by the factory system is inhuman the pristine rule of the husband over the wife must have been inhuman, too. If the wife can now base her supremacy upon the fact that she supplies the greater part, nay the whole of the common possession, the necessary inference is that this community of possession is no true and rational one, since one member of the family boasts offensively of contributing the greater share. If the family of our present society is being thus dissolved this dissolution merely shows that at bottom, the binding of this family was not family affection but private interest lurking under the cloak of pretended community of possessions.'[1]

Thus capitalism, either in the nineteenth or in the twentieth century was and is capable of removing some particular tasks that the family fulfils and of implementing these through the State. However, within the contradictions and irrationalities of capitalism, the family remains — in the colloquial sense — the most economic way of managing things. Yet there must be some reason for this.

If we look at the woman's work in the home, there is little to say about it from the point of view of political economy. Thus we content ourselves with the moralistic implications of the fact that it is a hangover from feudal patterns of work, as though that in itself made it somehow *worse* than capitalist modes of work. As it happens, the fact that it is more backward makes it neither better nor worse — unfortunately, it may make the task of its transformation harder. But its retention has its specific uses for capitalism. The woman in the home is performing socially useful work which has no commodity value; Marx comments on the nature of all such use-value work:

'Whatever the social form of wealth may be, use-values always have a substance of their own, independent of that form. One cannot tell by the taste of wheat whether it has been raised by a Russian serf, a French peasant or an English capitalist. We cannot tell by looking at the diamond that it is a commodity. When it serves as its use-value, decorative or mechanical, on the breast of a harlot, or in the hand of a glass-cutter, it is a diamond and not a commodity. It is the necessary prerequisite of a commodity to be a use-value, but is immaterial to the use-value whether it is a commodity or not. Use-value is thus indifferent to the nature of its economic destination, i.e. *use-value as such lies outside the sphere of investigation of political economy*. It falls within the sphere of the latter only insofar as it forms its own economic destination. It forms the material which directly underlies a definite economic relation called exchange-value.'[2]

Substituting for 'use-value' the phrase 'socially useful', we can see that political economy as such has nothing to tell us about the socially useful work of the 'housewife-mother' *except* (and the exception is all important) in its relationship to exchange-value modes of work.[3] As far as the relationship of socially useful work to exchange-value is concerned, we have a number of things to learn. I would just like for brevity's sake to point out one exemplary instance here. The person who is engaged in this type of socially useful work has very little to exchange. The products of her work are not for sale as are those of the peasant; and in addition she has little labour-time left to sell within commodity capitalism. The wife and mother thus has very little she can call her own — including her own labour-power. This feature of her oppression under capitalism distinguishes her from the slave, the serf and the peasant and from women in other forms of society. Under a system whose defining characteristic is that it reduces the majority of the population to have nothing to sell but their labour-power — hers, to a large extent, is already spoken for. Women have less valuable labour-power to sell and consequently get a bad bargain even if they put in forty hours a week at a factory. Employers are quick to point out that, given the degree of exhaustion produced by a woman's two jobs a woman's paid work cannot be as productive as a man's. The woman's labour time for this reason alone, is less valuable and must be sold cheaply. Equal pay and equal work opportunities are thus crucial anti-capitalist reforms, not just for abstract limited notions of justice, as we commonly think, but because they make the capitalist pay more for getting less. Even indirectly, they can help to make private capital pay for what happens to women in the home.

The socially useful work of women in the family lessens the value of their labour-power in the exchange-value capitalist mode of production. Women are thus a constant source of cheap and sporadic labour. But even in a direct economic sense, the family under capitalism does more than make the woman provide socially useful work and cheapen her labour-power for her extra exploitation when 'out at work'. In acting on behalf of her family as chief consumer, the woman takes a product out of the exchange system and redeploys it in a new socially useful way. The housewife thus has a very particular part to play — a part that excludes her from the dominant system and makes her indispensable to it.

As a consumer in the sphere of circulation she is particularly subject to the mystifying terms of the market place. It is in this area — via the medium of money — where like is exchanged for like and buyer is set only against producer that the notions of free and equal exchange and therefore of freedom and equality come in. If, as socialists bemoan, and reactionaries delight in, women are as a group a force for conservatism. it is not because some mothering instinct makes them want to preserve the status quo for their dependent young, but because as housewives and consumers they are trapped in the sphere of circulation from whence derives the bourgeois ideology of free and equal exchange which serves to obscure the real relations of production, to hide the fact that there are two sides to being a producer, that of the capitalist and that of the worker, and two types of buyer, a rich one and a poor one, a worker's wife and a capitalist's wife. As the area of private consumption, it is thus clear that the family itself will have a particular ideological role to play under capitalism, for it is here that the bourgeois language of individuality, freedom and equality is given some semblance of meaning: in the family home all are equal; as families, one is as good as another. Of course, neither proposition has any truth other than the truth of faith.

In a slightly different sense it is frequently pointed out that the family is in general a crucial ideological institution, for it is here that the next generation get their values. In our society, bourgeois values necessary for ideological submission through scarcely conscious consensus (so preferable to visible state coercion) are inculcated in the family. This is clearly true. But I would just point out that, once again, a greater part of this function could be dispensed with. Ultimately, the school may well prove a more efficient institution for some forms of indoctrination, and indeed its role has gained immensely in importance since the capitalist insistence on compulsory education and the school's ever larger share of the child's life as we extend its duration back into infancy and forward well beyond puberty. But having said that, I would point out that whatever the dominant ideological institution of a given mode of production — and it was definitely the church under European feudalism as it may be the school today — the family is never absent but only eclipsed. In the West today, perhaps the family could be eroded in this particular ideological respect, but in the first place a capitalist society has a lot to gain from its preservation here, and in the second, this is by no means its only function.

Indeed, the fact that the family is a crucial ideological institution under different modes of production must make us question it further. How does it operate as this? The indoctrination provided by the church or school is relatively visible — though even in these instances that factor by no means solves the problem. But in important ways the doctrinal role of the family is more elusive. I can only suggest here one or two thoughts that may be relevant and that touch on the larger problem of how ideologies are developed in class societies and how we might begin to use a dialectical materialist approach to this still neglected question in the particular case of Feminism.

The ruling class, be it feudal-landowner or capitalist-bourgeoisie, can only maintain power by establishing ideological hegemony to back up (express and obfuscate) its economic dominance. In the family this establishment of ideological hegemony operates in a number of ways. The family is, of course, a class institution and marriage a class affair. The child learns to live its race, class, ethnicity and nationality in the family. It also learns to live this in a way that is specific to the class hegemony of its particular society. In our case that is to say, it learns its own place within the terms of the bourgeois view, so that to an extent, and often with tension, even a working-class family, as a family, is liable to have a petty-bourgeois outlook. Only the advent of exploited *social* work in production potentially frees the working-class individual from this bourgeois-determined fate. Only the further assumption of Marxist political practice confirms the meaning of this incipient class consciousness.

But in the family the child learns to live not only the meaning of its class but also of its sex, male or female. In the family, (or its equivalents) the child acquires its place in the human order of things, learns to be a social being. As in all class societies, and thus all 'historical' societies, social relations are determined by an economic system of private property, the expression of any individual's social being will be within its terms. But, in a sense, while giving it its general expression and in different societies with different modes of production, giving it its very specific and particular form of expression, there is something that the system of private property has to give expression to. If we can make a comparison, in analysing diverse modes of production, historical materialism isolates class conflict as the form of social relationship which is dominant throughout civilisation or 'written history' as Engels puts it, so there must be some general principle of organisation within what has dubiously come to be described as the mode of reproduction. At the beginning of *The Origin of the Family, the State and Private Property,* Engels writes:

'According to the materialist conception, the determining factor in history is, in the last resort, the production and reproduction of immediate life. But this, itself, is of a two-fold character. On the one hand, the production of the means of subsistence, of food, clothing and shelter and the tools requisite therefore; on the other, the production of human beings themselves, the propagation of the species. The social institutions under which men of a definite historical epoch and of a definite country live are conditioned by both kinds of production: by the stage of development of labour on the one hand, and of the family, on the other. The less the development of labour, and the more limited its volume of production and, therefore, the wealth of society, the more preponderatingly does the social order appear to be dominated by ties of sex. However within this structure of society based on ties of sex, the productivity of labour develops more and more; with it private property and exchange, differences in wealth, the possibility of utilizing the labour powers of others, and thereby the basis of class antagonisms; new social elements, which strive in the course of generations to adapt the old structure of society to the new social conditions, until, finally, the incompatibility of the two leads to a complete revolution. The old society, built on groups based on ties of sex, bursts asunder in the collision of the newly-developed social classes; in its place a new society appears, constituted in a state, the lower units of which are no longer groups based on ties of sex but territorial groups, a society in which the family system is entirely dominated by the property system, and in which class antagonisms and class struggles, which make up the content of all hitherto *written* history, now freely develop.'

The two sides of production that Engels isolates here, not necessarily with reference to this particular text, have been redefined by Marxist feminists as firstly the mode of production (the area of labour) and secondly the mode of reproduction (the area of the production of human life, the family). This use of terms may be misleading as both are areas of production and both have to be reproduced. In our society, capital, for instance, has to be reproduced as well as human beings. Reproduction, like production, is twofold. It would seem better therefore to specify two aspects of a system of social relationships: an aspect dominated by class struggle and an aspect dominated by kinship relations.

Engels' account describes the situation in a way that makes it sound as though — through a revolutionary process which is nonetheless chronological — the organisation around ties of sex disappears as that around class struggle predominates. Certainly it is subsumed and certainly its particular expression will be determined by the nature of the 'area of labour', but I think it is important to stress that as a system it does not vanish. Kinship organisation exists even within the most complex and advanced social systems. And it is within this kinship organisation that women as a category are placed. A kinship organisation of social relations is larger than the specific family form through which it is expressed. The more complex the society, the less the laws that govern kinship will be explicit, they will be internalised and unconsciously understood, so for example, we know the rule that forbids incest without having to be told it and without external punishment descending on us if we offend against it. But the internal restriction and the self-punishment for breaking such taboos is as massive as any piece of legislation.

The kinship organisation that underlies a class system is only in part visible in some customs and some laws — laws of inheritance and customs of marriage, for instance. For the most part, the implications of the social relations set up by ties of sex or kinship are only 'known' unconsciously. In several diverse ways, this has a bearing on an analysis of the position of women and on socialist visions of a future family. Most obviously, the absence of women as a particular group from the class system has been reflected in their relative absence from the bulk of

228

Marxist theory; what we need in this context, is not so much an extension of historical materialism to include them, as a dialectical materialist understanding of the social relationships set up by kinship structures, an anthropology of kinship under capitalism and an analysis of the unconscious in which these structures are revealed.

In stressing kinship over and against the more usual socialist stress on the family, I simply intend that we should look to a general principle and isolate general laws which, of course, will be variously manifest as the basic kinship pattern takes on its form in particular families. Our current sociological accounts of various families in various classes, races and nations will have a reference point more relevant than merely a comparison with each other. What then are the features of kinship organisation that are crucial to the position of women and hence to any plans we may have for the future form of the family under socialism?

From the viewpoint of their kinship system, all class societies, that is, all societies beyond the small-scale ones that in Engels' terms pre-exist 'written' history, would seem to have been invariably patriarchal, variously patrilineal and frequently patrilocal. As these kinship laws are subjugated to class conflict in a gernal sense, so in the individual are they submerged and only indirectly accessible. They are the unwritten rules, the traces of laws no longer visibly transcribed, they are left as marks in the unconscious of each and every one. It is because its concern is with deciphering the unconscious that psychoanalysis is important.

Not surprisingly, many attempts have been made to amalgamate Marxism and psychoanalysis by theorists interested in questions of subjectivity, the role of ideology and the family. There are likewise many reasons why such efforts have been, at best, only partly satisfactory. One reason we might single out for reasons beyond polemics, is that they have not used a feminist perspective. A patriarchal kinship system will, at its most generalisable level, predicate a hierarchical structure wherein the feminine and, though not identical with it, the role of the female will be inferior. Women in their very psychologies of femininity embody their oppressed position within a patriarchal order.

It may well be that under socialism which begins the process of ending society based on the division and conflict of classes for the first time in written history, the organisation around sex ties is not overthrown. Indeed it is unlikely that unless they are seen and struggled against, these could simply wither away. Hitherto most socialist fantasies of the future family have righted certain wrongs, been wishfully egalitarian, destroyed private property as the economic expression of the subjugation of women that has characterised the family in all class-dominated societies. It would seem that as the family is only the phenomenal form of the kinship system, it is this latter and the patriarchal marks of it that we acquire in our unconscious which have

229

to be changed. In turn, clearly, the unconscious will not alter until kinship organisation is overthrown. Primitive matriarchy, like primitive communism, only helps us in our dreams of what we do not want, they stand as examples of alternatives to a history of father- and class-dominated societies. Ultimately, no-one wants to set up matriarchy against patriarchy, but a sex tie system which relates to patriarchy as a classless society relates to a class one would seem to be the direction in which our politics should be taking us.

Under capitalism women suffer a handicap in even selling their own labour power; where they have sold it, they suffer the same exploitation of it as the working class in general. The distinction which is certainly there is one of degree not kind and is conditioned by their other role as women, not 'workers'. Against the exploitation of their labour-power and appropriation of its products, men and women, whether directly exploited as individuals or not, have to organise and struggle as a class. Against their socially useful work in the home, as wives and mothers of a particular kind, which is the capitalist expression and use of one aspect of patriarchy, women, whether or not as individuals they are housewives and mothers, have to form a political movement as women. Nobody is exempt from the structure and implications of class nor of patriarchy. No women's liberation movement that denies the class struggle, and no class struggle that underplays the oppression of women, can be a fully revolutionary force. No analysis that ignores the basis of women's specific oppression is a revolutionary analysis.

NOTES

1. Engels, 1844, *The Condition of the Working Class in England,* p. 88.
2. Marx, *Contribution to a Critique of Political Economy.* Chicago: Charles Kerr & Co., p. 21 (my italics).
3. For this reason, amongst others, I would object to Margaret Benston's analysis of women's 'use-value' work in her article 'The political economy of women's liberation' — you simply can't have such a thing — and to most current theoretical arguments that seem to lie behind the tactical demands for housewife's pay.

12 'YOU'RE A MARXIST, AREN'T YOU?'

Raymond Williams

'You're a Marxist, aren't you?' This question would be difficult but not too difficult to answer, if only it ever got asked. But what happens instead of a question is, in my experience, something rather different. There is a kind of flat labelling with this term 'Marxist', which became increasingly common during the 1960s and is now a matter of course. I find, looking into my own experience, that I get described as a Marxist here and there in all sorts of contexts and with all sorts of implications. I looked myself up once in the *Anatomy of Britain* and found myself described as 'the Marxist Professor of Communications' and I thought: 'well, I'm not a professor, I don't teach communications; I don't know whether the first term of the description would be more or less accurate than the others.' Then again, I mix a good deal in what is known in the orthodox press as the extreme left, which is now composed of many different and in some senses competing organisations. There one very common tactic of argument is to say that somebody is 'not a Marxist', in much the flat way that is used from the other side. Or there is the formulation which has become very familiar (almost as familiar as that famous one from between the wars, 'it is no accident that . . . '): the flat announcement that 'this position has nothing in common with Marxism'. Inside the militant socialist organisations, the revolutionary socialist organisations, you hear this kind of argument all the time. People say it to each other about positions which, from the outside, get the one flat label 'Marxist'.

Now it used to be that the political position and the intellectual outlook which I broadly hold were called, with much the same flatness, 'Communist'. One would be referred to as a Communist whether or not one actually carried the party card of membership in the Communist Party or in one of the rival Communist organisations. There was a spectrum which was described as Communist. But that seems to have been replaced by 'Marxist' as this rather flat general term. I suppose the change is, in its most serious part, as recognition of the fact that the world Communist and Socialist movement has become ever more deeply divided, that there are rival centres of Communist and Marxist orthodoxy, of which the opposition between the Soviet Union and the Peoples' Republic of China is only the most obvious, and that it is then recognised that it is possible to hold many different and indeed alternative positions on the revolutionary socialist Left. But also I think it is a matter of academic accommodation. In the last ten or fifteen years some knowledge of the Marxist position has got into the universities, and it is then felt, perhaps from both sides, that Marxist is a more polite term than Communist, which might take us back to the days of the Cold War. Yet I often wish, in the description of some particular position, that one were still called a Communist or a Revolutionary Socialist rather than, flatly a Marxist, with all the difficulties that particular description seems to me to entail. I want to discuss some of these difficulties, but must first indicate some reasons for this preference.

For I am bound to say that when I look at the development of socialist thought, when I look at the dependence of many of the most creative periods in socialist thought on the whole experience of the working class, and on democratic and national liberation movements, moreover when I look at the whole temper of that thought and action and indeed, the temper of the best of what I know as Marxism, it seems to me wrong, in some ways fundamentally wrong, to have a whole tradition, or a whole emphasis within the tradition, reduced to being named after the work of a single thinker, however great. I want to make it clear, when I say this, that Marx is for me, as for many others, incomparably the greatest thinker in the socialist tradition; that his work seems to me still, in many of its parts, very much alive; and that in that sense no honour could be too great for him. Nevertheless, to specialise a militant tradition in which, literally, millions of men have participated, or an intellectual tradition in which thousands of men have participated, to a single name, has an emphasis contrary to what I think should be its real spirit. Moreover, the transition from Marx to Marxism is itself a matter of very complicated history and we have always to remember Marx's own observation that he was not a Marxist.

Now this false specialisation — this reduction of a modern mass movement to a single name, as if it were one of the old friends of academic or religious or intellectual schools — is very important. But it is nowhere so important as the issues to which it points, the controversies which it contains and disguises. We all have to try to make our position clear, in relation to those issues and within those controversies, and I also felt the need for some time to try to make my own position clear in respect of this particular kind of description. Back in 1959, in London, we had a founding meeting of the *New Left Review*. It was then a review edited by a different group of people from those who now edit it, although I see an essential continuity between that original foundation and its present work. But that meeting in 1959 was not only the matter of founding a review. Many people felt that some new political direction was needed and that in such a review a new political direction was being found. In the very particular circumstances of the late 1950s we were all trying to define this position. I spoke at the meeting and the definition I offered was that the two major traditions of socialism seemed to me to have broken down. This had become most apparent in the period since the end of the war in 1945, and was now inescapable. This fact that they had broken down imposed a new kind of challenge to socialist activists and thinkers, and in this sense it was reasonable to talk about the need for a new Left. The term 'New Left', with particularising capital letters, had not then been invented. Nor was it invented, at first, by those to whom it has since been applied. It drifted in. There is of course a certain modishness if a group announces itself as the New Left. There are periods when everything is described as 'new' in an almost obligatory way. The decade which is most conspicuous in this respect is the 1890s. The notion of self-announcement as 'new' or as 'modern' seems to me always very doubtful. But that there was need for a new direction, a quite new direction, I did not and do not doubt.

Now the two traditions which had broken down, I went on to define in this way. On the one hand, Stalinism. On the other hand, that inevitability of gradualism which you can call, in shorthand, Fabianism. Neither Stalinism nor Fabianism, which in the 1930s had seemed the two main competitors in the socialist political tradition, any longer offered us either an acceptable intellectual system or a viable mode of political action. So some quite new direction had to be found. The reason for feeling that Stalinism had broken down is perhaps the most obvious. It was a very great shock for a whole generation of socialists to live through from the 1930s to the 1950s with the steady accumulation of overwhelming evidence of all that had gone wrong with the Russian Revolution. But even more it was the sense that this had gone wrong not only because of historical accidents and historical circumstances but that there was something within the degeneration itself which related to a political system and a political theory and not just to a man. Indeed it was a sign that Stalinism was not ended in the society which had generated it, that it was reduced in their kind of discussion to something called 'the cult of the individual', or in certain other explanations to the machinations of a particular evil personality. For me at least, and I think for many others, there was a real if not inevitable progression from a mainline version of the dictatorship of the proletariat through the control of the vanguard party to the Stalinist regime which in its ultimate development was an outrage to everything that the Socialist tradition and indeed the best of the Bolshevik tradition had stood for. So it was not merely a case of leaving a sinking ship at a time of great stress. Indeed, many people had hung on through the periods of stress — had hung on to what they called 'a belief in the Soviet Union' — because the issue had posed itself in that way, that they should hang on, come what may, when the going was tough. This, after all, had been a real part of the history of the socialist and labour movements. But there was now a recognition that there was something more general than this. A particular kind of politics had played itself out, with a certain completeness. In a different situation it might have been limited, it might have gone differently, but still there was something in that kind of politics which one had to recognise had reached an effective dead end.

But then, as we saw this, we saw equally clearly that the apparently alternative tradition — that of Fabianism, the British Labour Party, the modern Social Democratic Parties — indeed the whole tradition summed up as the inevitability of gradualism was equally at an end. It had been a very acceptable tradition to people who had been living in the political democracies, who were well aware of the difficulties of starting a violent revolution and of the chances of exceptional hardship and indeed of repression if a revolution made in such circumstances was to be maintained. It was attractive also because it seemed to have a ready base in institutions which were already available. In Parliament, in public argument, by public education, little by little, gradually, but with a certain in-built inevitable tendency, a capitalist society would be steadily pushed back and replaced by a socialist society. Few people had really doubted the inevitability of that kind of gradualism. Why then did we feel that it had ended?

Well, first, there was the history of the 1945-51 Labour Government. Even more there was the reaction in the 1950s inside the Labour Movement to that experience. It was clear that certain major social reforms had been carried through in the early years of that postwar Labour Government, largely the inherited commitments of the Party. It was also clear that overshadowing and finally continuing these was the period of rearmament, the increasing involvement with the political economy of the United States, the movement towards NATO, the whole postwar military and political establishment in which the Labour Government had taken an enthusiastic and leading part, and against which the protests of parts of the Labour Movement had been quite unavailing. It was this double movement — a limited reform within a more powerful and opposite kind of development — which made me feel that to talk about the inevitability of gradualism was stupid and in the end vicious. It radically underestimated the historical process. Gradual changes might indeed be brought about by legislation and even more by changes in public opinon, changes in education and so on. But what this kind of politics really assumed was that there was not an enemy, there was only something out of date. Indeed this was a very popular interpretation: that the political, economic and social arrangements of England were simply hopelessly out of date and needed to be, as the word came through in the sixties, 'modernised'. As Orwell had put it: England was a decent family with the wrong members in charge; if you got rid of these wrong members you got rid of the old outdated institutions, and then gradually and inevitably you established a better form of society. It was all there as material to be worked on, waiting to be worked on, with a certain historical inevitability about it. But this was a radical underestimate of any real situation. Not only were there direct enemies who would defeat and absorb us: by violence, by fraud or by purchase (and the mode of purchase was widely used). Even more there was a sense in which the very changes themselves seemed the creation not of the society that had been foreseen but of a curious hybrid which might be a more dangerous because more durable form of the society which it had set out to change. It was not only, that is to say, that the gradualism was not inevitable; that it was not moving step by steady step towards a socialist society. It was that the very forms of the gradualism seemed to be ways of incorporating the movement which had set out to create a socialist society; indeed forms of conscious preservation of an unaltered, or only marginally altered, capitalist society. And this is where the reaction inside the Labour Movement in the fifties had seemed, to people like myself, decisive. We began to get alternative definitions of 'socialism' which did not envisage the transformation of the basic economic and political institutions of society. Socialism meant something rather different, we were told. It meant more kindly, more equal and more caring social relationships. What had been called capitalism was now called 'private enterprise', 'free enterprise', 'the private sector'. Most Labour spokesmen went along with this rhetoric of a 'free world'. But this was then the outlook and the programme of a fairly decent but also fairly modest Liberal Party. It had abandoned the analysis that the basic ownership of the means of production, distribution and exchange determined the character of the society or at least set limits to the possibilities of its social relationships. As such, in my view, it had abandoned the possibility of understanding or changing the modern world. And so, rightly or wrongly, people in my position felt that on the one hand Stalinism as a political mode had ended, and now Fabianism as a political mode had ended. There was no possibility simply of moving from one to the other, or even of thinking one was spending one's life usefully engaged in a debate between them. On the contrary, there had to be some different base for the socialist movement and a socialist interpretation of the world.

Now it was at this point, of course, that all the contradictions of the British Labour Movement itself, indeed of Western social democracy itself, became apparent. Well before the postwar period, the contradictory tendencies within the British Labour Movement and the Labour

Party, had been articulated many times. It was interesting that the 1950s ended with a debate on the retention of Clause 4 of the Labour Party Constitution — the socialist commitment — which on the one hand retained it liberally, representing in that sense a survival of the verbal tradition, but on the other hand, in practice, settled down to a programme conceived on quite other grounds, that of making capitalism more efficient and in sharing its profits building a more socially responsible society. Much earlier than that, indeed from the beginning if you read the history, there had been such dispute about basic asic principles. What I used to hear as a boy working in the Labour Movement in the thirties was that the British Labour Movement owed more to Methodism and what I knew I did not like, so I was quite prepared to believe that this was said as an explanation of the inadequacies of the Labour Party. But it always seemed, when I looked again, that it was said as a form of self-congratulation and the more I thought about it the less I saw that they had to be pleased about. Here was a nation of which two-thirds were working-class people, and it was still unpleasantly ruled by a stupid and vicious capitalist ruling class, with residual aristocratic pretensions. What was true was that the Labour Party owed a great deal to the method of self-organisation of the British working people, of which some aspects of nonconformist organisation were simply a part. And in this sense, as a movement, it was primarily practical. It was the self-organisation of very hard pressed people to maintain their lives, to better their conditions, and eventually as the eyes were lifted, to transform their society. The neglect of Marx could have been understood. The positive and complacent exclusion was a very much more serious matter for it was a deliberate exclusion of theory: not so much of this theory as of any theory; and the real reason for this was that in practice the Labour leadership shared the ruling class view of the world. They did not need theory; they had their world and there were only practical arguments about their place in it. But the specific and challenging theory which they excluded was Marxism. Now here we have to recognise that what Marx meant, what Marxism is, are properly the subject of intense controversy. In the last ten years, especially in Western Europe and North America, there has been an extraordinary revival of serious study of Marx. This has not been simply popular exposition but is the most searching and at the same time the most scholarly kind of enquiry that has taken place since before the First World War. The benefits of this in the long run are going to be very considerable. But in the position in which we have been since the war, when we have tried to identify the work of Marx and the Marxist tradition, in order, for example, to understand that contrast between Marx and Methodism in the sources of the British Labour Party, there has been a competition of emphasis, a competition of selections of what Marx meant, what Marxism really

236

is, and this has certainly not meant that there is brevity and clarity in the demonstration or in the argument. There is, of course, still substantial common ground. And in relation to this common ground, I find no difficulty in affiliating myself with this movement as a whole. The fundamental approach of historical materialism, as Marx defined it, seems to me to be profoundly true. Men make their own history within certain limits that are set by the conditions of their social development, conditions which are themselves profoundly affected by the state of their economic relations which are in turn related to a particular stage of the mode of production. But at every point in a summary like that there is in practice detailed and important dispute about what exactly is meant and implied. Nevertheless, if you hold that general position you arrive at an important general view of history, and especially of the development of capitalist society. You find a perspective on the relations between capitalist and industrial society, and on the relations between capitalism and imperialism. You find, moreover, that you have to believe that the attainment of a socialist society means the transformation of society, the movement from one whole social order to another.

Next, and decisively, you find you have to believe − and in this, from my whole experience, I was well prepared − that this transformation of society has an enemy. Nor just an electoral enemy or a traditional enemy, but a hostile and organised social formation which is actively trying to defeat and destroy you. Now this recognition of an enemy is something that the inevitability of gradualism had not allowed for, unless we are to suppose − and such complacent fantasies have occasionally occurred − that its policy of cunning permeation was a way of dissolving an enemy without him noticing. But the real question about an enemy was always this. Was this the kind of enemy who could be defeated by the normal processes of civil society; that is to say by the processes of political democracy, parliamentary democracy, trade union action, social organisation and so on? Or was this an enemy who had to be defeated by power, and in the last instance, if necessary, by actual violent defeat? If we look at the history it is clear that within the Marxist movement itself, and within the socialist movement much more generally, this has been one of the most fertile causes for dispute, division, splits and hostilities between different parts of the movement. And this is not, as it might seem, simply a question about strategy and tactics. At a certain point it necessarily goes back to some of the original formulations about the nature of the society, the nature of capitalism, the nature of the transition to imperialism, all of which can be interpreted in this or that way, to indicate that a particular contemporary strategy is correct. It is said that no solution which fails to include the violent capture of state power is either reasonable or honest. Or it is said that any solution which does so include the violent capture of state power is unacceptable because it is undemocratic. These are the positions around which so much of the debate has often rather abstractly moved. Abstractly because the debate often flourishes with particular intensity when neither possibility seems much in view.

Now as I think through the basic positions of historical materialism, the basic definition of capitalist society and its evolution, and then the need to supersede it, to go beyond capitalist society, so that a socialist society, as apart from isolated measures of a socialist tendency, demands the destruction of capitalist society; as I think through these three propositions and try to define myself in relation to them, I have no real hesitation. These are all positions from which I now see the world and in terms of which I try to order my life and my activity. Someone may say: 'it is where you stand on the third point, about the means of transformation, that really defines whether you are Marxist or not, whether you are Communist on the one hand or Democratic Socialist, Social Democrat, on the other.' Well, is it really so? This is where I search my experience as much as the theory. I grew up in a working class family, with a father who fought in the First World War, in an atmosphere in which militant trade unionism and a hatred of war, that amounted almost to conscious pacifism, were almost equally intermixed. When I look back I can see that this was the history of much of the Left in the thirties, that we were at once militant about the transformation of society and pacifist about war. But we were not allowed to live with those contradictions. By 1944 I, who had called myself a pacifist in 1938, was in Normandy. I remember a day when there was a counter-attack by an SS tank regiment and it did seem to me even then, even in that sort of circumstance, that a particular point in my life had in a way clarified and in another way been clarified for me. I found it important that they were the SS and not just German soldiers, still less the Ukrainian and other miscellaneous conscripts from the Hitler Empire who were usually put in front to absorb our attack. That these were the SS had very great significance. It gave a meaning of the kind I already knew, by report, from the Spanish War. Since that time I have never been able to say that the use of military power to defend a revolution is something that I am against. On the contrary I believe that a revolution which is not prepared to defend itself by military power is meaningless. But this, it can be said, is evading the question. Do you agree with *making* a revolution by military power? Yet here again, having seen the violence with which, when it matters, a repressive system is maintained, I can find no principle by which I could possibly exclude this. When I look at the history of the Chinese, the Cuban and the Vietnamese revolutions, I feel a basic solidarity not merely with their aims but with their methods and with the ways in which they came to power. If I found myself in Britain in any comparable social and political situation, I know where my loyalties would lie.

But of course we don't only find ourselves in situations, we also make situations. If we are to be serious about this question we have to relate our understanding of the society and the nature of our activities to the situation that we want to create, and in which we can act. And I am then very close to the development of the late sixties and the early seventies in North America and in Europe, where with the clarity of a new generation, so many people moved to direct action and beyond the first meanings of direct action to certain kinds of chosen confrontations with state power. I find it very difficult to say that this is wrong in some absolute sense. I see hypocrisy in the facile and orthodox condemnation of 'violence' in states wich have either established or maintained themselves by violence and which use it with barely a second thought against so many of the peoples of the world. And yet I do not believe that in societies with functioning political democracies, in societies with very complicated kinds of social organisation, these are the only or even the main forms of revolutionary activity. I believe the politics of confrontation is an inevitable response, within a particular balance of forces, to the authoritarianism of the characteristic modern state. And yet, commonly, it is not revolutionary activity. Indeed in some of its extreme forms it is quite clearly in a different tradition. It is in the tradition of one kind of anarchism or of terrorism, and at definite points, as it develops in that direction, I have to part company with it, because I think that it misunderstands the nature of the existing social struggle.

When the New Left was developing in many parts of the world, and particularly as it developed in North America, this kind of politics was often taken as the feature which most identified it: the politics of direct action. But here I think a very necessary distinction needs to be made. In North America the policy of direct action by students and others, like the policy of work in the community, was linked with a theoretical tendency which has also been widely identified with the New Left but which from the beginning I never shared and which, in my experience, very few other members of the British New Left shared. This theoretical position was that the potential of the industrial working class for changing society had, in western capitalist societies at least, been exhausted; indeed it may never, some said, have existed at all. And since this was so, other means of transforming the capitalist state had to be looked for; other 'agencies', to use the term that became popular in the sixties, other 'constituencies', other modes of social change. But as I said, I have never believed this. I believe that in Britain since the war the fundamental resistance to capitalist state power, whether the agency of that power is a Conservative or a Labour Government has been from the industrial working class. As I wrote some years ago, there would be very little resistance to contemporary capitalist society if it were not for industrial militancy, in all its forms of pressure and of course in strikes whether official or unofficial. Indeed, it was always true of the British New Left, as it was not of the North American New Left, that the industrial working class and its activities remained central. I am sure that this is now even more true. Nevertheless there is a combination of that kind of belief in the activity of the industrial working class with the methods of parliamentary pressure and of working towards a parliamentary majority, and this, I think, is not the position of the New Left, but more the position of the left wing of social democracy or the left of the Labour Party. And it is at this point that distinctions become necessary, although to the notions of Marxism.

What we thought we saw emerging in the 1960s was a new form of corporate state, and the emphasis on culture, which was often taken as identifying our position, was an emphasis, at least in my own case, on the process of social and cultural incorporation, according to which it is something more than simply property or power which maintains the structures of capitalist society. Indeed, in seeking to define this, it was possible to look again at certain important parts of the Marxist tradition, notably the work of Gramsci with his emphasis on hegemony. We could then say that the essential dominance of a particular class in society is maintained not only, although if necessary, by power, and not only, although always, by property. It is maintained also and inevitably by a lived culture: that saturation of habit, of experience, of outlook, from a very early age and continually renewed at so many stages of life, under definite pressures and within definite limits, so that what people come to think and feel is in large measure a reproduction of the deeply based social order which they may even in some respects think they oppose and indeed actually oppose. And if this is so, then again the tradition of Stalinism and the tradition of Fabianism are equally irrelevant. Simply to capture state power and set about changing that hegemony by authoritarian redirection and manipulation involves either unacceptable repression or is in any case a radical underestimate of the real process of human change that has to occur. And Fabianism, with its administrative measures, its institutional reconstructions, does not even seem aware of this problem at all, or if it is, regards it as a problem of the 'low level of consciousness' of what it calls the 'uneducated' or, like Stalinism, the 'masses'. But this is the most crucial underestimate of the enemy. Can I put it in this way? I learned the experience of incorporation, I learned the reality of hegemony, I learned the saturating power of the structures of feeling of a given society, as much from my own mind and my own experience as from observing the lives of others. All through our lives, if we make the effort, we uncover layers of this

240

kind of alien formation in ourselves, and deep in ourselves. So then the recognition of it is a recognition of large elements in *our own* experience, which have to be — shall we say it? — defeated. But to defeat something like that in yourself, in your families, in your neighbours, in your friends, to defeat it involves something very different, it seems to me, from most traditional political strategies.

So, I arrived at a position which at that stage seemed to me very different from Marxism, or at least from what most people said was Marxism, including many orthodox Marxists. And as I developed this position people said that I was not a Marxist. It doesn't really matter, as I said at the beginning, which label is adopted. But in understanding cultural hegemony and in seeing it as the crucial dimension of the kind of society which has been emerging since the war under advanced capitalism, I felt the break both from mainline Marxism and even more from the traditions of social democracy, liberalism and Fabianism, which had been my immediate inheritance.

So if I am asked finally to define my own position, I would say this. I believe in the necessary economic struggle of the organised working class. I believe that this is still the most creative activity in our society, as I indicated years ago in calling the great working class institutions creative cultural achievements, as well as the indispensable first means of political struggle. I believe that it is not necessary to abandon a parliamentary perspective as a matter of principle, but as a matter of practice I am quite sure that we have to begin to look beyond it. For reasons that I described in *The Long Revolution* and again in *The Mayday Manifesto* I think that no foreseeable parliamentary majority will inaugurate socialism unless there is a quite different kind of political activity supporting it, activity which is quite outside the scope or the perspective of the British Labour Party or of any other likely candidate for that kind of office. Such activity involves the most active elements of community politics, local campaigning, specialised interest campaigning: all the things that were the real achievements of the politics of the sixties and that are still notably active. But finally, for it is the sphere in which I am most closely involved, I know that there is a profoundly necessary job to do in relation to the processes of the cultural hegemony itself. I believe that the system of meanings and values which a capitalist society has generated has to be defeated in general and in detail by the most sustained kinds of intellectual and education work. This is a cultural process which I called 'the long revolution' and in calling it 'the long revolution' I meant that it was a genuine struggle which was part of the necessary battles of democracy and of economic victory for the organised working class. People change, it is true, in struggle and by action. Anything as deep as a dominant structure of feeling is only changed by active new experience. But this does not mean that change can be remitted to action otherwise conceived. On the contrary the task of a successful socialist movement will be one of feeling and imagination quite as much as one of fact and organisation. Not imagination or feeling in their weak senses: 'imagining the future' (which is a waste of time) or 'the emotional side of things'. On the contrary we have to learn and to teach each other the connections between a political and economic formation, a cultural and educational formation, and, perhaps hardest of all, the formations of feeling and relationship which are our immediate resources in any struggle. Contemporary Marxism, extending its scope to this wider area, learning again the real meanings of totality, is then a movement to which I find myself belonging and to which I am glad to belong.

Notes on Contributors

Bhikhu Parekh is Senior Lecturer, Department of Politics, University of Hull.

Victor Kiernan is Professor of History, University of Edinburgh.

David McLellan is Reader, Department of Politics, University of Kent at Canterbury.

S.J. Ingle is a Lecturer, Department of Politics, University of Hull

R.R. Eccleshall is a Lecturer, Department of Politics, Queen's University of Belfast

Irving Louis Horowitz is Professor of Sociology, Rutgers University.

Anthony Arblaster is a Lecturer, Department of Politics, University of Sheffield.

T.B. Bottomore is Professor of Sociology, University of Sussex.

Leslie Macfarlane is a Fellow of St. John's College, Oxford.

Neil Harding is a Lecturer, Department of Politics, University College of Swansea.

Juliet Mitchell was a Lecturer in English at Reading University and is now a writer.

Raymond Williams is a Fellow of King's College, Cambridge.